Her Texas:

Story, Image,

Poem & Song

Edited by

Donna Walker-Nixon
Cassy Burleson
Rachel Crawford
Ashley Palmer

WingsPress

San Antonio, Texas
2015

Her Texas: Story, Image, Poem & Song © 2015
by Wings Press
All rights revert to the individual editors, authors, and artists.

Cover art © by Malou Flato.

ISBN: 978-1-60940-423-9 (Hardback)

E-books:

ePub: 978-1-60940-424-6
Mobipocket/Kindle: 978-1-60940-425-3
Library PDF: 978-1-60940-426-0

Wings Press
627 E. Guenther
San Antonio, Texas 78210
Phone/fax: (210) 271-7805
On-line catalogue and ordering:
www.wingspress.com

Wings Press books are distributed to the trade by
Independent Publishers Group
www.ipgbook.com

Cataloging In Publication:

Her Texas : story, image, poem & song / edited by Donna Walker-
Nixon, Cassy Burleson, Rachel Crawford, Ashley Palmer-Boyes.
     pages cm
  Includes bibliographical references.
   ISBN 978-1-60940-423-9 (cloth/hardback : alk. paper) -- ISBN
978-1-60940-424-6 (epub ebook) -- ISBN 978-1-60940-425-3
(kindle-mobipocket ebook) -- ISBN 978-1-60940-426-0 (library pdf
ebook)
  1. American literature--Texas. 2. American literature--Women
authors. 3. Women--Texas--Literary collections. 4. Texas--Literary
collections. I. Walker-Nixon, Donna. II. Burleson, Cassy. III. Crawford, Rachel. IV. Palmer, Ashley.
  PS558.T4H38 2014
  810.8'0928709764--dc23
                                2014032916

The editors dedicate this book to the ground-breaking women who challenged the once-prevailing myth that women's art was of little interest, and that only men wrote or produced works of lasting value. Primarily, we pay tribute to the trail-blazing spirit of folklorist Lou Rodenberger.

The editors, authors, and publisher wish to thank the following individuals for their financial support of this work.

Rick Bradfield and Dr. Cassy Burleson
In loving memory of Lisa Campbell Bradfield.

Major D. E. "Ed" Burleson, U.S. Army, Ret'd.
In loving memory of Capt. Susan R. Burleson, ANC, USAR.

Dr. Casanda "Cassy" Maree Burleson
In loving memory of Dorothy "Dotty" Maree Bush Burleson, Jimmie Nell Bush Sutton, and AmaSue Freeman Madden (and with appreciation for Jasa Jerilyn Jordan and the "Girls of '65").

Earl Bush, Jr.
In loving memory of Mae Bryant Bush and Margaret Wells Bush

Dr. Jamie Carter, Jason Carter and Richard Montenero
In loving memory of James and Faye Huckabay, whose pioneer family founded Huckabay, Texas.

Drue Porter Parker
In memory of my brother James Patrick Porter, who died in October 2013 at age 62, and of our mother, Dr. Para Porter, the first woman to get a Ph.D. from Baylor University.

Dana Burleson Renschler and Richie Renschler
In loving memory of Bryant Edward Burleson.

Charles Rodenberger
In loving memory of Lou Rodenberger.

Anonymous donations in support of *Her Texas* were made:

In memory of two strong, determined women—Virtie Allard Joiner and Verlyn Walker. Also in memory Daniel (Gip) Joiner, Donnie Walker, and George F. Nixon, Jr. In honor of Timothy Hobbs.

In memory of Mildred Crawford, Virginia Stewart, and Donna Nafe, and in honor of Marty VanWagner.

In memory of Alford Stewart, Ernest Crawford, and Gerald Nafe, and in honor of Lee Crawford and Lee VanWagner.

In honor of Todd and Haley Nafe.

And with sincere admiration and deep appreciation for an anonymous donor from Waco whose influence for good has affected the world.

Contents

Poetry

Fiction

Lagniappe: An Editorial Extrusion

Introduction

Life in Texas might be described as a colorful tapestry, far from complete,
but in production for almost 200 years.

Lou Rodenberger—writer, folklorist, and Texas literary
studies pioneer—inspired us with this apt image as we began our
journey to weave together the diverse voices of 21st century Texas women. Our project continues the work of anthologies that
preceded ours, including Lou Rodnberger's and Laura Payne
Butler's *Writing on the Wind* (2005) and Diane Fanning's and
Susie Kelly Flatau's *Red Boots and Attitude* (2003). *Writing on the
Wind* opened a space for West Texas women writers to be heard
in all their rich complexity; *Red Boots and Attitude* accomplished
a similar mission in its collection of stories and poems gathered
statewide. In *Her Texas*, we've drawn inspiration from the stories
and poems of these and other fine anthologies, and we've also
included the work of songwriters and visual artists. The memoir
Lou was working on when she died provided us our title.

Chinua Achebe once commented that "until lions have
their own historians, the history of the hunt will always glo-
rify the hunter." Transposed from an African to a Texas literary
context, Achebe's words remind us that for a body of literature
to be vital and fully representative, it must relate experiences not
only from dominant or outside points of view, but also from the
points of view of insiders. Texas literature has been filled until
relatively recently with women imagined from male perspectives,
but women have claimed space for imagining women from female perspectives.

The premier issue of *The Langdon Review of the Arts in
Texas* contains an overview of Texas literature, "Texas Literature:
Past, Present, Future," by Tom Pilkington. In the same issue,

Lou Rodenberger reminds readers in "Sloshing Around in the Mainstream" that:

> Women writers have never been particularly over-whelmed nor impressed by what outsiders as well as Texas natives like to label as Texas myth. When their fiction is set in early Texas, the familiar characters often are reshaped from a woman's points of view . . . . Place for Texas women may dominate, but it may be East Texas or *la frontera* of those Tejanas living in El Paso and border towns. The range and cowboy life dear to Dobie and his admirers may inspire novels, but these staples of western fiction may be transformed into fiction with women ranch owners as protagonists and cowgirls competing as rodeo stars. The most talented of Texas women writers have earned their place in mainstream fiction in this new century. They may slosh around for a while, demanding recognition, but their place in Texas letters seems obvious and assured.

To provide the reader with a sense of who we are in context of Lou's characterization of Texas myth, as well as a sense of why we felt moved to open a space for the female lions of Texas to have their own historians, each of the editors will share some of her experiences and visions underlying the founding of this new collection.

Donna Walker-Nixon

Reading and storytelling loom big in the Texas mind. I came home from my very first day of school, held a book upside down, and proclaimed, "I can read now."

In second grade, the teacher asked what I wanted to do when I grew up. I said I wanted to teach but then felt guilty because I had lied—I wanted to write.

One of the first storytellers in my life was my mother's mother. We called her Mrs. Joiner since that's what Daddy called her; Mrs. Joiner meant grandma to my sisters and me. She told stories about her great-grandfather who served in the last battle of the Civil War under Dick Dowling. She said he fought Indians and belonged to the Texas Rangers. Tougher than saddlebags, he kept cooking while arrows flew all around. Wait! That just might be his brother—the stories are so similar that I can't remember who was who.

I loved Mrs. Joiner dearly, but I didn't pay enough attention to her stories. There was Aunt Sarah who hid from the Comanches for three days in what would become our back pasture. Again, I don't remember details. I don't know who Aunt Sarah was, and I want to retrieve the lore that Mrs. Joiner left behind.

Mrs. Joiner took advantage of the fact that I loved to read. So as not to hurt her feelings, I labored over her suggested reading list—*Little Women, Freckles, Five Little Peppers and How They Grew, Caddie Woodlawn,* and what I thought was the most boring of all, *Johnny Texas*. It's the story of a German family who settle on the Texas frontier. Scene and action loom big in it, but I had other stories I wanted to read.

As a grown-up, I now realize that the legacy of *Johnny Texas* extends beyond my own experience, even though my short story in this collection makes a reference to the novel. I bequeathed my copy to my niece Demona when at age 10 she expressed the same love of reading and discovery of the mind. She still delights in the book. Debby Everett, a high school friend, remembers her third-grade teacher reading *Johnny* aloud as separate chapter books. My former creative writing student Caera Thornton reports she received a copy of the sequel to *Johnny* on her seventh birthday when her family moved from Seattle to Texas. The big Texas welcome and the book turned this birthday into a day she cherishes forever. Johnny is embedded into our Texas lore. Sadly, few know that a woman, Carol Hoff, wrote this iconic story of a young boy on the Texas frontier. When I googled "Johnny Texas," I had to add the word *book*, or the first responses centered around the A&M Heisman winner, Johnny Manziel.

Although my conclusions are not statistically based, my experiences have shown me that women form a large part of the backbone of Texas storytelling and art, despite the fact that the existence of female mythmakers has all too often been overlooked. With intense pride, we want to continue the tradition of inclusion Lou Rodenberger understood so well.

Cassy Burleson

History remembers men. Edward Burleson was a North Carolina Methodist who died December 26, 1851—the month and day my brother was born—and was buried on my dad's birth date, December 28. As a child, Edward slipped a horse pistol from a saddle scabbard and shot an Indian between the eyes who was trying to scalp his dad. Before being Texas' vice president, he fought in 19 battles, leading the charge at San Jacinto. His last battle was in east Texas against a Cherokee named for a hat he was given by the president with promises of peace. Chief Bowles was killed without resistance. Edward had someone hand-carry the bullet-hole-marked hat to Sam Houston, who raged for an hour while the chief's people set out on the Trail of Tears to Oklahoma. Edward and Sam came from different worlds. Houston took a Cherokee woman as his second wife before settling down with his third wife, with whom he sired the editors of Baylor's first literary magazine, *The Violet*. Despite a summer of genteel education with his cousin Rufus, Indian Ed fought for a living and is in the painting of Santa Anna's capture at Washington on the Brazos. His first cousin Rufus C.'s mother gave Edward the only formal education he ever had. Rufus C. recruited students on horseback and was Baylor University's president four times.

So mine is a line of killers and drillers (soldiers, teachers, and farmers with oil and gas), including the Bushes on my mother's side. My mother, Dorothy Bush Burleson, maintained her wit, majored in library science, and married a soldier. She loved books, taught piano, smoked cigarettes, and persevered. Her mother, Mae Bryant Bush, played jazz piano by ear and believed that if your husband disappointed you or left you, or you got sick, you carried on like the Energizer bunny, clapping those cymbals and running the farms.

Even with acres and acres of work, art mattered to Ella May Cates Hawkins Burleson as she washed in an iron pot over a fire or wrung a chicken's neck. She told "true crime" stories while rolling my hair into permanent waves. Her mother's youngest brother ambushed their wealthy "Sunday Baptist" dad as he drove home drunk in his buggy. He had it coming because he beat them, stole their cotton-picking money, ran his horses through the gaps, and let the horses' wounds bleed. When her mother's oldest brother stepped up to be tried instead, Cates family land was sold to the Burleson family to pay for his defense. Legitimately found innocent, he scraped by with less land and fewer friends in Limestone County. My grandmother married Eddie Burleson, never learned to drive, and mapped her mind into a colorful tapestry with one art project after another.

Her husband's dad, Edward Houston Burleson, was 6'4" when he married a part-Cherokee woman less than 5 feet tall who was on the warpath until she was older than 100, thereby equalizing the Indian issue in our family and giving my grandmother license to lift her volume. Genes like these are a dangerous combination for docile marriages or anger management. But they can result in stories, images, poems, and songs as brave, brazen, and strong as Texas tornados and as gentle as rolling thunder. Our anthology is a space where contemporary female voices can keep breathing through decades to come.

Rachel Crawford

Growing up in Texas was a little like simultaneously inhabiting parallel universes—one of iconic myths and images and another of personal experience.

I was introduced early to a Texas of myth. By the time I could write my name, I could draw a wobbly outline of my state's distinctive shape. I visited the Alamo with my parents and came home with a rubber Bowie knife and a polyester coonskin cap. I got my picture taken with Big Tex at the state fair. I listened to Willie and Waylon and Jerry Jeff and Billy Joe and the rest of the boys. I read *Old Yeller*, *The Longhorns*, *Texas*, and *Lonesome Dove*, and I watched *The Lone Ranger*, *Hud*, *Giant*, *The Best Little Whorehouse in Texas*, and *The Last Picture Show*. I felt there was something special about being a Texan, something that had to do with self-reliance and horse-sense and grit.

Some elements of this mythic Texas appeared in my real life, and some didn't. I spent part of my youth in rural northeast Texas with my grandparents—children of sharecroppers who made it through the Depression and the world wars with enough money to buy twenty acres to retire on. They raised cattle, and when my grandfather put on his straw Stetson to walk out to the pasture, he looked a little like John Wayne to me. Rodeos and county fairs were part of ordinary life, and I showed up with my name on the back of my belt. Without feeling either corny or picturesque, I picked blackberries and fished with my grandfather and baked bread and canned vegetables with my grandmother. Older kids I knew baled hay for their allowance, and for my mine, I fed and exercised horses and cleaned out stalls. Nearly everyone I knew owned shotguns and rifles, and at least one pair of creased and dusty cowboy boots.

Life was different, though, in the Central Texas town where I spent the other part of my youth with my parents. Riding horses and working cattle happened mostly in books and movies, so the few kids who wore boots and cowboy hats looked out of place in a world of air conditioned malls. My parents and I lived in a house that had as much Eastern about it as Texan because my dad had just returned from service in Vietnam and Thailand, and my mother had grown up on a military base in Taiwan. I read *Jonathan Livingston Seagull* and *Zen and the Art of Motorcycle Maintenance* and watched *Hair* and *Easy Rider*. I forayed to concerts in Dallas and Austin and Houston. I spent time on my family's place in southwest Texas and admired the independent, idiosyncratic people who called themselves desert rats. They lived in old trailers or re-fitted metal school buses, and their values and ways of life seemed alien from those I'd known in either rural East or suburban Central Texas. I had all these experiences in my home state, but many of them felt a long way from any version of Texas I'd seen in movies or read about.

I felt even further away as a University of Texas student. My universe grew as I began to understand myself and my time and place within the vast contexts of anthropology and history and geography and literature, as well as the complexities of race, culture, class, sex, and gender. Texas began to seem smaller to me than it once did. Even so, the first time I tried to write, my story took place in that gigantic, mythical Texas I knew as a child. John Wayne would have felt right at home. I also found that the simplistic images of women from that universe—good girl/bad girl, good wife/bad wife, good mother/bad mother—pervaded my writing even though I knew better. It took me a long time to voice perspectives from less mythical and more individualized relationships with the real land and the real women and men of Texas.

I might not have had such trouble writing my first story if I had known a wider range of fictional representations. One of the things I appreciate about today's Texas literature is that it embodies the multiplicity and diversity and hybridity that should by rights spring from a state whose borders are drawn around so many different geographies and cultures. One of the pleasures of co-editing this anthology has been encountering writers who have known both mythical and actual versions of Texas, and who bring them together in stories, poems, songs, and images that represent the state's true complexity and vitality.

Ashley Palmer

In April 2006, I was set to go to Wisconsin. Four months married and, though I didn't know it at the time, one month pregnant, I had decided to jump off the cliff: we would move north so I could attend graduate school in sociology. But then, on tax day, the decision deadline for graduate programs at the time, I changed my mind. I came home from a double shift at the foster care home where I worked my second job, sat on the dingy matted carpet of our St. Augustine apartment while my husband slept in the other room, and frantically emailed Wisconsin and Baylor: *I've changed my mind. I'm going to Texas.*

And that was it; I ran away. Too young, too married, too pregnant—I ran us all away.

Four months later, I rode into Waco, Texas, with a baby in my belly and a husband at the steering wheel. The nausea I felt from the pregnancy overshadowed all other uncertainty of the move. I'd lived my entire life to that point in Florida—had left sugar sand and verdant land for the brown, drab interior of a state with few natural water bodies and a mess of cormorants and crickets.

And for Texans. At every meet-and-greet, I was asked whether I'd "found a church home." Women approached me in supermarkets to advise me on the care of my infant ("She really is too young to be out of the house already, Hon"). Older men talked to my husband and not to me. I'm certain it took me two years to make a friend, and when I did, it was with another non-native. "Oh, *Texas*," became our lovingly dismissive refrain for this surrogate home.

What had I run away to? Grad school was awful. Parenthood was hard; marriage, harder. I was lonely for water. And where were the trees?

It took a while for the extremes to normalize. In life, I was a sociologist of religion: I went to church to study, not to worship. I came away from school with a divorce decree, not an "MRS." Academia killed me; writing saved me. The Lone Star climes were equally drastic: it would snow in April and scorch in August. The bluest county in the state housed the staunchest Republican legislators. Boots with shorts. Tacos for breakfast. Two-step and teetotalling. Piety, propriety, and sobriety alongside dance halls, music festivals, and Shiner Bock.

But seven years in, with a "marital dissolution" behind me and a career change under way, I confessed to my former husband turned roommate (long story), "I think I've finally gotten used to Texas. I don't know that I quite consider it my home yet or if I ever will, but I know what it's like to be here; it's familiar now." That was an endorsement.

Somehow I've built a life here—piecemeal and ill-fitted, though it often feels, it is not boring.

Still, it's a fitful romance to maintain. We cannot decide whether to part from one another, Texas and I. Independent as she is, she doesn't much need me to stay. So I chase her approval all the more.

"Texas! I love you hate me! Texas! I hate you love me!" This is how we talk to one another and mostly from the road on the Austin-Waco stretch of I-35 where I spend several hours a week in commute these days.

But peace befalls us now and again, and we fit one another just right. Most recently it was in the queue for an inflatable art exhibit in Austin—*Air Explosion*, I called it to entice my kindergarten daughter. While I held our place in line, I sent her off with the other children to run around on the grassy knoll whose parents had likewise dragged them there on that 80-degree January morning.

The hippie-Santa Claus man in front of me turned to make small talk. "Is that your daughter?" He was nodding in her direction, yes—she, of uncombed hair and mismatched apparel, beads clipped to her head. "She looks like Janis Joplin."

"Really? You think so?"

"Oh yeah. Janis Joplin was a Texan, ya know."

No one else seemed to recognize it as a compliment when I shared the story. But I'll take it (Thank you, Bobby McGee). Texas calls one of us her own—this strong and free child, a thread in the colorful tapestry.

Her Texas:

Story, Image,

Poem & Song

Austin at Night

A Texas Photographic Sampler

Deana Newcomb

"Art is the objectification of feelings."
—Melville

I am a documentarian at heart. I love the ability to see the world through the documentarian's ultimate tool, photography. Perhaps this love began when I was a child and read *National Geographic* or an encyclopedia before bed. These publications allowed access to people and places I had never heard of and to nature I had never seen. Nature has always been my comfort and my inspiration, so it follows that I would use photography to document the object of my affection. The challenge is to produce a photograph that evokes the feelings I have about the subject whether it is awe, angst, or altruism. To this end, I use various digital tools including a Canon digital SLR camera, Epson Ultrachrome ink, and 100 percent cotton rag Moab paper. I hope they have done the job.

Morning on Fifth

Yield

Deana Newcomb

West Texas Power Lines

Giant Cloud

Capitol Scaffolding

CREATIVE

NONFICTION

Lou's Passion

Charles Rodenberger

Lou was one of the first women students at Texas A&M University. Professor Sid Cox, who taught folklore and Southwest literature, was a major influence in her later teaching career. Teaching courses in Folklore and Southwest literature as a graduate student fulfilled her desire to pursue this genre. Sid encouraged her to join the Texas Folklore Society and that led to meeting authors such as Elmer Kelton and Joyce Roach. She read and collected books in these genres by both men and women writers. Publisher Bill Shearer knew of her interest in women writers and chose her to edit her first book of Texas women writers. As she explains, this event became a *cause célébre* for her. Meeting and visiting with these writers and reading more of their writings led her to believe that they were as good as or better than men, igniting her passion about supporting them. Someone placed an excellent summary of her writings on *Wikipedia*. From the first book for Shearer Publishing, women were celebrated in *Texas Women Writers* and other collections edited jointly with Dr. Sylvia Grider. Her best-selling book was *Quotable Texas Women,* written with Susie Kelly Flatau and published and distributed by Glenn Dromgoole in several printing runs.

Teaching folklore became another passion. One of her classes celebrated the end of the semester by having a cookout at our home in Bryan with each one contributing unusual dishes like squirrel, possum, snake, and armadillo, along with folklore stories of all kinds. Most of her students kept up with her. We couldn't go out to eat in the Bryan-College Station area without one of the waiters acknowledging Lou as her or his teacher.

As she worked on her memoirs, I told her repeatedly to write the story, then go back and research to fill in with more facts, but she insisted on doing the research first. As ovarian cancer took her strength, we moved her files from her upstairs office down to her recliner and laptop. With files located on all sides, she looked at every letter, clipping and document from years back. Lou started filing newspaper clippings when she was in high school, and they filled filing cabinets in the office. As a result, this memoir only covers the first years of her publishing efforts. It is too bad that we weren't able to collect the later events. All of her files were transferred to Texas Woman's University, where they are available to researchers who can mine the details.

Lou and Charles Rodenberger

Her Texas: A Literary Critic's Memoir

Lou Rodenberger

Introduction

I can't imagine now that I had such nerve, but the need to know overruled what my mother had taught me about questions I had no business asking. I've never met a woman writer in Texas who did not provide material for a good story. The long-time professional writer Norma Patterson was one of the first. One fall morning in 1982, Bill and Kathy Shearer, my husband, Charles, and I sat in the writer Norma Patterson's old-fashioned living room in San Antonio, sipping champagne and getting acquainted. Norma was elated that her short story "The Boy Who Couldn't Be Saved" had been included in *Her Work*, the first original publication of the fledgling Shearer Publishing. As editor, I had corresponded frequently with Norma. Her informal, personal letters fueled my curiosity. I wanted to learn more about her career. How long had she been writing? I guessed from what I had already learned that she had been publishing for many years. If so, she surely must be past 80. I had to know. I turned to her sister, "How old is Norma, anyway?"

"Oh, my dear," she said matter-of-factly, "only God knows."

Nine years later, the headline on Norma's obituary in the *Dallas Morning News* answered my question: "Writer Norma Patterson Dalton dies at 102." She was 93 that fall day when I got my come-uppance for asking a question I should have known no one asked women of her generation. I was soon to learn that other Texas women in the first decades of the twentieth century seriously pursued careers as writers, but in biographical sketches, none lists her birth date or discusses her age.

A charter member of the Texas Institute of Letters, Norma Patterson published her first short story in 1912, six decades before I met her that fall morning of 1982. *Harper's, Good Housekeeping, Holland's, Woman's Home Companion, Saturday Evening Post,* as well as other popular publications, bought dozens of her short stories for the next five decades. Between 1930 and 1943, Farrar and Rinehart published eleven novels by Patterson, six of which became best sellers. Several of her novels appeared first as serials in *McCall's*, a popular woman's magazine in the mid-twentieth century. Although she wrote to appeal to women readers, her subjects varied from war stories during World War I to the rough-and-tumble life of oil boom towns. Several of her stories, as well as one of her novels, she wrote in collaboration with her husband, Crate Dalton, a Dallas attorney. Edward O'Brien, first editor of *Best Short Stories of America*, cited "What They Brought out of France" as one of five great stories to come out of WWI. Several of her stories were included in anthologies as early as 1918.

I would learn those facts about Norma later, but Norma's professional history represented more than the story of how a failed elementary schoolteacher became a best-selling author. On the day of our visit, she stood with me in front of a bookcase with glass doors where she casually pointed out her novels lined up on one shelf. On an upper shelf, curiously, were all of George Sessions Perry's works. I had to know the connection. She smiled and said proudly, "I was George's mentor." Norma was expecting luncheon guests, and our time for visiting was limited. Not until I began research for *Texas Women Writers: A Tradition of Their Own*, a history of women writers in the state, did the significance of Norma's declaration lead to need for clarification.

In her 1973 biography of Perry, Maxine Hairston verifies that Norma and her husband, during a visit in 1937, realized their friends George and Claire Perry were facing a financial crisis. Norma later described her reaction to her friend George, who was, she says, "turning out pages and pages of inspired beauty." The problem? Norma knew. Her observation: "Nothing sold. It seemed probable that nothing ever would. George was writing for George then."

Norma and her husband advised Perry to aim for commercial publication in popular magazines. So after six years of writing what he presumed the *Atlantic* or *Harper's* would see fit to publish but never did, Perry began to slant his essays for appeal to editors at *Saturday Evening Post, Redbook*, and *Cosmopolitan*. With the aid of Norma's literary agent at Curtis Brown Agency in New York, in the next two years, Perry sold a dozen stories, a novel, and was summoned to Hollywood to work on a movie script. In 1949, Perry dedicated his memoir of life with his indomitable grandmother, *My Granny Van*, to Norma Patterson.

Over the two decades since I met Norma Patterson, I soon realized that notable women writers abound in Texas. Because little had been written about many of these women, whom I discovered had contributed both insight into Texas culture as well as a much needed woman's perspective on Texas history and life, I began to think of writing a literary history of Texas women writers after *Her Work* was published. With the able partnership of three creative Texas scholars, I've edited or co-edited three collections, which I believe have contributed to expanding knowledge of the writing women in Texas. J. Frank Dobie would likely pigeonhole me as a "mere compiler." If I had known this old folklorist, who in his heyday reigned supreme in mid-twentieth century Texas writing circles, I most likely would have grinned and said, "You got that right, J. Frank, and the reward has been the pleasure of getting to know these writing women through correspondence as well as visits with many." I might also add that their stories, like Norma's, reveal lives of talented and often fascinating Texans, unknown to critics like Dobie perhaps, but contributors, nevertheless, to Texas culture and society. If J. Frank had bothered to notice the stories revealing the richness in the lives of successful Texas women writers in his time, he probably would have become intrigued. Dobie always knew a good story when he heard one.

One of our male friends, an engineer, told me with considerable emphasis that he never read what women write. He expressed a truth about most men readers in the state. Such a generalization does not apply to the many men writers, critics, and publishers who have been most valuable to my career as a "mere compiler." But knowledge of reading habits does explain why essays on Texas literature often cite few women writers.

Without purpose at first, but with a growing sense that women writers seemed to get short shrift, for whatever reason, in Texas critical literature, I have spent 25 years thinking and writing about what I have discovered. Definitive reading of works by male writers reveals to me that only a part of the story of Texas emerges in their often well-crafted fiction, critical studies, and histories. Extensive reading of novels and short stories and of nonfiction, including memoirs, essays, and histories by Texas women writers, convinced me that these writers add a needed dimension to what their male counterparts perceive as characteristic of Texas life. This study explores how, from their unique perspectives, women writers illuminate and even have fostered change in prevalent notions of who Texans are and what their intentions and purposes have been from the days of Austin's colony to today's diverse society. In discussions of selected works by Texas women writers, I have considered topics relevant to the development of the state's culture, beginning with the observations of those women passing through the state in the nineteenth century. Other writers prove how indispensable women were to frontier life. Many challenge Texas myth, including the development of the cowboy as icon. Motherhood and family life, politics and education, and folk life and storytelling all have provided material for "her story" of Texas. Tejana and African-American writers have now added dimension to the literary contributions of Texas women. What emerges from my connections with women writers are stories that confirm my judgment of their contributions to the Texas literary tradition.

As framework for my opinions, I have chosen a hybrid genre to explore the influence women writers have had in this state of many regions. I come from a family of storytellers, and many of my experiences with Texas letters always have seemed rich with possibility. So I share also, as memoir, many of the events that have led to growing knowledge and appreciation of the state's women storytellers. So although I have been chiefly concerned here with exploring women writers' points of view, I also share my own perspective as a native Texan. Many of my opinions originated earlier in scholarly research, but this work focuses on what women I have read reveal in what they write and in what I have learned through personal contact with many contemporary writers. I adhere to no theory of history or literary criticism, nor do I attempt to generalize without supporting my opinions.

I recognize that male literary critics, most accomplished in analysis of what Texas men write and in many cases of what women write, share with intelligence and insight the male point of view. Except for consideration of Larry McMurtry's carelessly titled, and somewhat carelessly written 1981 *Texas Observer* essay, "Ever a Bridegroom: Reflections on the Failure of Texas Literature," which has inspired so much point and counterpoint in Texas letters, as well as demonstrates ignorance of women's contributions to the state's literature, my discussion centers on women writers. This is not to say I don't appreciate the knowledge and illumination of things Texan that men, including McMurtry, have provided in what they write. As a life-long reader, I've read most major creative works, nonfiction and criticism by Texas men writers, many of whom are accomplished in their fields. But this work concentrates on a view of the state not yet much explored.

Life in Texas might be described as a colorful tapestry, far from complete, but in production for almost 200 years. In their short stories, novels, poetry, and nonfiction, Texas women writers illuminate the state's mythology and legend, share personal experience, and describe landscape in all of its regional diversity, where cultures are uniquely affected by climate and geography. The artist Georgia O'Keeffe's attraction to life in the West began when in 1916 she found Panhandle sunsets worthy of her artistic vision. These Texas women writers respond just as vividly with their pens.

Often the stories I treasure involve men writers' and publishers' interaction with women writers, although readers will find here little literary criticism or refutation of the story of Texas that men writers tell. Rather, this work attempts chiefly to examine the "rest of the story"—how Texas women shape their stories of the development of state politics and business, home and family, and the mythology that defines citizens as Texans and how I have come to know many of them. By examining my life for answers to why I have developed a deep interest in this subject and by sharing my stories, my interpretation of what women write, although far from definitive, I share here my perspective on Texas letters not yet examined.

Chapter 1

Probing memory sends me plodding through foggy terrain searching for landmarks that tell me where I have been. Suddenly, a vivid image arrests this fumbling process of looking backward, and the consciousness calls a halt. Why do I remember that moment in my history? And why do so many of those recollections focus on women, usually teachers, who in some never-before-examined way have become landmarks in memory searches? Conducting a search to recall motivations that shaped my personal history surprisingly has evolved into discovery of a motif that somehow influenced choices most of my life. Heroic women in life and fiction have provided both inspiration and motivation for choices I have made since childhood.

A quiet, dedicated one-room schoolteacher probably turned me into a lifelong reader. How I became a bookworm seems a miraculous transformation to me now. I flunked first grade. I apparently also flunked "reading readiness." My harried teacher that year softened her judgment of my failure by promoting me to "high first." Not quite five when I entered first grade, I was a lost child among 30 or 40 country kids divided into the first three grades. I remember little about that year, except that I waited on the front steps for my dad to drive in from town on a fall afternoon, sure my promised box of eight bright crayons would be in the grocery sack. Now it is clear that I spent that year coloring the animals and birds on handouts the overworked teacher gave out daily.

My parents taught in country schools most of their working days. Rural schoolteachers lived hard-scrabble lives in the early 1930s. Salaries came in the form of script from a bankrupt state treasury. Grocery and dry goods store owners became gamblers, taking that script, discounted, with the hope of receiving full payment when the state's financial situation improved. By spring, school teaching jobs became even more scarce. Time to move once again, although neither parent had jobs. Those Depression days brought out the pioneer survival talents of my parents, but it was a good year for me. At age six in 1932 in a one-room schoolhouse, I learned to read. Maybe my teacher, Miss Helen, saw future promise in this freckled, awkward child, whose marathon nosebleed (her last) led to an unscheduled holiday. Miss Helen cranked up her Model A Ford and drove the two miles to my house, where I am sure my mother rewarded her with a generous piece of her spectacular chocolate pie.

I found more than kind attention to my ailments that year. I found salvation in that one-teacher schoolhouse. Miss Helen made me a special project, taught me phonics, and turned me into a book lover. Then she double-promoted me. The next fall in yet another country school, my third-grade teacher testified to my new passion. He wrote in careful script on my report card: "Inclined to rush with school work in order to read." For the first dozen years of my life, I may have neglected school work to read, although I liked seeing *A's* on my report card. Nevertheless, my sister, two years younger, will tell you that I sometimes threw my book at her in exasperation when she pestered me to "go play." I don't remember any fancy Christmas doll, but I do remember the two best gifts I ever received—Anna Sewall's *Black Beauty* and Louisa May Alcott's *Old-Fashioned Girl*. Did my interest in what women write begin when I was eight? Certainly, it was then that I began to recognize women as heroes.

Then my own writing began. Open a beat-up blue composition book, still in my possession despite dozens of moves, and in
blue ink I have written at age 10 the title of my first "novel": *Little
Nellie's Adventures*. In five chapters and seventeen pages of wishful
writing, I adventure madly in my imagination through experiences
I had never had. Nellie enjoys plane and train rides, she "frolics"
at her grandpa's farm, and after riding Bolly the cooperative horse
and peeling potatoes with her grandmother, Nellie rides a bus
home. The end? Well, not quite. She assures the reader she will be
going back to the farm next summer.

In 1939, when our family left the Brazos River Valley in Palo
Pinto County where both my parents taught at Lucille, a three-
room school, "out on the owl-hoot" as my dad described it, we
settled once again at Cedar Bluff, better known as Last Chance,
where I had learned to read. This time my mother was teacher. After a year there as a seventh-grader, I caught a school bus the next
three years for classes in Cross Plains, population maybe 1,500 at
the time. Old English class notebooks, fading but still revealing,
recall for me those determined teachers, all young women, aiming
obviously to teach us how to write. By my junior year, in those days
when educators believed that eleven grades were quite enough to
educate young Texans, I was writing book reports on such novels
as Sinclair Lewis's *Main Street*. And yes, I emphasize in the three-
page review the importance of crusader Carol Kennicott to the
novel's development.

Often I thank fate for a move my parents made before my
senior year in high school. Both parents would be teaching at a
two-room school on a sandy road east of Hawley. My sister and I
enrolled that fall at Anson High School, an excellent school as it
turned out. Daily my sister Sue and I rode a boxy pre-war bus to
the county seat of Jones County. World War II battles dominat-
ed the headlines in 1942. I was only 15, however, and although,
the boyfriend I left back at Cross Plains would write from Rice
University that soon he would be drafted, WWII seemed "over
there," until the night I graduated in May 1943. More than a
dozen of my classmates left for the Marines or the Army the

next morning, several never to return.

My hero that year, however, wore unremarkable clothes and her hair in a bun, taught with a sternness that inspired action, and required memorizing one hundred lines of poetry and reading a dozen books. Leonora Barrett, who retired as senior English teacher soon after I graduated, wrote poetry and encouraged students to record their lives in daily entries in a diary (which she would read without comment).

Some said Miss Barrett had been in love with Larry Chittenden, known for his poem "Cowboy's Christmas Ball," written while he lived on his ranch near Anson from 1886 until the early 1900s. An adolescent crush, perhaps, since Leonora was born in the early 1890s. True, however, it was under her leadership that the annual Cowboy's Christmas Ball, once a regular celebration in Anson, was revived in 1934. Her diligence in reviving Chittenden's memory meant something quite different to me.

In retirement, Chittenden had financed a library in Christmas Cove, Maine, containing only autographed books. Likely this gave the nimble-minded Miss Barrett an idea for inspiring her classes to read. Students were denied access to reserved books in the Chittenden Library section of the school library until they presented evidence they had finished their required reading. I zipped through the book list. My diary records my first Chittenden Library selection, *And Tell of Time*, the post-Civil War novel by Texas writer Laura Krey. I could not know then that almost forty years later, in 1981, I would receive a personal letter from the distinguished writer. Laura Krey wrote that she regretted she could not submit a story for *Her Work*, a short story collection by Texas women writers that I edited for Shearer Publishing. Laura's excuse: she had a houseful of company. At the time, she was 91. Connections with past reading experiences have surfaced regularly in the years I have spent researching the lives of Texas women writers.

Anson High School administrators believed in suspenseful announcement. Not until after the three candidates for honors gave nervous short speeches on that warm May night in 1943 did

I learn I had been named valedictorian of my class. I look at my report cards with skepticism today. Could it be that these exemplary teachers I so admired rigged the grades? Surely, I didn't deserve A plus in Spanish and English that last six weeks, but my heroes thought I did. I carried the notion of women's worthiness as major characters in the drama we call life with me when I arrived in Denton as a naive, clueless 16-year-old to enroll as a journalism major at Texas Woman's University (then Texas State College for Women). My first publication in the campus literary journal, *Daedalian Quarterly*, a sketch describing bus riding in wartime Texas, focuses on a young mother with a fussy baby. Bus riders entertain the baby while this tired wife of a serviceman gets some rest. Obviously, early on, I admired women as participators in contemporary Texas life.

A new-minted journalist in 1947, 20 years old and semi-confident that I knew how to cope on my own, I spent almost two years as society editor of *The Kerrville Times*. A thick weekly at the time, the newspaper required my services as soother of advertising customers on Thursday morning when a typo in their ads annoyed them, errand-runner, composer of wedding stories as well as hospital news, and greeter of the public since my desk sat near the door.

Distinct images of the many who dropped in to visit with Sam Braswell, editor and longtime newspaperman, and his wife Cecilia, business manager, include the attorney who opened the door to comment that the "common people had won" on the morning after Lyndon Johnson, with a little Texas political hanky-panky, beat Coke Stevenson in the Senate race. Father Kemper, a Catholic priest who had lived in Kerrville many years, dropped by regularly to tell me his latest joke. Monte Hall, a Western movie star in town for a showing of his latest horse opera, teased and flirted as he sat on my desk waiting for Sam's attention. Often Junior Starkey, recently an Air Force pilot flying into Berlin, dropped in to visit with his brother, Rankin Starkey, the co-boss of the newspaper. One day, Junior Starkey, already engaged but still attentive, invited me to take a plane ride out at the airstrip he had built west of town on family property. In his wired-together single engine plane, I viewed Kerrville from the skies after I coped with a brief blackout when Junior decided to demonstrate his expertise at trick flying.

Memorable characters all, but the person I recall with greatest admiration came by almost every day to visit with Cil Braswell. I don't remember her name, but I do remember that her bright red coat, which she almost always wore, symbolized her bravery for me and for the town. Cil had told me sadly that this vigorous business woman with the indomitable spirit would die of cancer within a year. Maybe it was then that my developing notion that Texas women become heroic in tough situations began to take shape.

I left Kerrville in the fall of 1948 with great misgivings. I had lived in the Beehive, an elegant colonial style boarding house on Earl Garrett Street, where young singles just out of college usually landed. I learned to dance "Cotton-Eyed Joe," swam in the Guadalupe, picnicked at Garner Park, enjoyed San Antonio Symphony Orchestra concerts, and fell in and out of love several times. I find it hilarious now, humbling then, that the stack of rather modest pinup pictures the good-looking Aggie assistant county agent made of me one Sunday afternoon also included a photo of a jersey cow.

In retrospect, however, the most lasting impressions I have of Hill Country life involve heroic women. The young divorcee, Honey, who made it her mission that first summer to guide me over pitfalls she thought I would encounter sooner or later, offered friendship right away to a lonely kid. Miz B, proprietor of the Beehive, asked me how much I made that first day, and then—when she learned the tiny weekly salary I proposed to live on—set my room and board at $65.00 per month with the warning not to tell the teachers when they arrived. She charged them $75.00. Many of my friendships that year were with older women who provided guidance and advice when I requested it and, sometimes, when I did not.

An old notebook I resurrected from those early career days reminds me once again that I continued to write short stories, for my own satisfaction it is sure. I don't think it occurred to me to submit those stories to one of the popular magazines of the time for which they seemed written. By the fall of 1948, change seemed attractive. I enjoyed the good times in this Hill Country town, but I began to weigh fun against the fact that my measly weekly check of $22.50 was not likely to increase much in the future. At the time, my parents had drifted to West Texas near Lubbock, where they taught in a rural high school west of Levelland. The job opening at Levelland High sounded like a fit for my abilities, so I became a school teacher after Thanksgiving that year. My pay-check would double.

I had found my niche. In the new high school building, where we moved during my second term of teaching, planners had the good sense to include a corner laboratory for newspaper and annual staff. I supervised lively, hard-working staffers producing both the yearbook and *Lobo Lair*, a twice-monthly newspaper, and taught one section of journalism, as well as sophomore English classes. In the three years I worked with those loyal, fun-loving preservers of school history, my future jelled. Might as well yield to inherited genes. School teaching evolved from job into career those first years in Levelland, where I met my engineer husband, Charles.

Just before our daughter, Kathy, celebrated her first birth-day in 1954, Charles realized his engineering talents would be better appreciated in the aerospace field. We left the oil patch after brief stays in Odessa and Hamlin and moved to Fort Worth, where Charles went to work on the B-58 design for General Dynamics. In our six years there, once again, although I stayed home to care for Kathy and her brother, Mark, I began writing. My college membership in the professional journalism organization, Theta Sigma Phi, which later became Women in Communications, led to association with Fort Worth women writers in the local chapter. Television personalities, working journalists, fiction and nonfiction authors, and gifted socialites met monthly in members' homes. John Howard Griffin recount-ed his six-week adventure disguised as an African-American, which resulted in his much-reviewed story of the experience in *Black Like Me*. Member Betty Bob Buckley's talented teen-aged daughter, Betty (who would go on to appear on Broadway), performed at our Celebrity Breakfasts, organized to entertain women of prominent Texas men who were honored (and roasted) by the male journalists at their annual Gridiron dinner the night before. Hung over and sleepy, the newspaper reporters whom Steve Davis later labeled "literary outlaws" all showed up to perform skits from their program of the night before.

At our first breakfast, we learned how the gracious Lady Bird Johnson also could be a good sport. The evening before, several of us met her on the tarmac at Amon Carter Field. She arrived in a bright red coat, greeted each of us, and sat for a while in a reserved room visiting with us. Looking back brings astonishment still. Next to me, dressed casually in a black-checked cotton dress, Lady Bird's smiling, amiable friend introduced herself as Nellie Connally. In less than a decade, those two women's lives would intertwine dramatically.

As a senator's wife, Lady Bird attracted a number of prominent Fort Worth women to Colonial Country Club the next morning. Events that morning assured members of Theta Sigma Phi that the scholarship we had proposed to give to a future journalism student would be funded. Lady Bird had agreed to be interviewed by a panel of local journalists. One woman reporter, in modish dress and a jaunty white straw hat, admitted she had flown in from Amarillo especially to be part of the program. It turned out she asked most of the questions.

After the Amarillo reporter asked several questions, snickers from those sitting near the front threatened to interrupt the interview. Most of the audience soon joined in as the truth dawned. Seth Kantor, a local reporter, knew time for confession had arrived. With the help and exclusive knowledge of Theta Sig members Betty Bob Buckley and Alice Guenzel, who had originated the idea, he had dressed in drag and submitted to a classy job of makeup early that morning. With gracious good humor, Lady Bird accepted her role as butt of a bold—but what now seems to have been a misbegotten—practical joke. She joined my list of heroes that morning.

When the head of the Aerospace Department at Texas A&M persuaded Charles to join the faculty in the fall of 1960, life with its strange turns pushed me into a different world in the fall of 1963. The all-man world that was Texas A&M was forced to open doors to women students. I walked in. Now it is clear why I chose women writers as subject of my graduate thesis. I identified with Carson McCullers' adolescent tomboys Mick in *The Heart Is A Lonely Hunter* and Frankie in *The Member of the Wedding*. McCullers had recaptured early teenage emotional turmoil that I understood. For my master's thesis, I explored McCullers's techniques for creating characters, but one major theme surfaced. Her adolescent girls with the boys' names feel strongly that they don't belong, not to society nor with their peers. Remembering those years as a country kid in small town high schools, I could identify.

Another theme surfaces in memory when I consider why I chose Caroline Gordon for my dissertation study. Main characters in her novels always seemed to be men except in *The Women on the Porch*, which reviewers named as one of her lesser works. Although in a two-page letter she vehemently rejected my proposal to look at folk narrative in her work, I prevailed. No doubt in my mind, she depended largely on family saga for detail in many of her novels, and particularly her most praised novel, *Alec Maury, Sportsman*, a favorite of writer John Graves I am told.

What intrigued me about Caroline Gordon, perhaps as much as her writing, were accounts of her marriage in 1925 to the poet Allen Tate. She joined my heroes when I read of that stormy marriage. Many summers Tate dithered while she wrote her fiction and entertained their many friends. At their farm outside Clarksville, Tennessee, Robert Lowell camped out in the front yard one summer, and Edmund Wilson (with his current wife) made himself at home while Caroline managed food and clean linens with the dubious help of an often-inebriated maid. Katherine Anne Porter joined the melee occasionally. Before her final split with Tate in 1959, Gordon had published eight of the nine novels she produced. That she wrote at all during those years won my admiration right away.

My first essay to appear in print explored "Folk Narrative in Caroline Gordon's Frontier Fiction." Appearing in *Heritage of Kansas*, an Emporia State publication, in 1977, the essay appealed to L.L. Lee and Merrill Lewis, professors I had met at the Western Literature Association annual meeting in Bellingham, Washington, in 1976. The co-editors included the essay in *Women, Women Writers, and the West* (1979). Here, I think, my interest began to create both the knowledge needed for research in what women write and for me, the determination to learn more. For the next five years, I researched women writers of the Southwest, presented papers at several conferences, and began to establish a modest reputation for having some knowledge of the lives and works of Texas women writers.

Mockingbird Lane

Donna M. Johnson

(1) The babies are crying again. I lie awake and listen from my third-story bedroom above the nursery. I listen for sudden stops, the stifling of the air that feeds the volume. I hear, or rather feel, my mother moving below me. She is a tall, slim woman, but her step is heavy, so heavy it shakes the upper story walls of the yellow farmhouse where we live, so heavy I feel the weight of her exhaustion as she pulls herself into the nursery. She has made this journey several times a night since the twins' birth three months earlier.

The squalls amp up dry and furious: a good sign. I see her in my mind's eye changing their diapers. A gradual quiet descends: another good sign. At night my mother cradles one twin in her arms and gives her a bottle; the other baby feeds from a bottle propped on a pillow in the crib. She switches off the babies during the day so that each of them gets held during a feeding. At night, the one who cries longer and louder gets the comfort. That's the way it goes in our family.

I am almost asleep again when my sister Carol calls out, "I want water. Wa-ter." I groan. Carol is three years old and outraged that she has been banished from my mother's bed. "I want water." This will be one of those nights when my mother's bedroom, located between the nursery and Carol's room, becomes a fulcrum from which she swings between three ravenous sets of need. The stairs that lead from the second story to the first creak as my mother trudges down to the kitchen, then back up. I hear Carol again, "No, Water! No! No! No!" The twins cry out in unison, indignant at being awakened by the whim of their toddler sister. I feel my way down the steep stairs that lead from my attic bedroom. The light switch at the bottom of the stairs is useless in these descents, and ambient light from the dormer windows does not reach this passage. I aim for the dim gray light at the bottom of the stairs, a man-made twilight coming from the outside carriage light.

Carol screeches like a tiny banshee, "No, water!" I hurry to her room and flip on the light. She stands inside the crib, clenching the rail and pointing at my mother. "You did it. You did it," she says. Water runs off her hair and face, the front of her pajamas soaked. My mother holds an empty glass. It takes a moment to figure out what has happened. My mother says she can't take any more and walks toward the twins' room. I run after her. She reaches down and picks up one baby, tells me to grab the other. She settles into the rocking chair, lifts one of these clinging creatures to her shoulder and reaches out for the other. She breathes hard, like a horse pushed too far. I peel off Carol's wet jammies and pull a dry gown over her head. It smells of fake flowers. She locks eyes with me and asks for water.

I am 14. Most nights I roll over and go back to sleep, leaving my mother on her own. Except for those times when fear pulses in my ears. My mother is alone on the second floor with two new-borns and a toddler. My mother, who is hot-tempered and high-strung, who says she should never have had children.

The father of these girls, my half-sisters, is the traveling preacher with whom my mother had a secret 20-year liaison. He divorced his wife around the time the twins were born, but it was too late for my mother. He already was involved with the woman who would eventually become his second wife. Their daughter is the same age as my twin sisters. The preacher denied this at the time, but my mother knew, and I knew because she confided in me.

(2) I stopped looking at my mother around the time my sisters were born. This is not hyperbole. The topography of her face overwhelmed me. It was all there: my father's abandonment of her, the preacher's use and misuse. Betrayal, grief, exhaustion. Her need for forgiveness, so much need. I could not bear to look at her again, to really *see* her, until she was old and sick and I was well past middle age.

(3) My mother left for the first time when I was five. She left and came back, left and came back. Her appearances and dis-

appearances lacked rhyme or reason at the time. She said God counted on her to help the preacher spread his message. She did not say she couldn't bear to be apart from him. Or that she missed the excitement of playing music on stage as part of his traveling team. Thousands felt the power of Sister Caroline's backbeat. They stood in line after each service to shake her hand and thank her for all she was giving up to help spread the Gospel.

My younger brother and I lived with seven different families, all strangers, during the three years my mother traveled. There are things you learn as a kid living in other people's houses. You learn to accommodate, to move tentatively, to look for signs. You learn to shape and reshape yourself, your face, into something you hope will please. You learn to read a stranger like a map, always on the lookout for a wrong turn. You learn the necessity of moving on.

(4) "These rooms," the AAers say, and their voices go soft at the edges, "these rooms saved me." These rooms soaked in cigarettes and coffee, in the memory of gin and white powder and rocks and pills and all of the implements we used to stop the grind in our heads and the twitch of our sad strange bodies. The AA meeting rooms had kept me sober for six months, the longest I had gone without a drink or drug since I was 14, half of my 28 years. I felt like something life had coughed up on the beach, half-formed and all raw awareness. The urge to participate in the larger world, and for me this meant the urge to write, began to stir. I went to work for free at a small town newspaper outside Austin. And so it was that I found myself interviewing an artist and telling him how the frosted whites and blues of his painted fields invoked the smell of fresh cut hay, a smell I had always loved as a girl. "That's it," he says, his voice hoarse with excitement. I glance up from my note-taking, and a look passes between us, a look I have not seen since my friends and I used to stay up all night talking about God and music and writing. The thought occurs that maybe I can exist in the regular world ... without the jacked-up excitement of methamphetamine or cocaine. Maybe I can *exist*. Maybe everything will be OK.

Just as I am about to let my shoulders drop and feel a bit of that OKness, it's gone. The artist tries to catch my eye again, but I can't return his gaze. Slowly, inexplicably, the feeling of connection dissolves. I am overtaken by the knowledge that I am different, alien, and most important, ashamed of my alien self. I stutter out a question. He looks at me, and his eyes reflect something ... something in me ... something I don't want to see. There is a flash of recognition, and I know. I am no longer me but *It*. A mask of scales and misshapen features. A grotesque beast. I end the interview abruptly and bump past stacks of paintings on my way out. "Excuse me," I say. I'm sorry. I am so, so sorry.

(5) A woman spoke in an AA meeting about losing her mother. "My mother died when I was eight," she said. She told the story of how her father forbade her to grieve and how her mother's absence formed the overarching narrative of her childhood and how everything that followed became subplot. She didn't use these words, but this is what I heard; this is what I understood. She was small and blonde, the kind of woman who makes a career of wearing long gowns and attending charity balls, the kind of woman whose face does not betray her. I liked the stiffness of her white button-down blouses, her perfect, manicured hands. Here was a woman who knew how to cope with tragedy. She agreed to be my Sponsor, the person I would turn to when despair threatened my sobriety. The Story of the Disappearing Mother spilled out in one long breathless ramble the first time I called her. There was a pause ... and a long inhalation. "At least she came back," she said. "My mother died when I was eight." No matter where the conversation led during subsequent conversations, we always circled back to "My mother died when I was eight."

(6) My daughter and I are driving in our new car, a green Ford Tempo the color of gel toothpaste, the cheapest one on the lot. I am in the driver's seat. She stares straight ahead, her jaw set, her silhouette framed in the passenger window against a garish sunset. At 14, she is a super star kid who is finding the transition to high school difficult. She is often unhappy during her freshman year. There was another long argument before we left the house. A plea to go dancing at a local honkytonk on Saturday night, like

everyone else, of course. I am afraid, afraid of her genes and mine and her dad's, but I don't tell her. Instead, I say no, no, no. She hates me. She puts her face close to mine when she tells me. My hand swings through the air as if of its own accord, and I slap her.

I will never hit my child ... The rest of that sentence left unspoken ... *like my mother hit me.*

Riding in the car that day, I try to ease the tension between us. "Look at that sunset," I say. "Nature is so healing." These are my actual words. My daughter does not budge. Finally, I say I'm sorry. I say it out right, and then I say it again in different ways. "I'm trying to protect you." I am an intruder, looking for a way in. "I want you to be happy." I do not hear the plea in my voice. I do not understand how heavy my need for her happiness has become and how long she has carried it. Straight A report cards. Academic awards. Cheerleader. First Chair All City Band. A smattering of freckles. She looks like the girl I never was, never could be. She turns toward me. "People think you are a nice person," she says. "You are not nice. You are a monster." My hands lie heavy as clubs on the steering wheel.

(7) I was 23, and my daughter was five when we rented the house on Mockingbird Lane. Fully furnished with quiet, tasteful pieces, it was the sort of place I associated back then with people who read *The New Yorker*. Thick white walls, white carpet, white sofas. Tasteful, creamy-sink-your-teeth-into-it white. A person could feel clean in a house like that. There was a stone patio bordered by fruit trees and iris; a narrow strip of grass where I put the swing set, a gift from my mother; and a small dog kennel at the back of the house. The rent was more than I could afford as a single mom, so I took on an extra roommate. The house was worth it. It looked like the sort of place where people could be happy.

The meth addiction I nursed for three years took a back seat to drinking on Mockingbird Lane, and since it's easier to function with a hangover than it is strung out from speed, life moved in a more normal routine. I took classes during the day and worked nights as a waitress. On my evenings off, I went out. My daughter needed me at home, and I wanted to be with her. But when the sun went down, I jonesed for the easy intimacy of people I barely knew, people who bought rounds of drinks, shook their shoulders to the canned beat, and mouthed song lyrics with their eyes held open wide. She tugged at my hand. *Don't go.*

I read an article recently about a curious phenomenon called Alien Hand Syndrome, a neurological disorder that can occur after brain surgery or as a result of stroke or infection. The syndrome causes one hand to function on its own against the will of the individual. The rogue hand picks up an item, perhaps a cupcake or drink, and the other hand knocks it away. The two hands engage in a battle of wills that becomes so intense an individual will often call out, "Stop!" or "I'm not doing this." An apt metaphor for addiction if ever there was one.

I regretted leaving, even as I pulled the door closed behind me. I longed to fly back to her even as I slipped the key into the ignition and pulled away. Saint Paul had it right. "For the good that I would, I do not: but the evil which I would not, that I do." Oh wretched man that he was, that we all are.

In another time and place, a shaman or an exorcist might have been sought. And although I had witnessed the traveling preacher perform exorcisms or perhaps because I had, I turned to a therapist. She spoke in low, soothing tones and told me that my needs were not at odds with my young daughter's. "You need the same thing. You need each other." She said this so many times I began to forget that my conflict had not been with my daughter but with myself. Just before I left, she took me around back of her home office. There in a corner of her carport lay a nest of puppies, round and cuddly and old enough for adoption. I wrote her a check, hugged her and took a puppy home.

(8) I wake to stale cigarette smoke, a dry mouth, and the low intimate discussion of weather on TV. I push up from the white couch and rest on my elbow. Coors Lite cans, 8, 10, 12, some with ashes on top, rising from the cobalt blue tile of the coffee table, a deep sea of color bleeding into all that white. Tubes of light shoot through the wooden shutters. The brightness alarms me. It's late. My legs automatically swing off the couch and that's when I see

her, across the room, legs curved at the knee, a strand of long red hair whipped across the soft rise of her cheek. My daughter, my six-year-old daughter, asleep in a corner of the room, head resting directly on the carpet, pale arm slung across a nubby stuffed dog, a present from an ex-boyfriend's mother. I see her there, a synthetic universe in orbit around her; Barbie with her candy-colored clothes, shoes and cars, little ponies that glow in the dark. Was she still wearing her clothes, or was she in her yellow footy pajamas? The air becomes thin. *I don't know. I don't know.*

(9) Most of us have at the center of our consciousness moments large and small around which experience, memory and story coalesce. They become a filter through which we view the world and the mirror that reflects who we are. *I was five the first time my mother left. My mother died when I was eight.* My daughter, my only child. *Was she still wearing her clothes, or was she in her yellow footy pajamas?* She says she doesn't remember.

(10) Three things my daughter remembers about Mockingbird Lane:

1980: Sounding out the word *cocaine* as I spelled it over the phone.

1982: Sitting on the roof with her best friend Kris N., drinking Cokes into the night and watching as men stumble from the party inside, turn their backs, and pee into the bushes.

1983: Finding the puppy dead in the kennel.

Here's the thing, I could not remember the last time I fed or watered the puppy.

(11) In the early days of sobriety, I thought I could make up for the past by not drinking or using drugs and by taking responsibility for my actions. AAers call this making amends. I took my 10-year-old daughter to Kiddie Land, an amusement park we frequented when she was very young, and told her I was sorry that my drinking and drug use had disrupted her life. She said she didn't understand. I tried to explain that the chaos of our home wasn't normal, that normal people didn't have their electricity turned off on a regular basis, that perhaps dinner was served at regular times at her friends' homes, that normal parents didn't smoke weed at

their kid's birthday parties. "That's what you were smoking?" She looked puzzled. I groped for a better explanation and blanked. I couldn't think of the dead puppy or the night she fell asleep on the floor when I passed out or the times I went to the emergency room in the middle of the night. I couldn't remember the big ways in which I had failed her, and I couldn't figure out how to explain the effects of addiction to a kid for whom those effects constituted normal life. I settled for telling her I would do better going forward. I wonder if she remembers this. I wonder if she thinks I have done better. Twenty-five years later, it all seems naïve and inadequate at best, selfish at worst. There is nothing to be done.

(12) *I don't know what I was thinking.* This was what my mother said when I questioned her, accused her really of abandoning my brother and me. There was amazement in her voice.

(13) I am behind the wheel, and this time it is Mother riding beside me. We are on our way to a party at my sister-in-law's house. My mother almost never socializes with people who are outside her religious milieu. It makes her nervous. In the car that day, her hands twist and she has a caught look on her face. I tell her it will be OK and place my hand on top of hers. I tell her about my own discomfort in social situations, and then for some reason, I tell her about the artist and the creature that surfaced the day of our interview. She looks stunned. "That's happened all of my life," she says. "But I never knew it until now."

(14) People have always said I look like my mother. As a kid, I searched the mirror for proof of their error; the flat oval of my face—unbroken by the cheekbones that so define her face. *I am not her.* My skin poreless with no trace of line or wrinkle. The tip of my nose rounded instead of pointed. I ran my hand over my forehead, cheeks, and chin, relieved at what I did not see, and ashamed, too, of what felt like betrayal.

I have formed my identity over the years in opposition to my mother. Where she stayed, I left, one relationship after another. Where she left, I stayed. *I will never leave my daughter.* And yet I found a way. The snap, crackle, pop of meth and coke setting my synapses ablaze. The wet blanket of alcohol smothering the last spark. I was gone, gone, gone.

(15) It is morning in the yellow farmhouse. My mother and I rock in the big white ladder back chairs on our front porch, each of us holding a tiny twin to our chests. The white of a mockingbird's wing cuts through the deep shade of the live oaks that shelter this house from the Texas sun. The scent of cut hay, cow manure, pond water, dust, coffee, exhaust, and pecan oil ripen the air. One breath could sustain you a lifetime, if you didn't choke on it first. I inhale and tell my mother as best I can about the fear that keeps me listening at night, that causes me to get up and make sure everyone is still breathing. I tell her I am afraid the crying will push her over the edge, that she will place a pillow over each of the squalling red faces and hold it there. I tell her I am afraid of the silence that will follow. She stares at me from eyes that have sunk so far into her head they look like feral creatures peering out of a cave. She shifts forward. I am grateful for the weight of the baby she holds, grateful to be out of reach. She would never, ever, hurt her children, she says. What would make me think such a thing? The impenetrable presence of the live oaks mocks me. Why *would* I think such a thing? My head is thick with thoughts and feelings I know are there but can't find. I shake my head. I can't think of a single reason why.

The Man at the End of the Hall

Guida Jackson

I ask if he's in the States for good. He, being Scottish, pretends to misunderstand and answers he's here for good or ill. He speaks in that hollow, disconnected voice of someone who's lost a spouse.

He asks where I'm from, not that he could possibly be interested. It seems more polite than saying: "Why are you here, in this place?" The response is predictable. If you're asking a widow like me, the answer will invariably be: "After my husband died, I didn't need all that room." If you ask a widower, he might answer: "I don't want to be a burden to my kids," which is what the Scot says. The underlying text is: "I don't want to die alone."

When we pass in the hall, he asks where I'm from. Despite his civility, he can't muster a spark of curiosity in the melancholy blue eyes. Not that I blame him. There's nothing remarkable about an aging ex-teacher. Or about the drab High Plains I come from, born in my grandparents' house built in 1912 in a town that had existed less than 40 years when my relatives moved there. It was pioneer land, back then. While Scotland had produced world-famous economists and philosophers by that time, and this country's East Coast was thriving in the Industrial Age, my part of West Texas was just being settled.

The plains must seem particularly dull to the Scot, born on Bellville Street in Greenock, within sight of all that wild and ancient beauty. Greenock has been there forever.

I'm told that Scotland has 790 islands. My prairie has no islands, no beaches, no lochs. He grew up eating fish; I had to develop a taste for it as an adult. His home has dramatic towering tors. My land is so flat that you can see all the way from Claude to Washburn.

In the parts of Scotland I've visited, there are water and spectacular grandeur wherever you look, and he tells me he's walked over a good portion of it. As a member of a rowing crew, he traversed nearby Loch Lomond daily.

I've seen a few of those standing stones from Scottish antiquity. I'm told a particular one, the Callanish, dates back more than 4,000 years, ranking second only to Stonehenge. I could hardly take in the idea of 53 gneiss stones, part marking an ancient chambered tomb. How can I match that?

Still, I try. I tell him about the red bluffs above the Canadian River 20 miles north of Amarillo, where we used to picnic. I've read that people have lived in Scotland for so long, there's not an inch of landscape that hasn't been altered due to human habitation. Well, he should see the hills north of my town. OK, they're just undulating rises, but they're man-made. They're grassed-over quarries.

For millennia, people traveled great distances to dig Alibates flint from there because it was perfect for the tips of their spears. As far back as the Ice Age, even before the Great Lakes existed, Clovis Indians used that flint to hunt the Imperial Mammoth. Many tribes came to that spot. It makes me wonder about their communications system. How did they know, up in Canada, about a flint lode in the Texas Panhandle?

I wonder also: Did the whole tribe travel to the quarries? Such a trek took months. Surely, they shot game along the way. Someone had to dress the kill. They must have brought their women; otherwise, they might escape. Besides, men were still in awe of a creature who could bleed and not die; could bring forth out of herself a live being. Did they feel the need to belong to someone? Was the limbic system involved at all? Did they care for one another, or was it simply a matter of group survival? Did they ever know the ecstasy of bare feet against bare feet?

Now the Alibates Flint Quarries is a National Monument, the only one in Texas. They've dammed the nearby river and made Lake Meredith—a national recreation area which certainly wasn't there on that stark Dust Bowl prairie during my childhood. So people can actually fish, and this generation of kids can know what a fresh-caught fish tastes like.

I've often pondered the origin of those vast monoliths in Scotland. The canny Scots must have figured that one out. Yet I know where Texans could find some stones, too, if we dug deep enough. And I'm not talking about flint. I mean granite.

Part of my heritage involves mountains that not only aren't on the map but until recently, weren't even Googleable. But now we know that there are actually mountains on that unbelievably flat prairie.

I'm talking about the Amarillo Mountains, a range that lies *under* the Alibates National Monument and extends over the Texas-Oklahoma border. They were discovered by early oilmen, who were drilling through the sediment and hit granite.

If you're driving east from Amarillo toward McClean and Oklahoma, you'll see a few rounded humps in the ground. They're actually hints of granite mountains buried 100 million years ago by sediment that accumulates faster than you'd dream—try not dusting your baseboards for a few weeks and you'll see. The Amarillos are the northwestern extension of Oklahoma's Arbuckle and Ouachita Mountains that reach into Arkansas. They're buried under thousands of tons of dirt, layered like so many strata of consciousness. Some peaks are said to be 10,000 feet high. You'd have to dig down 2,500 feet just to come to the top of the tallest peak.

Recently, the mountains have begun shifting, causing a few earthquakes here and there. We have a metaphor here, I could tell the Scotsman: there's more going on beneath the surface than you could ever imagine. The land may appear flat and drab, but if you attend to the rumblings at its unfathomable depths, they could shake you out of your socks!

Although I desperately want to, I don't know how to make this fascinating to him, who's seen it all. Can a person possibly be worth knowing who springs from such bleak surroundings?

But I try. I switch to the topic of cowboys and Indians. North of my hometown, there are remnants of old walls built of adobe—the scene of the last battle before the Indians gave up hope and settled on Oklahoma reservations. He could read about the Battle of Adobe Walls, but he can't visit the site because it sits on private property, and the rancher takes a dim view of tourists cutting his barbed wire and tramping across his land.

Still, there are plenty of other remnants of the Old West, which, by Scottish standards, isn't old. North of present-day Amarillo was a place called Tascosa, one of the first towns in the Texas Panhandle, the others being Mobeetie and Clarendon. Tascosa was the Cowboy Capital of the Plains. In the old days, lawmen and outlaws moseyed through and, if they tarried very long, often became permanent residents of Boot Hill, the first cemetery. You can still read some fairly infamous names on the gravestones leaning among the buffalo grass and tumbleweed.

Tascosa thrived during the 1870s and 1880s until the railroad bypassed it in 1915. The last resident left was Frenchy McCormick, widow of Tascosa's first saloonist. She held out until 1939 when Tascosa officially became a ghost town. That same year, Bivins Ranch donated it, along with 120 acres, for a place called Boys Ranch for troubled kids. The old stone courthouse and 1889 schoolhouse are all that remain of the original. Anyone can see what's left who'd care to accompany me.

We could see the site of the 1886 shootout between the LS Ranch's Home Rangers and a group of rustlers called The System. Those who survived the bloodbath reloaded to kill again. The others took up residence in Boot Hill. Walk among the tombstones, and the wind almost sounds like their moans. I had the same very experience among the standing stones in Scotland. So much savagery, layer upon layer.

Or how about this for drama? Drive 18 miles south of my town across a featureless expanse and suddenly the land drops off almost a thousand feet in places. We're on the rim of the nation's second largest canyon, roughly 120 miles long and from six to 20 miles wide. It's the edge of our best kept secret, Palo Duro Canyon, the Grand Canyon of Texas, with steep walls of multihued layers of rock, like the one in Arizona.

There are hints of its presence from the highway heading west, on that gradual, steady climb from Fort Worth to Amarillo, which sits more than 3,600 feet above sea level. Ahead you'll see that abrupt dropoff called the Caprock. You probably won't believe what you're seeing.

The canyon is a good metaphor for woman: so many levels gouged out in the earth's heart, deep and mysterious, changing color with shifts of sunlight and moonglow. By day, the beating sun searches the crannies and crevices relentlessly and, like a wise parent who has spun off her children to make it on their own, never wholly lets go.

Like its larger counterpart, the canyon was carved out of the earth's psyche, formed by a river, in this case, the Prairie Dog Town Fork of the Red River. It initially winds along the level surface of the Llano Estacado (Staked Plains) then precipitously leaps off the Caprock Escarpment like a roller coaster.

In Jungian terms, water, a feminine quality, easily flows and changes course when encountering obstacles. But water also has enormous strength—witness its power during tsunamis. During the millennia, water has shaped the canyon's vivid formations, including caves and hoodoos, tall, thin spires of rock protruding from the bottom of arid drainage basins. One of the best known reddish hoodoos, or fairy chimneys, is Lighthouse Peak.

Centuries before cowmen took over the canyon, it was a favorite campsite for prehistoric people who sought water, food, and shelter from devastating winter winds. The first known inhabitants, dating back to 10,000 B.C., were big-game hunters of giant bison and mammoths.

This haven has been continuously inhabited, most of the time by Native Americans. Apaches lived there when Coronado visited in 1541. Next came Comanches and Kiowas, who had the advantage of owning horses stolen from the Spanish. They thrived in that protected canyon, away from summer's heat and winter's ravaging blizzards. It's peaceful there, perfect for camping. Its wildlife knows no fear. Once during a family campout, my late husband woke to find a bird perched on his nose!

Still, I hail from a violent land, just like the Scotsman. There's not a tuppence of difference between bloodthirsty savages on either side of the Atlantic, as Dachau and Andersonville bear witness.

In 1874 Col. Ranald S. Mackenzie routed the Indians and moved them to Oklahoma. Sound familiar? Something like the Clearances in Scotland, when English land barons, wanting land for their sheep, drove thousands of people into Northern Ireland. Mackenzie accomplished his version of this grab by capturing 1,400 horses and slaughtering them in nearby Tule Canyon, thus forcing the Indians to move out.

A couple of years after the Indians left, Charles Goodnight and John Charles Adair established the huge JA Ranch there. Cowhands threw dances that lasted for several days. My aunt used to attend because my grandfather's land backed up to the ranch, which extended southeast into Caprock Canyon. Both are now State Parks, the second and third largest.

But I digress. The Scot inquires where I'm from, but perhaps he means where I'm coming from. Specifically, I'm from the stock who headed west after the Civil War, meaning disenfranchised Rebs or Yanks whose forefathers may've sailed from Glasgow, to start over—much as Highlanders had to do when they were "resettled" in Northern Ireland. The Panhandle held promise for destitute war veterans: there were few trees to clear, no stones to dislodge before plowing. Flat land meant easy tilling for farmers. Grassland meant plenty of open-range forage for cattle-raisers.

There was one catch. Make that two.

The first was the absence of water in dry seasons, when the playa lakes quickly disappear. Sometimes, even creek beds dry up. Even to water the livestock, you'd need to dig wells, construct windmills.

The second was the wind, necessary to turn the windmills. Ah yes, the wind, the God-awful, whining, twanging, nerve-jangling never-ending wind!

Put the two together, and as soon as you plow, you get blowing dirt. On that flat prairie, the sand can easily travel from Colorado. Unless you live in the canyon, there's no place to escape the miniscule bits of silicone, sharp as needles. It stings the skin, scratches the cornea, stops the nose, kills the chickens, chokes the livestock. It gathers in piles against any structure. It buries whole

fences. In winter, it is merciless and punishing, driving snow hori-
zontally against helpless cattle, interring them alive unless they
keep moving.

There is where my forefathers chose to settle. Over generations, they'd made it this far, from the Atlantic Coast, through
the Cumberland Gap, across Kentucky and Tennessee, into Illi-
nois in wagons or Conestogas, and finally across Indian lands into
Texas, hauling plows and chifforobes, trailing cows, pigs, mules,
and squalling, snotty-nosed, bare-footed offspring. At times, they
must have felt as desolate as the land. Maybe they were too worn
out to go a step further.

Is that why my Scotsman ended up here, in Houston? Had
he, filled with the optimism of a cocksure youth, set sail with new
wife and wee bairn and promise of a fine butt' n' board and a better job thousands of miles from the comfort of aunties and gran-
nies? On arrival, had he found the anticipated job had evaporated
and his electrical training credentials were not recognized? What
bravery, what folly, to embark on such an exploit! Did he realize
there was no turning back, no hope of survival other than gritting
his teeth and digging in?

There were times when he was so hungry, he contemplated
taking his own life. But his family responsibilities weighed heavily. Suicide was not an option. He worked at anything he could
find.

Now look at him: he did survive. Over half a lifetime, he even
prospered, and most of his scars are barely discernable. But they
made him what he is. We have both been tumbled by the gravel
of exigencies, honed by grating relationships, tenderized by others.

Happily, he hasn't lost what makes him Scottish, including
his brogue and his indignation toward injustice. And I haven't lost
what made me a fifth-generation Texan, including my twang and
a certain amount of grit in my craw.

I wonder at his passion for Burns, like my late husband's
devotion to Eliot, whose *Complete Works* he dragged through three
tours in Vietnam, to remind himself of who he was. When I ask
if my Scot would have the same passion for Robert Burns if he'd

remained in Scotland, he answers in the negative. Scots become more Scottish when they leave home, he says.

So here we are, grown old and long of tooth, both weathered by days fervently traversed, living within walking distance of each other, both having nursed spouses to the grave, both groveling through our bereavement and scrabbling through the accompanying ailments, still alive, still hanging on. For what?

He tells me that initially, he moved into this place to die. I understand. I plan to remain independent until they carry me out feet first.

Throughout our musing years, we have come to similar conclusions about the end of things. Neither of us harbors any delusions about the finality of life, but we have come to treasure the present moment as all there is.

A cousin sends photos of his trip to the High Plains: a new owner is renovating my birthplace, our grandparents' house, which has stood in decay for years. He takes a panoramic view from a hill across the swale from the house: I can see the very room where I came into this world. The site gives me a jolt. The place behind my eyes burns, as if I had been crying for perhaps years. I am consumed with gratitude and grief. Gratitude, because the house, now a century old, is being given new life. Grief, that there will be no renovation for me. The town and the life I knew are gone, except in vivid memories. As I grow older, those images sometimes have more reality than the present.

My life since then is also gone. The things my late husband and I strove for no longer seem significant, whether or not we achieved them. I question if we could possibly have ever known true and abiding love, so engrossed were we on striving for ourselves and for our children. How shallow was our self-importance, our time-consuming goals!

Now, for whatever kindness I have done that deserves reward, I have been offered it: the Scotsman wants us to spend our remaining days together. We're done with striving. Over time we've become what we are at this moment. It is enough and always was, had we but known it.

My daughter wants to take us on a road trip to show him my past. His daughters offer to do the same—to visit Scotland. We consider these offers from the comfort of what he calls Shangri-la and know that our memories are reality enough. His home in Greenock has been replaced by a high-rise apartment. My birth home belongs to someone else now. The majesty of his mystical land, the bleak starkness of mine, can still be ours anytime we care to squander our precious present in reminiscence.

My Scotsman abandons his end of the hall, for good. I don't use the word, "forever," because I know better than that. "Good" says it all.

Let Her Roll

Christine Warren

For me, the Guadalupe River and music go hand in hand. Admittedly, I tend to assign songs to most places where I've invested any significant amount of time, but more than other phases and stages, this river conjures up a deeply personal soundtrack. Perhaps it is the fact that the Guadalupe is the darling of the Texas Hill Country, and we all know that good music springs out of the Texas Hill Country more abundantly than any other place on Planet Earth. (I'm pretty sure they've proven that to be scientific fact.) So maybe the two are predestined to be natural bedfellows. Or perhaps it is because I kick-started life on this river at the same time I was cutting my teeth on good Texas music. Regardless, they seem intrinsically cross-stitched together in such a way that they flow seamlessly as one entity through some of my most poignant memories.

My life as an elementary school girl in the 1970s in Dallas was good. I had doting parents, plenty of laughter, cute friends, and a pet dachshund named Dallas Alice who was named for a character in a Guy Clark song we would sing over and over again on road trips. The joy of my heart was time spent down in the Hill Country at my grandparents' vacation home. The house, nicknamed The Rapids, was located near the small town of Hunt and was not far from the headwaters of the Guadalupe River, which ran through the backyard. There was a steep 40-foot hillside that led down to the water, providing natural protection from routinely menacing floods. In the 1950s my great-uncle built a house for his third wife just about 10 miles down the road. When the river flooded, the newlyweds climbed on the roof and clutched hands until they were swept off and forcefully wrenched apart. He spent the night in a treetop while his new bride died in the floodwaters. The family waited anxiously for word of her recovery. Her body was found three days later 30 miles down river near Comfort, of which I'm sure the news provided little.

The river was never a threat in my mind. It was practically Disneyland for my cousin and me. We would tube the rapids under the Cypress trees, perform water ballet in swimming holes, fish for minnows with toothpaste on our toes, picnic on the gravel bar and skip rocks competitively until someone cried after losing too many times. Grown-ups would pry us out of the water for bath time, a routine tick-check, and then dinner. Afterward, we'd all drive around the country roads and count deer before coming home to eat homemade ice cream. It's hard to reconcile now that such a simple time existed.

Activity in the old house, which had been my great-grandmother's, centered around a fabulous screened-in sleeping porch with daybeds to nap near the breeze, a coffee table for playing cards, and a dining area. The wood-paneled galley kitchen stayed crowded with grown-ups preparing, whisking, and cleaning. I'd enter at one end to try to sneak a treat and inevitably get pushed and prodded down as if it were a factory line and then be unceremoniously spit out the other end. Cocktail hour was on the rock patio; dinners were served at the long table in the den.

There was always music playing—recorded music, just to be clear. Everyone in my family seems only to have been blessed with the gift of music *appreciation*. When my parents had control of the turntable, they played outlaw music. This was the prime era for songwriters like Willie, Waylon, and Guy Clark. We lived so close to the hotbed of the outlaw movement that we could feel its heat, and my parents listened to it all. Back then this music wasn't novelty; it wasn't hipster cool. It wasn't labeled alternative and, thus, deemed acceptable by rock fans who would otherwise never stoop to listening to country. It was quite simply the music of the moment. It sounded the way Texas felt, and we loved it.

Summer Saturday nights were the best. That's when we drove around the bend to Crider's Rodeo and Dance Hall, which was on the same side of the highway as The Rapids, alongside the river. It opened in 1925 and is the oldest open-air dance hall in Texas. As a little girl, I literally could not get enough of everything Crider's had to offer, namely the rodeos. I couldn't have comprehended it if you'd have told me that there were poor deprived people in other parts of the country who weren't experiencing nighttime rodeos in the summer as I was. They named the meanest bull Ambulance because he was responsible for sending so many people to the hospital. I thought that was the cleverest thing I had ever heard. In my mind, bull names at Crider's rodeo were the pinnacle of humor and the watermark for truly great comedy.

The dance was right after the rodeo, but I was too young for it, which nearly tore me to pieces. I was not shy about letting my parents know that not staying for the dance was the single worst thing that had ever happened to me. I'm sure it drained my parents, who were trying in vain to make a clean escape from the rodeo. Meanwhile, I went back and forth begging, negotiating, kicking, rationalizing, screaming, and petitioning to stay for the dance. *Just a little while ... pretty please ... you all are evil ... I mean you're the best ... pah–leeez can't we stay?* I watched longingly as couples whirled around the alfresco dance floor, two-stepping to the fiddles under the stars. It looked like the best time anybody had ever had in their lifetime, anywhere, *ever*. I couldn't wait to be old enough to stay for the dance at Crider's.

Unfortunately, a few too many revelers were known to peel away from Crider's under the influence, lose control at the bend, and wreck their vehicles in my grandparents' yard. I found it exciting to wake up and see a sexy sports car dangling on our splintered, ranch-style fence, while the grown-ups fussed about it and handled the residual logistics. My grandmother grew weary of the nuisance; at least that's what I heard adults whispering. There were murmurings about flooding becoming a headache. I'm sure they had solid reasons, but in 1980 my grandparents decided to sell The Rapids. I pinpoint this as the first great loss I ever knew. I was devastated and desperately sad it would no longer be a part of life. At that age, I didn't realize how life insists on many closures, many conversions. No one had died on me yet, no one had announced a big move, and no one had tried to break my heart. This was my first thing to grieve. I was nearly 10.

Of course, now I look back with gratitude and realize I had one hell of a good decade in that house on the Guadalupe River—even though I never got to two-step at Crider's.

Life went on. I drifted away from the river. We moved to London, then Tennessee, and while I would return to the Texas Hill Country every summer for camp, it was to a different neck of the woods. From high school in Nashville, I went away to college in North Carolina, married shortly after, and set up life in Boston where my daughter was born. She was a one-year-old in 2000 when we moved to Austin and I found myself back near my old Guadalupe River stomping grounds ... two decades later.

By this point I was in my 30s and had become passionate, if not actually skilled, at fly fishing. I'd learned how in Montana on vacations with my family and aimed to try my hand with Hill Country trout. People are surprised to learn Texas actually has the southernmost trout stream in the country. In the 1960s, some executives at the Lone Star Brewery decided to stock the Guadalupe River with trout. After a series of tweaks from biologists, the result is a 24-mile fishable stretch of river that ends near the historic town of Gruene, admittedly more famous for its legendary honky tonk Gruene Hall than for trout fishing.

I made a few pilgrimages down to the lower Guadalupe. Once I wandered into Gruene Hall on a random Sunday afternoon and instantly loved the female singer who was the opening act for the opening act. A New Braunfels local, she had a killer voice, striking blond beauty, and personality to spare. Months later, she would make it to Nashville. The world would come to know her: Miranda Lambert.

After so many years, I found it powerful to see the river again with its steep limestone walls and well-grooved trees curving over emerald green water. I've never seen another river with the same greenish hue. It's mesmerizing. Memories flooded back. There's something amorphously painful about revisiting a place filled with childhood nostalgia when you're not at your best, and at this stage of life, I was most certainly not at my best.

As much as I talked about trying to fly fish on the Guadalupe, daily life created obstacles—a stressful job, a young toddler, a crumbling marriage. As a child, I had all the time in the world but longed to be old enough to get into the Crider's dance. As an adult, I was old enough to get down to the river and fish but couldn't find the time. But unexpected free time was coming my way.

It was Labor Day when my ex-husband confirmed he wanted a divorce. I wasn't blindsided. There had been talk throughout the summer, including a mutual Hail Mary attempt at reconciliation. Shutting down a marriage is rarely a linear process, progressing decisively from point A to point B. More often it winds, twists, stops cold, then lurches forward to its end.

I recall the vague sensation of being underwater. Things were happening fast, yet everything seemed in slow motion. Voices were muffled. I didn't respond with the typical triage one would expect. I didn't call girlfriends to huddle around me with an afghan throw, a bottle of Chardonnay, and all the supportive indignation they could muster. Instead, I packed an overnight bag and drove down to the Guadalupe. I'm not sure how long I trolled up and down River Road before I checked myself into a La Quinta on the service road of I-35. My head throbbed violently. I needed air, but I was kicking my way to the surface too fast and suffering some sort of emotional version of the bends.

Even at the time, I knew how comically desperate it was to languish in a low-budget chain motel on the interstate surrounded by nothing more than a remote control and fast food take-out bags. So I pulled myself together and made it to over Gruene Hall to see Charlie Robison perform. I'd seen him there before, knew all the words. I watched the crowd, full of life, dancing and singing along with the band. My head pounded with each drumbeat as I ached to enjoy myself. I didn't enjoy myself at all, but Robison's crumpled appearance, honky tonk lyrics, and screw-it-all-beer-guzzling attitude were a poetic way to survive one of those days simply meant to be survived.

It took a year or so, including some false starts, but all-in-all, I blossomed from there. I dragged friends down to float the

Guadalupe by day and see live music at night. The river became a source of true recreation. I started researching gear I would need to fish it by myself. I questioned local fly shops, read discussion boards online. I joined the local Trout Unlimited chapter, a conservation group responsible for restoring a river that in a way was restoring me. Once I was ready, I waded into the river on my own, cast my line onto the water, and fished.

I had a few nibbles here and there, but I couldn't bring anything to the net. I needed more instruction, local expertise. I asked my parents for a guided day on the water as my Christmas present, and a few weeks later on a freezing January day, I floated the river with a fishing guide. He taught me well. After all my years playing on the Guadalupe, and all my years fishing on other rivers, I finally caught my first Texas trout. I celebrated that night in Austin at the legendary Antone's, where I saw Will Hoge perform. My toes stayed frozen from the day on the river, but the show was red hot, and I was soaring from the fishing and the music.

Things flowed along brilliantly from that point into spring. My daughter was thriving, which made everything else hum. I fished the river regularly and met new friends at Gruene Hall for live music and cold beer. I was writing more and more, and people seemed to want to read as much as I could put out there. And then, on pitch with everything else that was going so well, a guy from Alabama came onto my scene.

Our first date was to a music festival in Live Oak, Florida, where we camped near the Suwannee River, saw incredible music, flirted shamelessly, and laughed around a campfire. You could have knocked me over with a feather duster when my old hero Guy Clark took the stage, playing several of the hits I listened to as a girl with my parents. We had a fantastic time, and the momentum rolled on from there. Our second date was Memorial Day weekend in Austin, where we started with a Junior Brown show. The next morning, we drove down to Gruene and spent the day along the river. There's something joyous about revisiting a place filled with childhood nostalgia when you're falling in love. The river was aglow, and the fact that he seemed to appreciate the whole scene made me appreciate him even more. That night we saw an electric Cross Canadian Ragweed performance at the River Road Icehouse that had us singing and dancing at the front of the stage like a couple of high school sweethearts.

From our earliest days in Florida and Texas, and then later, trout fishing in Montana, ours is most definitely a romance born of rivers and music. It's a theme we couldn't shake if we wanted to. That's just where we tend to find our luster. But for me specifically, the Guadalupe is a river of second chances, a repository of personal history, harmony, and hope. Not to mention, it's still the best place for an old-fashioned, honky-tonking Saturday night. I may have ventured off course a while, but just as the river keeps on rolling, the music keeps on flowing. You see, the band still plays at the oldest open air dance hall in Texas. Apparently, it wasn't a certain *age* I was waiting on to dance at Crider's under the oak tree alongside the river. It was love.

Lotería: La Rosa

Mary Guerrero Milligan

Grandma's house is now a barbershop. I drive past wondering if I should take my son in for a haircut. I decide not to because he is very particular about his hair and this doesn't look like his kind of barbershop—a barbershop on a downtown San Antonio side street with a red and white pole in front. And yet I haunt the house. My spirit has walked past the barbershop pole through the shop's walls past the hair clippings and scissors to my grandmother's kitchen.

I return again and again, as a little girl, to her kitchen. Standing in front of Grandma's kitchen table, I see her sitting with her two neighbors, lotería game boards in front of them. It looks like a grown-up birthday party, but Grandma says that Mexican bingo is *not* a children's game.

Playing for pennies, each player has three or four game boards and a handful of pinto beans for markers. The deck of cards is in the center of the table, face down. Grandma turns them over slowly, one at a time. I love looking at the different lotería cards. Each picture coloring my otherwise black-and-white memories. I stare at each beautiful picture, as real to me now as then. The brightly colored sandía still makes my mouth water, so perfectly ripe and juicy. Even now, whenever I pass a fruit vendor selling watermelons, I wonder if they could possibly be as sweet as la sandía in Grandma's kitchen.

I try to be patient as I wait for number 48, la chalupa, to be called. Will she be called this game or will I have to sit through another until I see her again? Lovely and graceful in her narrow boat, I long to squeeze between her fruits and flowers and join her in her travels. Where is she going? Will she ever have room for me? Her card, more than any other, is alive for me. I can hear the gentle ripples as her boat glides through the water. Once when I touched her picture, my finger came away moist.

I often walk by the San Antonio River and, sometimes, when the water is especially calm, I can see the faint ripples of a narrow boat that has recently passed. Where is la chalupa going? Is anyone riding with her? Will she ever let me join her?

In Grandma's house, I am stripped of all that time has given me, able to revisit my earliest memories. Today I am waiting for a new lotería game to begin. It is a hot, sticky afternoon, but Grandma is refreshed from her nap and ready for a long session of bingo. Anticipation makes everyone silent. Except for the steady hum from the fan in the corner and the shuffling of the cards, the room is quiet and still. Pete in his tank-top undershirt and his wife Andréa in her brown print house dress watch my Grandmother carefully as she shuffles the cards—once, twice, three times. Placing the cards face down in the middle of the table signals the start of a new game.

The first card called is:

La Rosa

Waking up heavy with sleep in my grandmother's bedroom, I hear the sound of bells. The room is cold, but I am warm deep beneath the covers. The house is dark, except for two candles flickering on the altar in the next room. I can see Grandma's silhouette. She is kneeling in front of the candles, as still as her statues on the altar. While the shadows dance around the altar, I begin to doze, when I again hear the sounds that woke me up.

I know what it is: clip clop clip clop jingle jingle jingle. Wide awake, I throw off the covers, my heart pounding with excitement. "Quién viene? Santa Claus? Con reindeer?" Christmas Day is almost two weeks away, and I don't understand how this can be happening. Shivering with cold, I try to see out the window by the bed. The window is foggy from the cold, and I wipe it with my sleeve, making my arm feel wet and chilled, but I don't care. I will see Santa tonight.

"No, no mija. Son los caballeros. Van a cantarle a la Virgen," answers my grandmother. Now that I have rubbed the mist from the window, I can see the horses clearly. Two rows of black and silver riders wearing huge sombreros ride slowly past us carrying guitars and trumpets. I hear their soft strumming intermingled with the horses' hoof beats against the paved street.

As the riders shrink into the night, Grandma explains that today is the day we sing las Mañanitas to la Virgen de Guadalupe. Before sunrise the riders will serenade la Virgen in front of the church. She tells me how special today is for la familia in Mexico. As I begin to get sleepy, I listen to her stories about visiting la Virgen with candles and roses. She reminds me that spring will soon be here and that her garden will be filled with many beautiful roses and, if I want and if I am good, I may choose any of her roses to give to la Virgen and to my teacher at school. Under the covers again, I drift back to sleep as the dawn begins to creep behind the office buildings, and the church bells begin to ring. I think about the rose bushes sleeping outside the bedroom window that will soon be filled with roses and I am not disappointed that it is still almost two weeks until Christmas.

The roses are long gone, yet their scent fills my mind. I walk through her garden, down her street, trying to recapture my lifeblood, but I stand in the middle of a parking lot. I am a barbershop ghost, searching.

Downtown was Grandma's neighborhood. We walked everywhere: to her work at El Teatro Alameda, to the Cathedral, to eat at El Bohemio, to visit the local curandera or to shop at El Mercado. An impatient walker, she refused to acknowledge traffic lights, racing across streets. She'd never wait and would walk against the light regardless of the traffic. I'd ask her why we were risking our lives. She would point to the red "DON'T WALK" and remind me in Spanish, "Yo soy Mexicana y ... I—don't—read—English."

On bad weather days we'd take the Shopper's Special. Paying a nickel, we'd ride the slow-moving bus as it crawled its way through town. It was entertaining to listen to the passengers on the crowded ride: fast-talking viejitas, loud talking muchachos, English, Spanish, crying babies, giggling school girls in their Catholic school uniforms. And as soon as we were off the bus, Grandma would argue about how much faster it would have been to walk.

I loved our walks together. Grandma was not a silent walker. She talked as fast as she walked. No light conversations or playful chatter; instead, a steady catechism about the way I should live my life. While I explored her neighborhood, she'd explore my heart. Even now the noise, the color, the smell of downtown take me back to those walks.

<hr/>

Another cold, early morning. It is a little after sunrise when we enter El Bohemio. My mother and I have joined Grandma an hour earlier to help her finish cleaning the office buildings across the street. Now all three of us are ready for breakfast. The aromas remind me of my hunger while the mariachi music from the jukebox keeps me awake.

This morning Chorte is our waiter. He is my favorite as well as a friend of my grandmother. With an easy smile and a gentle manner, he shares his daily story with us. They are usually funny, and I eagerly await his new tale. I order my regular El Bohemio breakfast: one barbacoa taco and one chorizo con huevo taco. As we wait for our tacos, we sip our coffee. I drink some of Grandma's coffee in her small glass creamer. She always drinks sugary coffee with lots of milk. It is warm and sweet.

But this morning I don't like Chorte's story. It's about catching a pigeon in the park for last night's supper and I can't believe any of it. That he was able to catch it, or that he would want to or that he, my dear friend, could ever do such a thing. I try not to cry or show the pain I feel inside, but Grandma senses it and doesn't approve. After he leaves, Grandma is angry with me. She points out that the pigeons in the park are food to him, not pets, and that in Mexico where she and Chorte are from, people sometimes have to do worse. But what is worse than eating the park pigeons that come to you because you will feed them? She reminds me that barbacoa is a cow and chorizo is a pig and that farmers feed their animals lovingly right up to the time of their slaughter.

We finally get our tacos and now I am mad at Grandma for telling me that my wonderful breakfast might be some little girl's pet so I begin to eat my taco like a gringa. I take big bites right down the middle of the taco, eating it like a sandwich until it is split in half. Grandma watches me with growing displeasure. Telling me that I am eating it all wrong, she shows me the Mexicana way. She squeezes one end tight with her fingers to keep the juices in and bites from the opposite end. I laugh to myself as she demonstrates the proper way.

———————

I try to retrace our walks: to the Cathedral, El Bohemio, back to her home. But like a puzzle with missing pieces, the picture is incomplete. Standing in front of her bedroom window, amid the long-dead rose bushes, I knock against her window, hoping to wake her up, but my hand goes through the wall.

An Uncommon Proposal

Betty Wiesepape

Ransom Filmore Holland took Vera Kate Bruner to be the mother of his five children on December 24, 1913. It was not the kind of wedding young women dream about. No courtship, no matching gold bands, no long white wedding dress—only a hurried buggy ride to purchase a marriage license and stand before a justice of the peace before the Smith County courthouse closed for the Christmas holiday.

When Kate and Ransom arose at dawn that cold December morning—she to build a fire in the cook stove of the boardinghouse she managed, he to bring the cedar tree he'd cut the previous afternoon into the parlor so the children could decorate it while he went to Tyler—neither had any idea they would be man and wife by sunset. Whenever family members asked them in years to come how their marriage came about, they said it was a "business arrangement."

If pressed for more details, Kate might have admitted she noticed the tall Southerner with the Alabama accent the first time he stopped in for a home-cooked meal at the Tyler boardinghouse. Standing six feet four-and-a-half inches tall, Ransom would have been difficult to overlook, especially for Kate, who stood only a fraction more than five feet in her stocking feet. But it was not Ransom's height so much as his posture, grooming and easy Southern manners that made him a favorite with boardinghouse staff. Whenever he came to town, his face was shaved, his shoes were polished, his khakis were starched and pressed. Before he came inside, he wiped his feet on the doormat and removed his felt hat. These were things a woman like Kate Bruner would have noticed, but she would have dismissed any attraction she felt the instant she found out Ransom was married.

Short and plump with a plain-looking face and prematurely white hair, Kate was not a woman who attracted attention.

Nevertheless, she kept her distance from her male clientele so none of them got the wrong impression about the kind of business she was operating. But avoiding Ransom Holland was not easy. He was well-read, well-spoken, and quite the talker. Every time Kate came near his table, he attempted to engage her in conversation.

Kate felt more at ease around Ransom when his brother came to the boardinghouse with him. Webster Holland, who was closer to Kate's height than Ransom's, wrote gospel hymns, and on occasion, Webster would sing one of his hymns while Ransom accompanied him on the upright piano in the boardinghouse parlor. From the brothers' conversations, she learned Ransom's wife, Margaret, was expecting a baby. Kate couldn't help the pang of envy that stabbed her stomach like a knife when she found out Ransom and Margaret already had four children. All Kate had to show for five years of marriage were two locks of fine blond hair she'd cut from the heads of two still-born babies.

Once Kate determined all Ransom wanted was an audience for his stories, she began to feel more comfortable in his presence. She even started calling him Rance, the name he said he preferred, and she began to look forward to the Holland brothers' trips to Tyler—to deliver a load of cotton, to settle accounts at the bank, to stock up on groceries for their families.

One day in February when the brothers came to town to buy seeds for planting, Kate gave each of them a packet of snapdragon seeds she'd collected to take home to their wives. Rance thanked Kate and promised that the next time he came to town, he would bring Margaret along so Kate could meet her. But that never happened.

The next time Rance came to the boardinghouse, he came alone, and he'd lost so much weight Kate almost didn't recognize him. His shoulders were stooped, and his eyes had a hollow look about them that Kate recognized immediately. She was a young teenager the first time she'd seen that look on her father's face after he told her that her mother was dead, and for the better part of a year after the deaths of each of her babies, she'd seen that same hollow look each time she walked past a mirror.

Kate knew, even before Ransom told her, that something tragic had happened to someone in his family. Shortly after giving birth to a healthy baby girl, Margaret had developed an infection that resisted all his aunt's and sister-in-law's home remedies. Then on top of the infection, she contracted German measles. By the time Rance summoned a doctor, Margaret was so weak and the infection so advanced that she didn't respond to treatment. Margaret died when baby Ruth was 13 days old, and for the last seven months, Rance had been trying to be both mother and father to five children younger than the age of 10.

"I've tried. Lord knows I have, but I can't do this by myself," he told Kate as she set a platter of fried chicken on the table. "I can't take care of my children and work enough to put food on the table. I need someone like you to help me."

Kate, unbeknownst to Rance, had a hearing problem and thought he was about to offer her a position as housekeeper. As she made her way back to the kitchen, her mind was racing to think of a way to turn him down without hurting his feelings. Even if Rance could match her salary at the boardinghouse, which she doubted, she couldn't afford to give up a job that included free room and board.

As soon as Kate returned to the table with a bowl of mashed potatoes, Rance continued his one-sided conversation. "You can cook. That's important, and I've known you long enough to know you're a good woman. And you're a good listener, and I'm lo ..."

"Excuse me," Kate interrupted. "I have biscuits to take out of the oven."

When she returned with the biscuits, Rance pulled out a chair and motioned for her to sit down, but Kate ignored the chair and hurried back to the kitchen for a bowl of cream gravy.

"So how about it, Katie? Will you marry me?" Rance blurted out the proposal before Kate could take off for the kitchen again. "I need someone to help me take care of my children, and you need a husband who can make you a good living."

A husband?! Kate was so surprised she almost dropped the bowl of cream gravy in Rance's lap. Not only was his proposal sudden, it was frightening. She'd read magazine stories about passionate love between men and women. Before she married Mr. Bruner, she'd even dreamed that someday, such a thing might happen to her, but it hadn't. She had respected her first husband, a man many years older than she, but she had not loved him the way Rance obviously had loved Margaret. Kate had never even called Mr. Bruner by his first name, not even when they cuddled together beneath the quilt from her hope chest.

"Face it, Katie," her stepmother had told her, "you could do worse than Mr. Bruner." And because Kate was approaching 30 and because, more than anything, she wanted to have children, she had said yes to Mr. Bruner's proposal. Now five years and two still births later, she was a soon-to-be 35-year-old widow with prematurely white hair who lived in a single room in the boarding house she managed.

Rance was honest. He didn't pretend he loved Kate. He said it was too soon after Margaret's death for him to love anyone. He was offering Kate a "business deal." These were his exact words, and they sent Kate scurrying back to the kitchen without giving Rance an answer. He waited a while, gazing out the window at nothing in particular. Then he placed a dollar bill on the table, picked up his hat, and departed the boardinghouse.

Almost as soon as Kate heard the front door close behind him, she began to have doubts about her decision. She knew she could do worse than Ransom Holland. As soon as word got around that Ransom Holland was available, women would be lining up to take advantage of his business deal. But what if she accepted his proposal, and after they married, Rance met a younger, more attractive woman? That was something Kate had not had to worry about with Mr. Bruner, but she was three years older than Ranson. And what about the children? Kate had never even met Rance's children. The baby would be easy enough to win over, but how would the nine-year-old boy and seven-year-old girl react to someone taking their mother's place so soon after her death? Margaret had only been dead seven months. That was sure to set tongues at the Baptist church to wagging. Not that any of that mattered now. It had been more than a month since Rance proposed marriage, and he had not been back to the boardinghouse since. Kate doubted she would ever see him again.

We can only imagine the look of surprise on her face when she unlocked the front door of the boardinghouse and saw Rance standing on the porch with his hat in his hand. No one knows exactly what transpired that Christmas Eve, except that sometime between his arrival at the boarding house and their buggy ride to the Smith County courthouse, Kate told Rance she had changed her mind and would accept his proposal. What they did the rest of that day will forever remain a mystery. Kate must have returned to the boardinghouse to pack up her belongings, and she probably had to give notice and arrange for one of the other employees to take over as manager. Rance still had to stock up on groceries and purchase something to put in the children's Christmas stockings. All we know for certain is that it was well past dark when Rance and Kate arrived at the farmhouse in Bullard.

The corners of my Aunt Lucille's mouth always curved into a smile when she told what she remembered of that long ago Christmas. Rance's Aunt Catherine, who had moved into the house to help Rance with the children shortly after Margaret's death, had departed earlier in the day to spend Christmas with relatives in Ellis County, leaving eight-year-old Lucille and 10-year-old Otho in charge of their younger siblings. The children spent the afternoon stringing popcorn, cutting paper snowflakes, and hanging foil stars and tinsel streamers until every branch of the cedar tree held something that sparkled. Only the angel with the white hair and silky white dress remained in her box on the settee because neither Cile nor Otho were tall enough to place her on the topmost tree branch.

When it began to grow dark and their father still had not returned, Cile fed the children the cornbread, milk, and stewed apricots that Aunt Cath had left for their supper. Otho helped two-year-old Hugh put on his pajamas and listened to his and Aline's prayers, while Cile rocked baby Ruth to sleep and placed her in her crib.

Cile eased the door to the girls' bedroom closed and tiptoed down the hallway to the top of the stairs before she realized her feet were bare. If her mother were alive, she would have sent Cile back to the bedroom to fetch her slippers before she caught her "death of pneumonia." But Cile didn't want to take a chance of waking her baby sister, so she ran as fast as she could down the stairs and into the parlor, where she sat in Margaret's sewing chair and tucked her mother's flannel coverlet around her bare feet. Cile didn't know what pneumonia was, but she knew she didn't want to catch it. She knew what death meant. It meant God took you far away from the people you loved and never let you come back.

She ran her fingers over the wooden arms of the chair where Margaret's hands had rested. Cile felt closer to her mother when she sat in the rocker, but she rarely got to sit there. The rocker was Aunt Cath's favorite place to sit, and Papa had said they should be respectful and let her sit wherever she wanted to sit—because Aunt Cath was doing them all a favor.

"She's not doing me any favors," Otho said, scrunching his freckled face into a pout. Papa scolded Otho, but Cile silently agreed with her brother. Aunt Cath mostly just sat in the rocking chair and told Otho and Cile what to do. Cile didn't dislike Aunt Cath, but she was glad their great aunt was spending Christmas with their cousins in Ellis County.

Cile was sound asleep when Rance pulled the buggy to stop at the front gate and he and Kate came quietly into the house. Kate waited in the parlor while Rance carried her suitcase and trunk to the upstairs bedroom. She was bending over the Christmas tree to inspect the children's homemade decorations when Cile opened her eyes. With the light from a nearby lamp illuminating Kate's white hair, Cile thought, in that moment between dreams and reality, that the Christmas angel had somehow gotten out of her box and come to life.

Kate and Rance rose early the following morning, Rance to bring a load of firewood into the house and fill the children's socks with nuts and oranges and ribbon candy, Kate to make pancakes for their Christmas breakfast. Then Rance went upstairs to wake the children. When everyone was awake and seated around the Christmas tree, he went to the kitchen, took Kate by the hand, and led her into the parlor. "Look what I brought you for Christmas," he said to the children, "a new mother."

And as if the baby Ruth understood what her father was saying, her face lit up in a smile, and she held out her arms to the woman who henceforth would be known as Mama Holland.

If this were a fictional story, this would be a good place to end, but real life doesn't stop at happy endings, just as all step-mothers are not wicked. The marriage that began as a business arrangement endured for more than 40 years and produced three additional Holland children. During those years, Rance and Kate, like most married couples, endured their share of hardships and heartaches—drought, crop failure, the Great Depression, and a fire that destroyed their house and the only existing picture of their first Christmas together. They sent one son off to fight in WWII and buried their youngest at the age of 29.

The relationship between Kate and the Holland children began as love-at-first-sight because of their desperate need for one another, and over succeeding years, the bond between them grew even stronger. Kate never referred to them as her stepchildren, and they never referred to her as their stepmother or to her and Rance's children as half-brothers and sisters. Their son Hugh, who was a two-year-old the Christmas Rance and Kate got married, said he was never sad that his birth mother died because he had the best mother a boy could have.

I wish I could say that Rance grew to love Kate as much as he had once loved Margaret, but he did not come to a full realization of how much he loved Kate until she was dying. Then he sat for hours beside her bed, talking to her and holding her hand. After she died, he told people that he had been a fortunate man because God had blessed him with two wonderful wives.

Before Kate became ill, he only talked that way about Margaret. He talked so much about her, often in Kate's presence, that

I hoped she couldn't hear what he was saying. He wanted so desperately for Margaret's children to remember their mother and for her grandchildren to know something of the woman whose DNA they carried that he never quit showing pictures of her and telling how beautiful and talented she was. As a result, Margaret took on mythical proportions and became like a goddess or fairy princess who served as a measuring stick for her female descendants' looks and accomplishments. None of her daughters were as pretty or as sweet or as accomplished as their mother, and as each granddaughter came of age, her picture was compared to Margaret's.

In the image of Margaret that is embedded in my brain, she is a lovely young woman in her 20s, wearing a white Gibson Girl dress with leg-o-mutton sleeves, and she has the same dark brown eyes and hair I had when I was a bride of 20. But it was Mama Holland, the short, plump middle-aged woman with beautiful white hair who taught me to embroider, to shell peas, to churn butter, and to lift an egg "oh so gently" from a hen's nest. She's the grandmother I remember, when the family gathers in my living room and I look up to the top branch of the Christmas tree and see an angel wearing a halo atop her snow white hair.

My Memorial Day

Frances Brannen Vick

There are three graves that lie together in Lake Jackson Rest-wood Cemetery that always carry two flags on Memorial Day. One belongs to my brother's grave, and one belongs to my father's grave. There should be one on my mother's grave, too. Her sacrifice was as great.

I have my mother's copy of *Best Loved Poems of the American People*. It is both painful and uplifting to read through it and look at the notes she left on some of the poems. One of the most painful to read is "I Have A Rendezvous with Death" by Alan Seeger, where she has written, "The last poem I heard my son give, December 11, 1944." And she has added what my brother said after reciting it: "Woman, you didn't know I was an Alan Seeger man, did you?"

He apparently was trying to prepare her for whatever might come when he went overseas and into action. And it did come, on May 9, 1945, in a bombing raid on a supposed kamikaze base, when ground fire brought down Crew 17, Patrol Bombing Squadron 102 in their PB4YI, with my brother Andy on board. He lies out there somewhere in the deep of the Marianas Trench.

In "Bingen on the Rhine" by Caroline Norton, where the "soldier of the Legion lay dying in Algiers," my mother has bracketed the following lines:

> Tell my sister not to weep for me,
> and sob with drooping head,
> When the troops are marching home again
> with glad and gallant tread,
> But to look upon them proudly,
> with a calm and steadfast eye,
> For her brother was a soldier too,
> and not afraid to die.

I have always assumed she meant for me to read that and act accordingly, which I have tried to do down through the years, but I find it harder to do so in my older years than in my younger. The tears come much easier now.

My mother—Bess Brannen—died in 1958, at age 53, 13 years after my brother was shot down over Marcus Island in the South Pacific. She battled cancer from 1953 until her death, which my brother Pat says was really caused by a broken heart. I can't argue with him. However, it left the task to me to be the one who represented the family at different monument raisings and such in later years. True to the admonition to "not weep for me," I carried out those functions to the best of ability in my mother's stead.

When my father, Andrew Brannen, was approaching his death in 1977, he asked my brother Pat to arrange a military funeral and said he wanted it to be a joint funeral, since there had never been one for Andy. My father had been a Marine in World War I and World War II, and although he was a schoolman through and through, having taught and been an administrator for more than 35 years, he felt deeply about the Marine Corps. It also apparently bothered him that no funeral had ever been held for Andy, although the tombstone had been erected, which gave all the appropriate information.

There had been no funeral because the telegram that came said Andy was missing in action, although my mother knew from the beginning that he was gone. My father held out hope, until the war was over in August, that Andy had been captured and was a Japanese prisoner of war. I guess that by the time the final telegram came, they thought it was too long after the fact to hold a service.

The funeral was to be arranged through the local American Legion Post, the one named Andy Brannen American Legion Post 306 for my brother. My brother Pat made the mistake of asking our father if he wanted Marines to be the honor guard, which our father said "yes" to with alacrity. As Pat said, from then on our father told everyone to be sure to come to his funeral because it was going to be a real show, complete with Marines. Pat said it took some doing getting the Marines there, but after he told the colonel in Galveston that our father always said the Marines took care of their own, he agreed to be there with an honor guard. As Pat writes, "The Marines showed up on time and, true to Dad's promise, they put on an outstanding show. The captain joined Mother and Andy in style, with a half-dozen sharp Marines as sideboys."

My father had received four beautifully printed commendations from the French government for service during World War I that I had framed and displayed in our home where Dad was living during his last illness. We took those to the funeral and displayed them beside his casket. The honor guard was duly impressed that they were doing duty for a Marine who had served in five major battles during World War I and in Pershing's Honor Guard afterward. I am impressed, too, after going to the sites of those battles and reading about them and seeing what he had to do.

Blanc Mont was particularly hard to visit. That is where my father had been wounded, and looking up at the chalk white hill and the distance between where the Marines jumped off and the top, it was nothing short of a miracle that Pat and I were standing there together looking at the ground over which our father had dodged bullets years before we were born. He should never have lived through it. So many didn't.

His lieutenant, John Overton, a Yale track star he admired tremendously, had not made it. He had been killed at Soissons. My father wrote that the last he saw of Overton in the charge across the sugar beet field, "He was walking backward and trying to shout something back to us. He carried his cane in the left hand and a .45 pistol in the right. The din and roar was so terrific that I didn't have any idea what he was saying, but interpreted it from his expression to be some words of encouragement. He was soon down, killed."

My father spent that day in a sunken road, far out in front of the other troops, unable to move without getting shot at by German guns. Late in the evening, he was able to find some Marines in a ditch and crawl over to them. They were relieved some time after midnight, so he again escaped death. John Overton is one of the ones he remembered on Memorial Day. I was always told that had I been a boy, my name would have been John Overton, so he became a hero to me, too.

I remember my father wearing a red poppy in his lapel in the old Memorial Days when those poppies were sold with the funds going to the disabled veterans. The history says the poppy money was for the orphaned children and widows of the veterans, so perhaps that was so. In any case, the red poppies were prominent around the house during those years. I do not see them now.

My own personal memorial day, as was my mother's, is May 9. On the Sunday closest to that date, my mother always had red roses put on the church altar in honor of her son who had fallen in battle. I do, too, although the altar guild picks the flowers to use, and I have added my father's and my mother's names to the remembrance, along with Andy's. I expect my children will do the same. Although we lost Andy all those years ago, he has never been forgotten, even by nieces and nephews who never knew him. Nor has their grandmother, whom they never knew, either.

Two of my granddaughters bear her name, as does a school in Lake Jackson, Texas. She had heroically pulled herself together enough to make a very big difference to students in her care. I have a nephew and a great nephew who bear Andy's name. My son wears an Andy Brannen hero bracelet. So none of them have ever been forgotten, nor the sacrifices they made. And particularly not on Memorial Day.

Blue Hole

Susie Kelly Flatau

Looking forward, I fly forever; looking backward, I never land. And somewhere in between, life is framed in frozen moments—moments when Mother Nature invites us to linger for a bit in her sacred spaces, asks us to pause, to appreciate her purity. If we are open to this invitation, we enter nature's diaphanous world of beauty and design—a world from which we are never turned away, a world within which we forever feel her grace.

We hear her melodies as they float upon gentle breezes. We sway to the songs of her lullaby leaves. We dance to the beat of her bongo raindrops. In close harmony with her graceful offerings, we glide through time—forever flying, never landing.

It was in my youthful innocence that I first found faith—found it when I soared upon an illusory updraft high above the Blue Hole. It was during that childhood flight I discovered the unconditional gift of grace—a gift of memory that I will carry forever.

After the long drive from League City, Daddy maneuvers our car alongside the chipped concrete picnic table that will be home base for a week. When he cuts the engine, I reach for the door handle to escape the car's trapped heat. Immediately, I let go of the handle when Mama clears her throat—two, quick staccato notes. I know that warning. We all do. It is her unspoken signal for the three of us—Bubba, Sharon, and me—to freeze what we are doing and sit still.

I sneak a sideways glance at my older sister, who sits sandwiched between Bubba and me, as she squirms. She is careful not to touch either one of us. Me? I fidget and lift one leg and then the other from the plastic seat cover that has grown soft and mushy from the Texas heat.

We wait for what feels like an eternity, as Mama puffs on her cigarette. When she exhales, I watch the corkscrew eddies of smoke float up and out of her window. I stare at Mama's short, cropped brown curls that swirl in all directions just like the cigarette smoke. I want to shout for her to hurry up. But I know better. We all do.

When Mama finally turns around, her speckled gold and green eyes hold each one of us—first me, then Sharon, then Bubba—in place. She says nothing. We hold our breath. We watch. We wait for the tightly pressed, ruby-red seam of her lips to come unstuck. When that seam finally splits, Mama frees us with her words. "You kids go on and play, but do not let me catch you in that creek!"

"Yes, ma'am," we reply in chorus. Bubba kicks open his door and dashes off toward the other boys—Laddie, Tommy, Lynn, Mike, and David. For a moment, I don't move. With my hand still on the door handle, I watch them race uphill into a thicket of trees and underbrush, all the while shouting and shoving one another. Sharon scoots away from me and out the opposite door. She shuffles over to the concrete bench and sits down, slump-shouldered, already bored. I look beyond Sharon and find my body held spellbound by the mystical lure of the distant cypress trees and creek.

The spell is broken only by Mama's voice. "Get out of the car and go play, or you can help me unload the food in the trunk," she says.

I pull up on the handle, push open the door with my right shoulder, and plant my bare feet onto Texas Hill Country earth. The ground feels hard and lumpy, crumbly yet solid—so different from the sandy soil of my hometown in the coastal plains. As I run to the creek, oyster-colored rocks prick the tender flesh of my feet. Here and there, I hopscotch along clumps of short, spiked grass—their soft bristles poking up between my toes.

A muffled buzzing draws my attention upward. I scan the sky but can find no telephone wire, no electrical line. And so it is that I am introduced to the invisible spirit that lives at Cypress

Creek—a spirit that ushers me closer and closer to the murmurings at the water's edge.

In a burst of power, I cross the pockmarked earth, and in six,
maybe eight long strides, I finally reach the creek's sloped bank. I
want to wade in, to let the water wash over me. But Mama's words
ring in my head, so I merely gaze into the creek's green-black water, imagining another world—an *other-world*—that offers the
promise of adventures. And in that very moment, my young mind
mingles with the soul of the Blue Hole.

I drift off into a make-believe world. I drop to my knees
and kneel upon the bank. When I plunge my hands into the cool
water, I notice that beneath the surface my palms and fingers look
whiter, fatter, slightly off center from my wrists. I stare beyond my
swollen fingertips to study the mosaic of smooth river rocks in
hues of chocolate and tea and milk. They look like stone eggs scattered in random chaos. Carefully, I lower my entire arm into the
chilled water. I wrap my fingers around one large stone and bring
it up out of the water. Cradled in my palm, I study the stone. Then
I turn my gaze back to the creek's surface, where rope-like ripples
of water shimmer away from me.

With the stone safe in my hand, I sit down at the creek's edge
and dangle both legs into water that feels like liquid velvet. I look
across the creek and begin counting the wrinkly-looking cypress
trees that cling to the opposite bank. When I have counted 13
trees, I turn my attention back to the one tree on my left that rises
above me. Its tangled trunk of roots—like a knot of fat and woody
ankles—seems to rest upon the water's surface. I imagine how the
roots that continue deep into the creek anchor the towering upper body of the tree to the world below. I study the tree's peeling
bark before I raise my eyes to the other cypress giants. High above,
I notice finger-like branches thick with feather-thin leaves that
reach across the creek to form a canopy—a canopy through which
I glimpse patches of blue sky that look like shards of translucent
glass. And then ... Grace happens.

My six-year-old-other-self flies to the tops of those trees,
through the shards of translucent glass, and into the world beyond.

I hear the wind; I feel the sun. I smell the pureness of the sky. And when I taste eternity, Grace suspends my young body and holds me aloft. I am not certain how long I ride this reverie, but it is broken only with the whoops and hollers of my brother and his pals, with the music from the transistor radio sitting on the concrete table, with Mama yelling for me to return to our campsite.

I do not want to leave the magic of my newfound world— the world beside the water, beyond the treetops. But somehow, in that moment of forever as I listen to the Blue Hole, I hear the promise of a life of adventures. Filled with a sense of trust, I rejoin the others.

Nearing the campsite, I see that everyone is busy. The adults are chattering away, setting up the chairs and tents, preparing the food for our first meal. Bubba and his friends are gathering twigs and broken limbs for firewood. Sharon is drawing in the dirt with a stick. And the marble-filled voice of Louis Armstrong can be heard on the transistor radio.

———◆———

More than five decades later, I have grown stronger from years of loss and gain, from years of pain and joy. I have come to know that moments of purity found in nature are neither crafted nor created by the hands of man. I have come to know that the cycle of seasons will forever be infused with immortality. And I have come to know that to be touched by Grace, all one must do is to pause.

This wisdom is found in the ripples of an echo from a family vacation during the summer of 1958. And so it is that today, when life calls for calm, I need only close my eyes and listen once again to the splendor of that shallow creek moving sleepily alongside ancient cypress trees. I need only listen to the notes of my mother's deep-toned voice, to the notes of my father's quiet stories. I need only to replay that childhood vacation at the Blue Hole along Cypress Creek.

Stall Rest

Gail Folkins

Guided by pressure from my right calf, the reddish-bay quarter horse I rode glided sideways across the dirt, his front legs crossing and rhythmic as a dancer. The limp in the gelding's stride came sudden and discordant, a wrong note in our lateral movement.

"He's off," Grace, the riding instructor, said. I walked the horse, Tesoro, across the covered arena to where Grace stood in her tall boots. I tried not to see the concern on her face. We coaxed him forward one more time to be sure, revealing uneven strides to the left from this smooth-gaited horse. I hopped off and guided the stirrup leathers up the English saddle and loosened the girth, our work finished for now.

At the barn, I replaced Tesoro's bridle with a halter and ran my hand down his front left leg, his tendons cold with no obvious swelling. Many cases of lameness in horses originated in the foot—maybe it was related to the new shoes he'd had earlier that week, something easy to fix. I picked up his hoof and soaked it in a shallow bucket of saltwater, coaxing a bruise that wouldn't show. Although it was late October in Central Texas, the breeze blew warm through the barn door, no hint of the cold ahead.

On a warm day months earlier, sunshine lured me out of the arena and into the smell of fresh-mowed grass. *Tesoro's not a trail horse*, Grace warned me when I first started riding him, though I'd been determined this show horse could learn a new job. Over time, I introduced him to walking outside the arena, going farther each ride until we passed the barnyard and stepped into an open field of live oaks and diving bluebirds.

Today, Tesoro's gait was closer to a prance than a relaxed walk, even though he had few reasons to jump around, the wind calm and no rumbling farm machinery to speak of. I poked my stick-straight hair away from my eyes and further under my helmet. At the gated entrance to the open field, the horse stopped altogether, black-tipped ears pricked at something I couldn't see or hear. Before I could nudge him forward, the horse spun around in place like a carnival ride until we faced the opposite direction.

My ankle, braced in the stirrup, didn't keep up with the rest of me. I felt a dull ache through my boot, but the horse's refusal to go forward fired me up more than whatever had happened to my ankle. I bumped Tesoro with my calves, sending him forward against the doubts he'd had about the field and our direction. He walked past the gate in steps slow but willing, my reins and legs tighter this time.

We didn't go far, just enough to prove we could handle the unexpected. Back at the barn, I stepped off the horse, my ankle showing no swelling or bruising, no evidence of a pull. I brushed off the injury and made the best of things, something I'd become better at since losing full-time work this past year—a collection of part-time jobs helped keep expenses in check. Owning a horse, a decision driven more by faith than logic, was a situation I'd wrangled by leasing Tesoro to another rider and working on Sundays. The ankle would be fine, no need to have it looked at. The job situation, too, would work itself out.

Through the middle of 2011, the nationwide jobless rate hovered just above 9 percent. A larger yet less often discussed group consisted of the under-employed, those engaged in part-time work through an inability to find full-time jobs or with limited offerings in their chosen fields. Tracked in a 2011 Gallup poll, the underemployed made up a broader group of 18 percent, moving as best they could from one part-time venture to the next. Grace offered me additional work at the barn, a means of holding onto the horse and of giving me time to find a longer-term solution.

In search of a concrete fix after soaking Tesoro's foot produced no results, I stood across the barn aisle from Dr. Pruitt, a veterinarian who specialized in large animals, to watch the horse move.

"Turn him left," the vet, a tall man in a black cowboy hat, told his 20-something assistant, a man in jeans and scrubs. I wondered if the assistant was studying to be a vet, just as my college roommate at Washington State University had. Unlike many other job fields, opportunities for large-animal veterinarians remained strong.

The vet pointed out Tesoro's footfalls, how his left front shoe rang out lighter on the unforgiving cement because the horse put less weight on this particular foot. "It's definitely the left front," he said, moving his hand up and down the horse's leg and finding no more swelling or puffiness than I had. "We'll block him," he said, meaning he'd numb each part of the leg to isolate the site of the injury.

After wiping the ankle, called a fetlock, with iodine, the vet made a small injection near the hoof to numb the horse's foot. Based on my unsuccessful saltwater soaking, I wasn't too surprised when Tesoro trotted across the hard surface just as lame as before, the right front foot ringing out extra loud.

The vet worked up Tesoro's leg two more times with no change, the horse's footfalls staying uneven and his head bobbing, a sure sign of lameness. I wondered how serious this injury might be if we'd have to wait until the numbness reached his shoulder to find out.

The fourth injection came with more iodine and a site just behind the left front knee. The assistant trotted Tesoro, whose footfalls all of the sudden sounded even, his head still.

"We look for a significant difference," the vet had said earlier. His interest in the horse's strides told me this was the change we were after.

The vet felt the thick ligament at the base of the knee and followed it down to the horse's fetlock before coming back up again. "It's a pull high in the leg," the vet said, indicating the back of the knee.

"Is the injury age related?" I asked, wanting to know if there was more I could've done, if the 18-year-old horse and I should have been working differently.

The vet shook his head. "It's a common sports injury," he said. "It could happen at any age, anytime." He gave me some supporting remedies, an anti-inflammatory oral paste for any mild discomfort the horse might experience, along with a yellow heating gel to alternate with ice on the leg itself.

"He'll need stall rest," the vet said. "Six weeks. You can walk him by hand about 10 minutes or so a day, but that's all."

Along with the paste and alternating hot and cold leg wraps, the biggest remedies of all would be time and immobility. I was glad for an answer and at the same time unsure how Tesoro, who had access to a small pasture each day, would respond to staying inside. The horse-racing industry has revealed how difficult recovery can be for horses like 2006 Kentucky Derby winner Barbaro, who survived surgery to an injured hind leg but not the long-term standing needed to heal. Tesoro's injury wasn't as significant as Barbaro's, yet he was still an athlete made for motion, now out of work.

A few months after I turned my ankle, I walked down to the creek that sculpted a ravine through the forested backyard where I'd grown up in Washington state. Each visit, my brother and I hiked the slope of the mountain, a walk I hoped to repeat this trip. A short stroll on my own, damp leaves cushioning every cold step, was a test to see if I could make it up the initial slope.

After crossing the creek, I put my fingers in the clear water before I started up the steep grade. On the even ground near the creek, I felt fine, my ankle protected by the stiff sides of my hiking boots. Once I started up the incline, my ankle nudged me. Ignoring it, I climbed straight up the hill. The established trail hid beyond a covering of branches and leaves, an obstacle course prelude to a smooth dirt path. Through this thicker brush, pain tinged every stride. I wasn't near the main path, yet I couldn't go any farther, my hike on hiatus.

I applied for jobs in Washington state, drawn to my first version of home, wood stove memories enough to warm me from the rain and cold. I applied as a corporate writer, an editor, a teacher, and a journalist at my hometown paper, but nothing stuck; whether due to competition, my address a few thousand miles away, or my scattershot approach, it was hard to tell. The more I tried to force things, the less happened.

During the height of the economic downturn, the state of Washington's unemployment rate hovered just above the national average. New positions anywhere were sparse and more difficult to find; a steady gaze was needed to look beyond what the current climate offered.

The eye, not the leg, was the first thing I noticed when I led Tesoro out of his stall several weeks into his recovery. From the left side, he looked fine, his red-tinted coat dirt and dust-free from his time inside.

His right side, by contrast, was a horror movie, an eyelid torn and hanging across his eye with eyelashes perpendicular to the ground rather than horizontal. I wiped away the blood on his face while Tesoro stared from his over-exposed and already large eye, hopeful for a red and white-striped peppermint.

Shocking as the eye looked, the sudden movement that must have caused it wasn't. During the first week, Tesoro had been happy staying inside with extra hay, but by the third week, he'd grown agitated during our 15-minute outings, walking faster out of the stall and toward the grass I led him to. With cold fronts sharpening the air, the slightest sound set him off—a diesel truck, another horse strolling by, things that shouldn't have turned his head.

On a recent walk, a metal noise from a horse trailer sent Tesoro airborne, with all four feet off the ground and me gripping his multi-colored lead line, flying the 1,100-pound horse like a kite. Once his feet touched down again, his two-beat trot steps looked even and straight, no head bobbing to speak of. I watched, fixed on this unsanctioned movement and what it meant—that the horse was recovering. I was just as anxious to get back to work. Though the horse looked fine, I tempered our enthusiasm with the vet's careful advice. I'd have no one to blame but myself if I jumped in the saddle too fast, if the leg didn't heal.

Dr. Pruitt arrived on Thanksgiving Eve to look at Tesoro's eye. Without a word, the vet produced purple thread and a pail and directed me to lead the horse into the washing area. He sedated Tesoro with a shot that made the horse sway and brace his four legs like a drunk, his head drooping.

From the bright light the vet's assistant shone, Dr. Pruitt cleaned the eyelid, blood dripping in the pail and making puddles on the rubber mats where we stood. The precision of the work made the scene bearable. The vet stitched two rows along the eyelid, first an inner portion and then a careful outer row. By the time he was finished, the purple thread lay on the inside, making it hard to tell anything had happened.

"You're a plastic surgeon," I told Dr. Pruitt.

"It'll take a while for the swelling to go down," he said. The vet showed me the eye ointment I'd use, how I'd pull back the lower eyelid and slip a thin layer of goo on top of it.

I considered the eye treatments I'd add to the leg wraps I placed on the horse's injured leg each day, alternating between hot and cold, new injury and old.

I sat in the doctor's office, doubtful of my ankle injury and whether I should have made this appointment in the first place. The tissue paper covering the exam table crinkled, as did the pages of the months-old magazine I read to keep my mind quiet. I'd waited out this injury, feeling the ankle only on rare occasions when I used it the wrong way. I wasn't searching for a pain fix, but for some assurance I hadn't missed a step along the way, that keeping off of it for a while had been good enough.

My husband also had a foot injury, a fact I shared with the doctor when he burst into the room with a simultaneous knock and opening of the door. "All three of us have ankle injuries—my husband, my horse, and me." I set down the magazine while the doctor flipped through my chart and smiled, probably at the mention of the horse.

"What are all of you doing," the doctor said, more statement than question.

I shrugged. "The vet said it wasn't related to age," I waited for the doctor to say an old ankle injury didn't have anything to do with me being in my 40s, that it was a random event rather than a constant one. "You have a lot of movement," he said instead, rotating the foot.

"It's pretty specific to riding," I said. "I just wanted to make sure there wasn't anything else I should do."

"I don't recommend surgery." The doctor handed me a piece of paper with the name of a sports medicine office. "It's probably a ligament," the doctor said. "Sports medicine can help you strengthen the ligaments around it."

The doctor left before I had a chance to put on my shoes and leave the well-lit room with its aging magazines. I stepped on the ground with both feet, my ankle revealing no discomfort, no indication its twinges would last forever.

I managed my collection of part-time jobs, glad for them and at the same time on the lookout for something new. Aware of my freedom of movement but its charm worn thin flitting from one gig to the next, I weighed my options. The aging VW Beetle I drove added new rattling sounds as if it, too, were tired.

Although national rates would remain high for both the employed and the underemployed, the months to come would indicate slow economic growth, more people working on faith the coming years would be better.

The air was cold yet sunny the day the vet and the same assistant who'd been along for the eye stitching returned to see Tesoro's progress seven weeks after his leg injury. The assistant's eyes widened in surprise at how good the horse's eye looked, a dot of purple thread the only sign of an injury. "The eyelid is the tiniest bit thicker, but it's still healing," the vet said from beneath his hat.

The assistant led Tesoro on the hard winter ground outside the barn to inspect the horse's gaits. The horse danced on the end of the lead line, making the vet grin. "There we go," he murmured, as if this were a good sign.

Tesoro trotted up the hill in footfalls both even and loud. "Come back down," the vet told the assistant. "I'm very pleased," he added, which I knew meant something. The assistant played with Tesoro's nose, giving him a hard time just as the horse had meddled with him. The horse's forelock moved in the breeze, sharing a rare view of the white star on his face.

"Another 10 days and you can ride," the vet said, as if reading my mind and having us wait a little bit longer, just to make sure.

Two weeks later, I brushed Tesoro like usual, the only difference the black neoprene boots strapped on his front legs for ankle support. With the saddle blanket and saddle in place, I slipped the bit into his mouth for the first time in almost two months and led him to the riding arena. He didn't flinch when I stepped onto the mounting block, standing still while I slid my weight onto his back.

With the ball of my foot poised in the stirrup irons, my right ankle didn't twinge once, the paperwork from the doctor filed away in my home office for now. I rode Tesoro around the arena at a walk, the horse's strides long, fluid, and best of all, even. We'd save faster gaits like the trot for days to come to build up the horse's condition over time, the same slow steps I'd take toward a more certain livelihood. Clouds moved outside the open arena, patient in their float to someplace else.

A Cowgirl's Life for Me:
The Tale of a Texas Gal's First Roundup

Paula A. Reynolds

"Adventure is worthwhile."
—Amelia Earhart

Up before the first fingers of light could tickle our pillow-cases, my sister and I would greet the Saturday dawn on a beeline to the television. With the rabbit ear antennae angled just right, we'd patiently watch the litany of 1960s cartoons, and then … finally … the beloved King of the Cowboys, Roy Rogers would appear. Handsome Roy, faithfully accompanied by his Queen of the Cowgirls, Dale Evans, would outsmart yet another ne'er-do-well, usually upon his trusty steed, Trigger. Imaginations saturated with all-things-cowboy, my sister and I would gallop outside to begin our self-scripted reenactments of western adventure.

The cowboy life, the western way, the romance of life on horseback: these were certainly part of the fantasy of my childhood, yet they never found their way completely out of my visceral longing for reality. Fast forward to early 2008—I was reviewing an email from singer/songwriter/author and friend, Mike Blakely, which boldly proclaims "The First Annual Romp, Stomp, and Chomp Round Up" upcoming in April. A quick perusal, and I frantically fired back a reply to Mike that read, "I'm IN!"

Westward Ho

"To have courage is to have the life you want."
—R.C. Jonas, cowgirl, 1904

The home front secured, lesson plans in place, one last check of things packed, and I was finally ready to hit the trail west. Anticipation is a beautiful thing and must undoubtedly release endorphins that ignite some lesser-used synapses in a pleasing way; however, its evil twin manifests in errant little worries…. "Am I sure I can handle this?" "A stampede string … do I really need whatever that is?" "I haven't ridden much in the last 30 years." I offered myself half-hearted reassurances as I coerced the duffle zipper shut.

The roundup was held on a historic 80,000-acre ranch about 43 miles south of Alpine, Texas. as an active cattle ranch by a team of brothers, the spread was made up of the vast, rugged beauty beholden to deep West Texas. A roundup is held two to three times a year, and a couple of the brothers, along with a handful of kindred spirits, meet up for a few days of living the cowboy life. The idea was hatched to offer this experience to folks like me who'd always pined for it or who missed active ranching. Throw in some great nightly campfire music (ala Mike and Jeff Posey), a real-deal chuck wagon and cookie, a list of cowboy necessities (like a stampede string), and well, pard'ner … there ya have it.

Cargo loaded, we pointed due west on Interstate 10 under a low scud sky and settled back for hours of Texas vista and talk. Somewhere west of Ozona, the green, rolling terrain of the Texas Hill Country transitioned to stark flat lands accentuated by mesas. The scenery transitioned again as we left Alpine; ruggedly handsome, mountain-bordered, cactus-dotted plains flecked with roaming cattle filled the view. The realization hit in a vivid way that I'd be on horseback, up close and personal with those doe-eyed bovines—very soon! My anticipation grew palpable as Highway 118 poured us deeper into dramatic desert vistas.

We were the first to arrive. The ranch house was a quaint white structure, circa 1920s, accompanied by a *new* bunkhouse— an old shed reborn as three guest rooms. There was a huge watering tank, or pila, which provided a reflection pool for majestic Santiago Peak to the northeast, and scattered pens were situated easterly. Horses settled and goods unloaded, we eased back with a cold drink in hand. I scanned my surroundings—endless frontier that included no noticeable signs of man—accompanied only by the serenade of the lonesome wind and an occasional bird. I reveled at the raw elegance of this vast Texas sanctuary.

The solitude was interrupted by the distant rumble of vehicles with soon-visible clouds of dust verifying the others had arrived. Trucks, horse trailers, and assorted equipment preceded the cast of characters who would soon become highly admired teachers and new friends. We exchanged hearty greetings, and I was welcomed warmly. No doubt, though, the boys sized me up as the wanna-be cowgirl who had yet to show her mettle. After we'd unloaded our gear, we quieted our stomachs with a cold-cut dinner as the morning wake-up time was debated. The evening ended with soft campfire songs beneath a three-quarter moon hung delicately over Santiago Peak.

Day One—Tired Takes On a Whole New Meaning

"You must always do the thing you think you can't."
—Kathleen Harris, cowgirl, 1910

I never sleep deeply in new surroundings, and the first night kept the record intact. Work awaited, and our trail boss, Von Box, roused the bunkhouse at 5:45. I stretched with relief; the anticipation of the unknown fringed with tangible excitement held sleep at bay anyhow. Bumbling in near darkness, I donned what I hoped were appropriate cowgirl duds and made my way to the house. Two of our cowboys, David Aguilar and David Alexander, had prepared a hearty breakfast and inviting coffee. Hmmm … two nice looking men in cowboy attire preparing me breakfast? Not a bad deal so far! The caffeine was kicking in, and I listened intently as Von discussed the day's work. First order: gather up iron panels and haul them to the No. Three pasture for pen building.

Being the novice (and only female) cowpoke, I felt a healthy uncertainty on my place. Heaven forbid I become a hindrance, but I sure didn't want to just observe. By now, the fellows were west of the pila, everyone busy loading panels—except me.

Shoot. I high-tailed it over, made a feeble attempt to move some brush, then grabbed onto the trailer as it lurched forward. Wind and dust cradled my face as I joined the cowboys' banter.

We arrived at the No. Three to unload and I ventured to help, but it was an eager group, these fellows. All were extraordinarily polite, but I quickly sensed they wanted to protect the lady. Understood. But I needed to prove myself. I wiggled my way in, latched onto a panel and helped move it in place. Heavy indeed—no doubt a 150 pounds! I went back for more and despite attempted help insisted, "I've got it." This was a litmus test, and I'd gained a little ground by the time we completed the unloading. The remainder of the morning found us laying pens with cattle strategy in mind. I helped straight-wire the pieces together, twisting-tucking-cutting rhythmically—I finally felt useful. Pens intact, our reward was a welcome hot lunch.

Post-lunch, our steeds were saddled. I was assigned Mike's older gelding, Red Man. Being my first saddling job since 1970-something, I asked Mike for some quick tutoring. Cinch secure, stirrups adjusted, bit in place—done! However, we'd trailer into Pasture No. Three's 9,000 acres, so horses were loaded and I jumped in the back of the pickup with several others. Von asked if I had silk long johns on or if I brought moleskin (other things on that list!). "Nope, but I'll be fine!" He smiled … sympathetically?

As our posse reached the first rise, the panorama unfolded. Santiago Peak to the north, Nine Point Mesa to the east; rolling, rock strewn hills, brush-choked draws, three-dimensional mountain vistas spread out like something I could before only imagine. Surely I was watching myself in some great western. Our consort split, and I rode with Von, David A., and his teenage son Storm. I noted a few cows here and there; we'd return for them tomorrow. However, I had now become acutely aware of the motivation for Von's sympathetic smile. A very painful open sore had developed on my left knee, not to mention that my inner thighs felt like they'd completed a Thigh Master marathon. No problem … I'd deal with it. Cowgirls don't complain, and I wasn't about to break the creed.

The cow search continued as we individually rode and scanned the vista; however, I'd begun feeling noticeably weary. Von and David rejoined me, and my haggardness betrayed the "I'm fine!" response. Von suggested a break, surely for this cowgirl's benefit, and we found a tank with a few scraggly shade trees. Oh, how I hoped the boss didn't think he'd gotten stuck with a sissy. The others eventually joined us, and we shared stories of where the stealthy bovines were hiding as we stole a few more minutes of respite.

Daylight was signaling its end, and it was time to return to headquarters. A cold beer was golden elixir and a warm shower pure paradise at the end of that first day. Tired, sore but happier than happy, I joined my new friends for our first chuck wagon meal as a million stars came to life overhead. Two new cowpunchers arrived just in time for chow—a family friend of the Box brothers and rancher Mike Speights.

A satisfying meal, another round of campfire song with Mike and Jeff as the moonlit night gently cradled the Peak … such sweet ending to an extraordinary day.

Day Two — Wanna-Be Becomes the Real Deal

"A cowgirl gets up early in the morning, decides what she wants to do, and does it."
— Marie Lords, cowgirl, 1861

The gentle morning light roused me, but I decided to lay low a minute more. Von's voice broke the silence—"Hey Paula, you alive in there?" In fine cowgirl fashion, I managed a hearty "Barely," and hurriedly threw myself together. Greeted by the chilly morning air and appetizing aromas, my senses perked. A warm chuck wagon breakfast and campfire coffee awaited—my rewards for being awakened periodically from 4:30 on by our cookie's busyness.

The early morning sun warmed the land as the drovers pulled fresh horses from the corral—Cooley, a black gelding, was mine, and we saddled up. The morning sky had transitioned from soft aquamarine to ever-increasing cerulean as we encountered various delays. Searching to be useful, I couldn't offer much as stubborn horses were loaded. A stuck tailer and other complications occurred, but were finally conquered. We entered the highway for our short ride south-final destination the furthest reach of 9,000 acre Pasture No. Four. The boss offered apologies for the late start. "No problem," I imparted with a smile—and genuinely meant it.

Time to mount. I felt amazingly more comfortable today. Von lent me silk long johns, along with a square of moleskin for blisters. Oh, the difference! Gracias, boss. I'd definitely pack these items next time.

Four of us diverted to ride the fence line to the south corner while the others branched out to the west and southwest. The team rode this fashion to cover the expanse, each rider accountable for scoping out and pushing cattle northward. I fell into formation; I wanted to bring in some cows.

Cooley and I ambled on—it felt incredible, amazing, almost surreal. Under an endless blue sky brush-stroked with wisps of cottony white, I took in miles of untamed landscape colored in unending shades of grays and blues. Dots of green vegetation broke up the montage as if someone randomly scattered broken emeralds across the terrain. Bursts of firecracker red blossoms crowning the ocotillo cactus added their exclamation to the picture; they appeared to float in mid-air, gray spindles melting into the background. Purples and blues coloring the vistas seemed to blend and fight, calling out, "Look at me ... me first!" I felt a sense of comfort as I scanned the horizon, the landmarks of this vastness now recognizable. I also felt a sense of aloneness unlike any I'd ever felt. It was not adverse, though—quite the contrary. My utter joy was interspersed with only a few fleeting moments of worry ... not so much anxiety-invoked worry, but some embedded caution found in urbanized townsfolk. I brushed it off quickly and crooned "Don't Fence Me In." If Cooley's stubborn gate was any indication, he was not impressed.

As the last strains of my serenade faded, I did a double take. On a small ridge due north, I spotted a black cow … or was it a bull? Who cared … it was mine! We were first on the scene as we raced, Cooley-style, toward the prize. We crowned the last ridge, and it became painfully obvious that a brushy draw was the gauntlet between this cow and me. I studied and plotted, anxious to capture my find. This is cowgirl doable, I decided as we headed into the most permeable looking section. "We've got this, Cooley!" I admonished, ducking wildly as over-anxious thorny limbs did their best to show me a thing or two. In short order, we were in one impassable, mean pocket of a West Texas draw with only one option—dismount and back out on foot, blast the thought of "Rattlesnake!" or "Crazed javelina!"

Retreat accomplished, I picked off the larger souvenirs collected in that tangle, and we headed west down the draw until a sand bar greeted us as safe ferry to the ridge. Maybe we still had a chance.

My cow appeared … along with several riders nearby. Well, at least we'd given it a determined try. A sprinkling of other cows congregated, as well. Reunited with my team, I replayed the adventure in the draw.

"A cow and those calves came up out of the draw," Jeff remarked. "You must've stirred 'em up." A satisfied smile crossed my lips, I gave Cooley a pat, and we spurred our rides to push the gathering herd.

Secured in the pens, a fine cloud of dust and animated cow-speak rose to announce excitement at rejoining relatives and friends as the herd settled in. A couple of bulls jousted and bullied, hoping to impress the less-than-interested females. We watched impatiently, wondering the status of the unaccounted-for riders. The fence-sitting patter grew old, and it was decided to ride northeast to assess things, as well as to assuage our restlessness. We'd ridden a short way when a column of dust swirling sunward appeared and the spectacle came into view—a splendid parade of cows and calves, 150 head at least, coming our way. Scattered riders trotted alongside, heee-yahing and whistling encouragement and obedience, their colorful wild rags whipping about like victory flags.

Pen work awaited as we downed the last gulps of our trucked-in midday meal and buckled loosened chaps. The rodeo began as man and beast played little games of Chicken, the goal being to load a small herd for transport. I was the cowgirl cork as I hovered at a gap, whooping and hollering and waving my hands wildly overhead. Guess it worked. Not one cow slipped through.

Our next agenda was to separate calves from cows. A blur of cowhide, dust, and cowboys set the scene, and I wanted a part of it. However, the pen was already overcrowded, so I observed and learned, overriding my desire … this time.

Things got a little more western as we flanked, vaccinated, and branded calves in a whirlwind of boots, sweat, searing iron, and hypodermics. I was invited to vaccinate, and I stepped up to join the fireworks. Vaccination tutoring would come later, though—the holler to help brand clipped the air, and I stumbled forward, grabbing a fiery iron that glowed like hell's fury. I hesitated, not quite sure about the action awaiting me. Based on observations, I assured myself the calves seemed fine after the work-overs, and I advanced on the flanked calf, coached on each move. Boot on the calf's hip to steady him—firm pressure for an adequate brand—a gentle rocking motion to guarantee the mark was solid. Five—10—15 brands into it, and I've found some finesse.

"Still want to vaccinate?" More cowgirl schooling: syringe sideways, puncture the flesh under the foreleg, avoid the muscle, and inject. The scene was a choreographed dance. We stepped around, aside, and sometimes right on top of one another—from delicate ballet-like moves to rough-and-tumble slam dancing—but we got the job done with no serious mishap.

The last of 34 braying calves were ready to release. Leaning over to Mike B., I said, "I want to throw a calf or whatever that's called."

"Really? You mean you want to flank a calf?" My steadfast smile and stance made it clear I meant business, and Mike shouted to hold off releasing the calves. They chose a smaller fellow and gave me the how-to: one hand under the rear flank, another wrapped around the front leg … lift and bring him down as you follow. Done! After some cowboy whoops and high-fives, the obliging little guy shook us off and trotted back to his peers.

Our overtly tired, dirty, hungry, and happy crew returned to fill up on a warm meal, then lingered in the glow of the welcoming campfire. A lullaby of winsome cowboy song pacified the night as the almost-full moon washed our surroundings; the land appeared soft, its jagged edges melted to velvety richness. The desert's eve-ning breeze had awakened and it was time to trade places with the doings of the night. G'nights were exchanged through yawns, and I crawled into bed feeling abundantly blessed.

Day Three: It's a Done Deal

"If anyone told me I could be this content out west, I wouldn't have believed them."
—Elizabeth Clayton, cowgirl, 1887

A luxurious stretch, eyes barely open—and I bolted upright with a start. It was light already, and the clock showed 7:15. Mo-mentarily panicked, I remembered the day's lighter work granted a later wake-up call. Sure hoped I hadn't blown it.

Swiping the last tasty breakfast morsels from my plate, I cen-tered my hat and ran to find my compadres readying horses. Dun-nie was my mount, and we joined the others to load for a quick ride to the pens where the almost 200 cattle from the previous day's work remained.

Strategy decided, our company formed a funnel to expedite a cohesive exit from the pens. More whistling, clapping, and huh-yaws kept the beasts moving, and we transitioned into an absolute-ly beautiful cattle drive—point riders in the fore, swing and flank riders managing the sides, drag riders keeping the aft in shape. We moved comfortably, each position ebbing and flowing in need and attention to the herd. They plodded along mostly willingly, constantly talking—some singing to themselves, mothers berating their playful calves, others calling out for company. One bull was a self-assigned leader and seemed to chant as he piloted the way north. Euphoria washed over me—I felt like a real cowgirl. I could anticipate the movement of the cattle, the moves of my fellow riders. We worked as a tight team—ready to jump into action, assist, or get out of the way.

To my left, a few cows acted jailbreak suspicious. I gave Dunnie a little nudge, just in case, and … one rebel cow bolted toward the mesa. I reacted instantly; this cow was in my passel of dependents, and I wasn't about to let anyone down. I spurred Dunnie, decided my strategy in split-second fashion, and rode fast at a 45-degree angle to the cow's trajectory. We slowed when I sensed we could close off the cow, and—the renegade was ours. It was a nice victory trot back to the formation, and the boss, riding swing, offered a long distance congratulations.

Four or five vehicles stopped along the highway to watch and take pictures. I chuckled … that literally was me a couple of years ago. I imagined their conversations; for whatever reasons, I hoped they noticed it was a girl on this beautiful dun gelding.

With the herd secure in the northern pastures, we began the ride back along a well-worn dirt road. Full of light-hearted contentment, many broke into full-fledged, wind-whipping gallops. Pulling forward, Dunnie and I bolted like a tumbleweed in a blue norther—hooves pounding, limbs flapping, the wind rushing past my face. I let out a whoop, feeling exhilarated like I imagined any cowpuncher of days gone by felt after a successful drive. Tiring, we slowed to a trot and caught up to two other riders.

Appetites appeased with a rib-sticking lunch, it was time to begin the pen work at headquarters. The final group of calves was large … very large … and did not look kindly upon being roped and wrestled to the ground.

Each cowboy in turn fashioned a loop and took aim, hoping to effectively anchor a calf for quick flanking. "Who's next?" queried David Aguilar. "I'd like to try, but…." Never afraid of a wild bull, rattlesnake, or novice cowgirl, David set out to show me the ropes ... literally! A western rope can be harder to coil than a kinked garden hose, and I struggled. David admonished, "Loop is large and the pointing finger on your swinging hand aims for the target." First throw ... fair. Recoil the rope, a few more pointers, and ... second throw. Better, but not productive. One more shot, and I'd get out of the way. Determined swing, pinpointed aim ... throw! It landed right behind the target's heel ... and I froze. The wary calf stepped back—right smack dab in the middle of my loop! "Pull! Pull! Tighten the rope!" Immediately I had a very unhappy calf on one end and spirited cowboys helping me on the other. Finally flanked and worked, the hapless calf shook off the dust and sauntered over to join his friends.

The freshly worked cattle were slowly let loose as we fell into drive positions for a 30-minute ride toward the Cuchilla Trap where we bid adios to the herd. As we basked in the satisfaction of a job well done, the late afternoon sun reflected the warmth in my heart.

I gazed west over the ranch house as the sky transitioned to that juncture of day and dusk when the sun's low beams leave the would ensconced in a fairy dust wash of color and feeling. I sprinted for the closest rise, anxious for the best view. A land-locked sea of colors and texture surrounded me as the sun dipped into a blanket of wispy clouds whose arms extended upward as if they had spent the day waiting to be an escort to the other side. I desperately wanted to ensnare the beauty. A camera, though, is inadequate to capture a moment that imprints an overwhelming soul reverberation amid such glorious creation.

A full moon snuck up behind me as I contemplated my existence. There was a brief moment of illuminated duet as the sun retracted the last of its energy and the moon shook off low clouds in preparation for a big night. Another beautiful light appeared; the campfire was full and inviting, and a group of festive folks gathered 'round. I left my desert sanctuary for the earth-bound light below.

The evening continued on a celebratory note as Mike and Jeff served up tunes that covered a gamut of emotion. Snuggled in a warm quilt, I felt as content as any worm in a cocoon ever had. The now-full moon illuminated the gift of this gathering, shining upon a circle of faces that, like me, had set the rest of the world aside.

The music had quieted, talk had slowed, and the moon had covered at least half of this night's work. I held out to the very last, but my heavy eyelids betrayed me. Time for us remaining few to wish sweet dreams and head for our bunks. The moon glow tucked me in as I nestled under the covers to greet blessed sleep.

Day 4: Happy Trails to You

"The land is beautiful and hard, like life itself."
—Pearl Morgan, cowgirl, 1900

Von offered the night before to escort me to a high ridge to catch the sunrise, and there was only one answer to an offer like that. A 6:20 wake-up knock, and I plundered the covers aside, hollering "I'm on my way!"

Atop the rise, the truck bed was positioned east and I found a fine seat on the toolbox. Watching the low eastern light, I momentarily swiveled west and was met with a gasp-evoking sight. A dreamy egg yolk moon caressed by silvery clouds rested momentarily atop a mesa; the ethereal scene was stunning. It quickly eroded, leaving me awed and feeling honored.

The wafting overcast disappointed Von, but its multi-layers added dimension to this continually evolving 360-degree theatre. It was like watching a watercolor of pastels that were static for only a breath, always rearranging for yet more spectacularity.

We talked amid interspersed silence. It was comfortable, though, and almost necessary for digesting the scene. Our conversation revealed that Von was a man who loved and respected this land and the creatures it sustained. Qualifications, I decided, for a real cowboy—along with not fearing hard work.

We returned to a hub-bub of activity. Jumping right in, I

helped ready the horses, then somehow re-stuffed my goods in the pickup. Goodbyes began to this very fine group of now-revered friends who just days ago were complete strangers, and we bid farewell with hopes of finding ourselves together once more, riding south to begin again. I caught the gate as we departed this piece of West Texas heaven. A tinge of sadness lingered as I latched it for the last time and looked north.

Gender

Sarah Cortez

I am sitting in the front passenger seat of a large white van in a gas station parking lot. McBroom and I have been waiting several hours for prisoners from warrant raids to be brought to us for transport. So far, our prisoner count is zero. We fall into our routinely easy banter, the tit-for-tat chain-yanking that cops excel at. Then, in reply to some stray observation, he launches into his reasons for females being excluded from police work, fire fighting, and the military—the triumvirate of public service, in which he's been employed throughout his entire life. I see his freckles color with his vehement rationalizations. Because I like him, I listen. I've never seen this side of him, and we've worked together on plenty of special assignments, like today's.

When you're viewed as an outsider, moments like this can intrude into the already-complicated mechanics of a working relationship. Moments that reveal startling glimpses of prejudice and anger, as well as humor or pluck. I prefer the out-and-out 'fessing up; better to meet an enemy head-on than try to grapple with unvoiced attitudes and the oily pastiche of false politeness. Besides, like I said, I like McBroom; he likes me. He just doesn't like my gender in a uniform. It's that simple.

———

I remember the first time I was told I couldn't do something I had set as a goal for myself. I was 28 when a sharp-eyed, exquisitely-dressed headhunter with careful posture told me that I was too old to change from teaching high school to a corporate career. I could tell by her level stare that she believed it. I didn't. I enrolled in a master's program in accounting and almost tripled my salary in that first job in a new industry.

———

McBroom's thin-lipped exegesis of females' incompetence in the military leads into a recitative of all the female soldiers who asked him, as their West Point topography instructor, into their tents to examine their boot blisters during finals. These females were stark naked when he showed up, and, if he's to be believed, he promptly left the area after a careful scrutiny of their *feet*. All these years later he is still incensed over the fact that they thought they could bribe him with pussy to pass the map-reading course. But, hell, who knows, maybe they just found his thick patch of strawberry-blond hair and blue eyes attractive? Some girls might be attracted to a sturdy white boy with muscles honed by years of bull-riding and a genuine East Texas twang.

<hr />

But today, it's insanely important to me to convince McBroom that I have never slept with anyone to get anything. His belief that a female cannot make the grade on her own ability but must resort to sexual bribery is archaic to me, but to him, and to so many others, it is a reality shored up by disastrous examples like the West Point story he has just related. I hear myself say the words, "Mc-Broom, I've never slept with a man to get something career-wise," but I know he doesn't believe me. He can't.

If I allow myself the luxury of caring long-term about what McBroom, and so many others like him think, then the whole apparatus of my *life-as-career* halts. Why? Because there is no way for light to penetrate the blinders surrounding their logic: females are incompetent; I am a female; therefore, I am incompetent. This is especially true within the sacred trinity of public service: military, fire, police, beyond which nothing worthwhile exists. Careers in medicine or education might be better accepted by parents, but when it comes to action, danger, *proving yourself a man*, there is *only* this trinity. And, if you are a female like me, who craves danger (on the job), then you will have to be 10 times better than any male, and you'll have to pretend you don't know you're better, smarter, faster, more detail-oriented, more tactically sound, have better handwriting, smell better, make more arrests, clear more cases, write more citations than any of the males you work with. And remember, if any of them notice, then they'll hate you for it. So you'd better be sly; you'd better be preternaturally unobtrusive. You'd better hope your sergeant isn't overheard bragging about your arrest stats or case clearance rate. Make sure no one knows you've been to college or like opera. And don't ever let yourself speak about your home life or what you did before becoming a cop.

And what about the ideologies floating around in this century that men and women are equal? Can perform equally well at jobs? Deserve the same pay for the same job? How do these ideas fit into the conservative world of policing in a smaller agency, where most of the men were raised expecting their "little ladies" to wear frilly dresses and stay at home to cook smothered pork chops for dinner? No wonder these poor guys don't know what to make of females in trousers and tactical boots, females who prefer the thrill of a good arrest or the simple satisfaction of an air-tight investigation completed with warrants issued. We aren't the girls they grew up with, and we sure-as-hell aren't the girls they wanted to marry.

What about us females who fit no one's expectations? Not McBroom's or those like him, not those of tradition-bound females who think we're just looking to get laid or snatch someone else's husband? So it all becomes in a strange, if not perverse, way, a matter of convincing members of both the sexes that the job is all that matters. That the whirly-gig of life-as-career takes precedence over any type of affect. That danger is a better lover than anyone else—at least, on-duty.

Let me clue you in on something else. There is no equality between men and women on the streets. Men are stronger; women are meaner. Men are disastrously short-tempered; women communicate better. Men are better initially at B.S. and they sustain it longer; women carry grudges and never stop hating someone once they've started. In fact, I myself prefer working with men. Men are less neurotic, less backbiting. Every time I hear the story of another female cop who is sleeping with fellow male officers or doing her nails inside the patrol car, I feel personally disgusted.

The burden of diminished expectations from all the male officers increases by one more cemented brick, sealed by the mortar of whispered "I told you so's" that I'll never hear out loud, but will have to attempt to overcome by the sheer dint of exceptional work product veiled in silence.

So, if you're another female who wants to become a cop and come out on patrol to play with us, keep your mouth shut, your trousers zipped, and your nail polish at home. Here, everything is dead serious, even when we laugh at jokes you don't yet understand. And McBroom and I will continue laughing, even though I'll never convince him through logical conversation that I am that different kind of woman he can't understand. I like him; I'll cut him some slack. As he'll probably do for me, for exactly the same kind of reason.

On Forgiving

Leslie Jill Patterson

adj., (of a thing) easy or safe to deal with: *If you'd like to look a couple of pounds lighter, black is a forgiving color.*

By the time I met Tyrone, I'd studied all of the affidavits and memos his defense team had gathered from several Texas Youth Commission workers, who warned that Tyrone was capital-T Trouble strolling down the street. None of them had seen him in over a decade, nor could they remember his name or any particular offenses he'd committed while in custody, but when they saw his photograph, they recalled his flimflam smile, the kind that made you forget his explosive temper seconds before he swung a fist. Which might have been a sparring tactic he'd honed back in the day, when he was five and his uncles taught him to "dogfight," pitting him against other kindergarteners in a makeshift ring in their living room and casting bets on the outcome. He was a quick and certain study: all these years later, he'd beaten three of his "baby mamas" as well as the one wife he truly loved. Days before the homicide, Tyrone's most recent girlfriend filed charges with the police, accusing him of beating her with a box-fan until she'd fallen unconscious. Twice. I knew he'd killed two adults—while three children and one infant howled in terror as he fired the gun, again and again, until it ran out of bullets. The infant was his. Prison officials at county lock-up where he'd been housed ever since thought him so dangerous they wrote him up when they found a "weapon" in his cell: a single staple, which he had used to slit his wrists. The judge overseeing his case summed up everyone's impression: he set Tyrone's bail at $1,000,000.

When the guards brought Tyrone into the private client/ attorney room at the county jail, he wore orange prison garb but wasn't shackled at the belly and the ankles as other defendants had been. His eyes, wide and brown and wary, overwhelmed his narrow face and undercut his notorious smile, which he flashed right away. As his defense team introduced a couple of student attorneys and me, he nodded at each of us, polite but dismissive. He wasn't sure we were anyone he needed to impress. I'd heard he would put on a show—all hood slang and profanity, a rooster cocking the walk. Certainly, his orange pants were slung so low on his hips, I thought they would slide to the floor, and he had a way of zigzagging his chin and jacking up one shoulder that seemed pretty street to me, white woman that I was. Despite his swagger, though, and my expectations of a "killer" physique, Tyrone was rawboned—knobby elbows and lean as a starving coyote. Striking, in a fierce sort of way.

His family and friends swore Tyrone's sense of humor could spike a funeral into a New Year's bash, and sure enough, to my surprise, he could crack a joke. When he found out I was divorced, he said, "You need him bounced? I got people. I can make some phone calls." We fell quiet, stunned. One of our team's mitigators, Rob, involuntarily looked overhead for a recording device. Our client couldn't afford to land in the newspaper again for another in-house infraction—this time, attempted murder for hire. Max, the team's attorney, looked at me and swiped a hand across his throat: *let's garrote this conversation.* But then Tyrone's face cracked open, all teeth, and he said, "I'm kidding, man. White people, you so serious." Then he proceeded to run down a list of vocabulary words we used that he found hilarious—we had to stop appreciating him all the time, for one thing. What kind of hokum word was that: *'preciate.* "Bullshit," he said. "Stop talking like damn honky psychiatrists." I'm saying, he had us unstitched pretty quick.

Halfway into the meeting, though, Tyrone quashed the comedy routine and sobered up. He turned to Max, the type of defense attorney known at the courthouse as a "gunslinger" because you don't want to square off with him in front of a jury. Recently, Max had represented Calvin Solomon—a man who pled guilty to the shooting deaths of a family he didn't know: a man, his pregnant wife, her teenage daughter, even their dog. A ringer for the needle if ever there was one. But Calvin skirted death row because Max's efforts led a jury to settle on Life Without Parole instead, an outcome unheard of in Texas if a capital charge goes to trial. Sitting next to Tyrone, Max looked like a mafia mechanic. Two considerable gold rings lent his hands a Vito Corleone respectability, and he weighed a solid 250 pounds. I'd seen him break in two, one after the other, a stash of ballpoint pens made from recycled cardboard, simply by gripping them to write. He wasn't the type you looked at and thought: *sensitive.* Or: *Let's talk.*

To Max, Tyrone said, "You read the Bible?"

Max showed no expression. His empty face suggested he might need to admit something I'd seen a character confess in a Steve Yarbrough short story: *There are lots of books in this world I haven't read, and among them is one called the Bible.* But I knew Max was a devout Catholic. He'd shown me his church when we drove around town one afternoon. I figured he'd cracked a Bible at least once.

Tyrone asked him again. "You read the Bible?"

Max couldn't or didn't know how to react. He stared at his client. Maybe he was trying to calculate where this discussion was headed; maybe he thought the question was a con. Honestly, it seemed pretty suspicious to me. I'd had my fill of men sidling up to religion for my benefit. When my ex-husband found out I'd lost the ability to have children, he'd said, "See, even God knows you shouldn't be a mother." When I'd answered, "You don't believe in God," he'd said, not missing a beat, "Yeah, but you do."

"I read the Bible," I finally offered, though I rarely owned up to my spiritual beliefs since they hadn't served me so well. Too, in Texas, for the most part, if you're a Christian, you're also a lot of other things I didn't want people assuming about me. Republican, for one. Both a Muslim-hater and, by bogus association, an Obama-hater. Sometimes in Texas, there's a triple-digit heat to Christianity which makes it unlikely that devout churchgoers, the kind who brag about their convictions, can chill the

Old Testament wrath and show compassion toward people who haven't earned it.

Apparently, that attitude is catching. See what I just did in that previous paragraph? I myself cast Tyrone as the type of person who didn't deserve understanding. *People who haven't earned it:* I was talking about him and the other defendants the team represented, right?

Tyrone sized me up, nodded. "All'ight," he said, "you know what I'm conversating then."

I shook my head. "No. What are we talking about?"

He leaned forward in his chair and clasped his hands in front of him, as if they were shackled, and pumped them in the air. "The Bible say we got to honor our parents. It don't say if they nice to you or deserve it."

Everyone in the room stiffened. By that point, we knew that Tyrone's mother, when she paid attention to him at all, thrashed him regularly between the ages of four and twelve, with an orange utility cord and always for petty offenses like having untied shoelaces or eating his cereal incorrectly. At night, she burst into his room while his was sleeping and whaled on him without waking him first because, rape-baby that he was, she should've had an abortion. In the darkest moments of our investigation, when we needed something to make us smile for God's sake, we joked about putting her on the witness stand first, wearing a T-shirt that said, *Exhibit A.* By the time Tyrone turned seven, he tried to hang himself, an obvious cry for help that CPS ignored, sending him back home after his allotted days in the county-run juvenile mental hospital. When we confronted his caseworker—we'll call her Exhibit B—she'd shrugged. "That kind of thing happens in black households all the time," she said. "A dime a dozen."

Tyrone's biological father, Manny Wilson, who had allegedly raped his mother, denied Tyrone from day one and was now a junky, whom Albert, our private investigator and the most resourceful man on our team, couldn't find for nearly a year. Manny's name wasn't listed in any phone books. He didn't have even the slightest cyber footprint. Finally, Albert and Max tracked

Manny down by knocking door to door at the apartments where Tyrone's grandmother heard Manny lived. She didn't know the name of the complex, only that it was near the Dennis the Price Menace Liquor Store. Since we'd found him, Manny had called Rob several times, weeping and begging to see Tyrone, who had said, *No way, no fucking way.* And Rob and Max—ever vigilant and earnest about their jobs as Tyrone's defenders, and both of them large men—had thrown up a wall, their bodies prepared to block Manny's efforts to visit his son in lockup if it came to that.

Tyrone stared in my direction. Not exactly a direct beam, but canted to the right. Or maybe I was the one diverting my gaze.

I nodded my head. "That's what the Bible says."

He looked at Max, then leaned forward a little more and turned again toward me. "It say you got to forgive in order to be forgiven."

I nodded.

"I've been thinking on that," he said, his hands pumping the air. "I need my kids to forgive what I done, so I need to forgive my daddy."

Max propped his forehead against his fists and stared down at the table. I knew, from previous interviews with other defendants, that this was the stance Max took whenever he thought he might tear up but, by God, wasn't going to. His cheeks puffed, and his face turned red from the effort.

Tyrone looked at me, his eyes square on mine now. "That right?"

"That's what it says," was all I could manage without my voice cracking.

"Okay." Tyrone nodded. "Okay."

"You don't need to worry," Max told him. "We aren't letting Manny anywhere near you if that's got you troubled."

Tyrone made a gesture that looked like a rap groove or maybe a Crips sign—his fingers crimped as if double-jointed and his hand flicked, scooping the air. "I'm gangsta with that," he said.

Rob cocked his head to the side, as if he were deaf and simply needed to angle his ear toward Tyrone in order to understand him. *How's that? What?*

I looked around the room for an interpreter.

Max parked his big fists firmly on the table. "That's right. Manny isn't getting anywhere near you. No worries."

Tyrone jacked up his chin. "I'm gangsta with that."

Max's brow wrinkled. "You want to see your dad?"

The rap grove again. "Fuck it," Tyrone spat at him.

"Okay, okay." Max held up his hands, palms forward, signaling everyone to halt. "No visits from dear old Dad."

"Fuck it. I'm gangsta with that," Tyrone shouted

It felt like we were trapped in that Progressive car insurance commercial where the elderly guy keeps talking in some sort of jazz-speak—*Okie-McSmokey Skiddlely-Doo*—till Flo shakes her head and admits, *Yeah, still no idea what you're saying.*

"You want to see your Dad," I tried. Decisively. Not a question, but a statement of fact.

"Fuck it," Tyrone said again, but calm this time. He settled back in his chair and flashed his smile.

Max nodded and wrote a note on his legal pad. "Got it. We'll set that up." He looked a little sheepish, then with a zigzag of his own chin and a shrug of his shoulders, he added, "Fuck it."

Laughter snorted from my mouth. The hopeless, egregious ineptitude of a team of middle-aged, middle-class, overly educated white people representing a young African-American man from the hood lit up the room. Everyone howled. A real New Year's hullaballoo.

Though it wasn't funny. Not at all. In the county where Tyrone would be tried, African-Americans comprised only two percent of the total population. Most of them weren't registered voters—why would they bother in Texas?—so they wouldn't receive a summons. If they owned a car and received the call via their vehicle registrations, the six-dollars-a-day jury salary was a pay-cut they couldn't afford, and so they wouldn't appear. Even if they did, during *voir dire*, when the prosecutor asked if anyone

had experienced a negative run-in with the law that might pre-
vent them from taking seriously every police officer's testimony,
the African-Americans would likely all raise their hands and be
dismissed for cause. Tyrone's jury of his peers would look a lot
like his defense team.

When we got ready to leave, Tyrone hugged my neck, said,
"No shit, you're divorced?"

I nodded.

His face turned dark, like he was getting ready to kick some
holy ass on my behalf, getting his game on. "He didn't hit you,
did he?"

I shrugged. "He was smart. He had alternative methods."

Tyrone squinted, leaned toward me. "You behaved?" he
asked. "You didn't deserve it?"

Which sounds like a horrifying question given its implica-
tions and Tyrone's history. Then, again, it was the same question
I'd asked myself for years. And it was the same question society
implied whenever they argued that women stick around cause
they like it.

"Angelic," I said. "A real saint."

"Serious now," he said, smiling again, "I got people. What
you say his name was?"

I grinned. "Nice try," I said.

"Fear of God and all that," he promised.

I nodded. "Sure: repentance, forgiveness." But in my head,
I was thinking what a damn shame it was I hadn't taken my
husband's last name when we married. That way, he'd be easier
for archangel thugs to hunt down and knock unconscious with a
box-fan. At the very least, I wouldn't mind my ex bumping into
Max or Rob or Albert in a dark alley. Out loud, I said, "Only, my
ex is agnostic. He doesn't believe in any of that."

"Yeah—" Tyrone paused, "—but you do."

At that moment, his face staring at me was the that of the
little boy whom TYC workers recognized from a second-grade
photo—a kid smiling, all flash and bravado, because he didn't
want anyone to notice the case of ringworm so thick it covered

his arms and torso, because he didn't want anyone to suspect how his cousin and his cousin's friends ran a train on him in the family garage every afternoon. What I know about forgiveness today I learned from murderers. If I was going to tell Tyrone's story and tell it true, I'd have to forgive his mother, and her mother before her, and her mother before her. Forgiveness lies at the bottom of a rabbit hole deep and dark, and once you dare to jump in after it, all you can do is fall.

Collared by the Jaguar

A Profile of Kay Sutherland (1942-2002)

Catherine Rainwater

The deserts of the American Southwest provoke intense emotions. Fear. Disgust. Awe. Delight. Reverence. Enchantment. Among all possible responses, indifference is rare. Barren and worthless to some who pass through it, the desert is to others such as the prize-winning naturalist writer, Ann Haymond Zwinger, "the pivot point of a compass, ... the center of the universe—a place to dance, to hoot and holler, to rearrange mountains, to count the rollicking stars at night."

Kay Sutherland was the hoot-and-holler type, always the mountain-rearranging type. Spellbound by pictographs and petroglyphs encountered in the Chihuahuan Desert, she called this sun-sated land of scraggly creosote and prickly pear both beautiful and sacred. For half her life, she visited rock art sites across the world. Her favorite, 32 miles northeast of El Paso, Texas, Hueco Tanks lies at the geographical center of the prehistoric Jornada Mogollon region. At one time or another, Kay probably walked through, climbed over, crawled under and squeezed into all of the area's approximately 60 rock art sites.

Explorer, student, scholar, and teacher, Kay was a woman whose mind and heart traveled the same road. She spoke of her work with spontaneous, rejuvenating joy, inspiring friends and students to join her on educational treks to El Paso, New Mexico, Belize, Mexico, Guatemala—wherever she could learn more or teach others about Southwestern rock art or the Mesoamerican cultures that influenced it. I never tired of the pleasant stream of her conversation that ran sometimes above ground, public and professorial, and sometimes below, in the more personal, introspective current connecting friends.

"The more I learn about all this," she once told me, "the more it changes the way I think."

Throughout the 14 years I knew her, Kay often proclaimed herself an atheist. She required evidence of a higher power, and she hadn't seen much. Time spent among indigenous people, however, had eroded her skepticism. Strange figures in the desert, picked and painted on rock in arrested motion, fired an inner quest for the ineffable. In her notes, recorded June 29, 2000, not long after attending a sunrise ceremony with Mesoamerican tribal elders at Hueco Tanks, Kay reluctantly calls this mystical phenomenon "god," but as in many of our conversations, she seems dissatisfied with the word. She wanted a word that captured the beauty and the power of the desert. The beauty is subtle—many observe it without appreciating. The power is not subtle—I've hardly known anyone to miss it, though not all are favorably impressed. I have felt the surging power of the desert. I've felt, paradoxically, immense and shrunken as sun-energy and earth-energy meet in a supernova at the solar plexus. Lightness in the head and shriveling of the skin—both seem to indicate, "Out here, what takes anything from the sun, gives back."

The prehistoric artists of the Jornada Mogollon left behind images limning their existence under a pitiless sun in a nearly waterless country. Their goggle-eyed storm gods, step-fret designs, and rain altars are nouns and verbs in a desert language that Kay set out to learn. "The first time I saw a collared jaguar," she admitted, "the first time I crawled into a secreted rock shelter and discovered a painted red mask staring at me, I was hooked." Somewhere on the outskirts of El Paso, she became a willing desert captive, a nexus for a mysterious power she could not name. This power that flowed through the Jornada people flows through us today beneath the sun that brings their ancient art to eerie life.

At Hueco Tanks, three towering piles of rock rise 450 feet above the plain. Inside enormous hollows—*huecos*—precious rain collects to become a year's supply of drinking water. Living creatures have slaked their thirst at these tanks for 11,000 years. Pioneers in the 19th century wrote "Watter Hear" so others might not pass it by unnoticed. Hueco Tanks is both a geological and an archaeological anomaly. The only source of water for miles around, it also features the largest concentration of Indian painted masks in North America. Over the years, Kay developed a theory about these masks and several of the other Jornada Mogollon glyphs that would revise portions of the history of the Southwest.

Around 400 CE, Mesoamericans arrived in the American Southwest as missionary traders in search of turquoise. They brought new religious concepts, new items to exchange, and new technologies. Over the next 1,000 years, Mesoamerican contact with the hunter-gatherer societies produced the Hohokam, Anasazi, and Mogollon cultures. We can only wonder, Kay remarks in her book, *Spirits from the South*, what the Mesoamerican missionary traders, with their rich cultural background and monumental architecture and productive agriculture, thought of the Jornada Mogollon's nomadic foragers, who painted or pecked the symbols of their beliefs on stone surfaces, who lived in the earth, who scratched, sometimes desperately, for food in a harsh climate. One wonders, too, what our foragers thought of our *spirits from the south*, "who appeared one day carrying wonderfully colored plumage and copper bells for trade, speaking of pyramids and storm gods and feathered serpents and collared jaguars and masked dancers and Twin Heroes, the movements of the sun and the stars, and seeking turquoise to carry south.... Whatever they thought, between them, they started a revolution."

During a thousand years of contact, the Jornada Mogollon assimilated many aspects of Mesoamerican culture. They changed from hunter-gatherers into agriculturalists, growing primarily corn. Their art relates how they adopted portions of Mesoamerican cosmology and incorporated Mesoamerican designs into their own frames of reference. Their hunter deities took on features of the Tlaloc, the goggle-eyed Mesoamerican storm god, and evolved into a multitude of masked, ceremonial dancing figures. Some of these figures retain horns and other symbols suggesting the preservation of their hunter-gatherer values. Over time, the borrowed Tlaloc figures changed as well, potentially forming an index to stages in the cultural confluence. Gradually, the desert people developed what is nowadays known as the Jornada Mogollon Style of rock art.

The masks at Hueco Tanks exemplify this style. There are two kinds of masks: "outline" masks with almond-shaped eyes showing pupils, triangular noses, and semi-circular mouths, some with teeth, that occur in large, open areas near Tlalocs and animal figures; and "solid" masks with blank, ghostly eyes that appear among other masks in small, isolated niches. Among the thousands of images at Hueco Tanks, approximately 250 are masks. In Cave Kiva, eight spectacular undulating masks convey a haunting illusion of motion. In addition to the Tlalocs and Tlaloc-inspired masks, there are horned and plumed serpents, collared jaguars, caricatured faces, geometric designs, dancing figures, people wearing elaborate headdress, masks with conical helmets, cat claws, X designs and symbols of animals and plants, including corn. Prototypes of these images adorn Mayan temples and ruins throughout Mesoamerica. Unsurprising in a culture organized around a desire for control of rain, much water symbolism appears in both pictographs (painted figures) and petroglyphs (etched or picked figures).

From 1971 to 1986, Kay and a succession of colleagues painstakingly recorded rock art throughout the Jornada Mogollon region. She studied archeological accounts of it. She weighed the evidence for its estimated age. She pondered theories of how and when the distinctive Jornada Mogollon Style emerged. By the mid-1980s, she suspected that some Jornada Mogollon rock art was much older than archaeologists had previously determined. Although she would have to wait another decade for solid proof, a few of the figures at Hueco Tanks already had convinced her she was right.

Although Kay was particularly fascinated by a few of the key figures—the Tlalocs and the masks—her goal as a cultural anthropologist was not to focus on any single motif, but to analyze groups of images in their geographic, iconographic, and ethnographic contexts. A significant obstacle in the study of rock art, however, had always been the lack of any scientific means for determining its age, an essential component in the assemblages of artifacts that archaeologists and anthropologists construct. Thus, mid-summer of 1995 found Kay ecstatic. Over the past couple of years, chemists at Texas A&M University had developed technology for dating painted glyphs containing carbon pigments. Kay had arranged with Texas Parks and Wildlife for tests at Hueco Tanks as soon as she learned they could be done, and the results showed several figures at Hueco Tanks to be even older than she had estimated, perhaps by 300 to 400 years. At last, Kay had hard evidence to show that Jornada Mogollon Style developed centuries before, not concurrently with Pueblo cultures. Indeed, further carbon-dating confirmed its origins perhaps to be as early as 200 CE.

"With the new dates come new understandings," Kay explained. "I think what we will now find is that contact between the Mesoamericans and the Late Desert Archaic peoples a few centuries after Christ triggered a prolonged fusion of two world views." Moreover, the rise of this new culture "proceeded in lock step for ... seven centuries ... before it culminated in the Puebloan culture." At last, Kay could argue conclusively that the Jornada Mogollon Style masks at Hueco Tanks are, as she had believed prior to their carbon-dating, prototypes of the katsina masks of the Pueblo Indians' masked dancing cults.

Kay seemed unable to imagine anyone's lack of interest in this fact, or indeed in anything concerned with rock art. Once she struck up a conversation about it, most people would feel at least a little of the contagious passion that had gripped her the day she spotted her first collared jaguar. More specific dates allow for better interpretation within the contexts of other rock art, other artifacts of physical culture, or the cosmology of the era. There are "whole books" in these glyphs, she proclaimed, books illuminating the Jornada Mogollon's transformational encounter with Mesoamericans.

Kay described the Jornada Mogollon region as a "diffusionist frontier." As the desert dwellers assimilated Mesoamerican culture, they exerted their own powerful influence in the region.

Kay saw Hueco Tanks as the geographical center, as well as the ceremonial center—a Mecca—of the Jornada Mogollon. Hueco Tanks provided water and protection from the sun; it was located on the turquoise trail; there were pithouses and a small pueblo in its vicinity. The most important icons of a new, syncretic religion— the masks and Tlalocs—are more numerous at Hueco Tanks than at any other site. She argued convincingly that the first katsina dances might have occurred there.

Even today, Indians with Mesoamerican spiritual roots are particularly drawn to Hueco Tanks. Energized by the results of the carbon-dating, Kay hoped some of them could help her de-code the specific meanings of rock art figures, and so the next phase of her work began to unfold. In 1996, she formally estab-lished a nonprofit educational organization called Rain House. Promoting a philosophy of "simple living and complex thinking," Rain House would facilitate communication among groups of all sorts—Indians and non-Indians, scientists and non-scientists, professionals and laypersons, educators and students—in short, anyone who could teach or who wanted or learn something about the Mesoamerican heritage of the Southwest and, espe-cially, about rock art. Various projects were supported intermit-tently through gifts and grants, but consistently by Kay's own personal funds.

News of Rain House spread through written word and word-of-mouth, the venue most likely to attract native people. Kay her-self was becoming a "diffusionist frontier." Forever an optimist, she was nevertheless astonished at the number of tribal people who appeared from near and far at the earliest workshops in Tularosa, N.M. They brought a new dimension of knowledge to bear upon Jornada Mogollon rock art in general, and Hueco Tanks in par-ticular. The tribal people she consulted agreed there are "books of information in the glyphs" on subjects ranging from agriculture to medicine and cosmology. White Bear Fredericks of the Hopi Bear Clan assured her that the Hopi had once traveled to Hueco Tanks and that the Bear Clan's origins could be traced to the collared jaguars there.

Other Native people also were eager to help her interpret rock art. They included a Mexica/Tolteca elder named Tlakaelel and his apprentice, Acacio Oltehua Acatecatl, and Don Allehandro Cerilo Perez-Oxlaj, a Quiche Mayan priest. Professor Eduardo Diaz (Universidad Nahua and Juarez University), a scholar of Mayan cultures, was another of several valuable resources. Tlakaelel, Acacio and Don Allehandro set out to teach Kay not only what they knew, but *how* they knew. Thus began another phase of her extraordinary life.

Kay understood she was the trusted recipient of uncommon gifts. Fluent in Spanish, with graduate degrees in Latin American studies and anthropology as well as extensive field experience among native cultures of Nicaragua, El Salvador, Belize, Guatemala, Paraguay, and Mexico, Kay was prepared intellectually to receive what was offered. She also was humble and willing to listen. The Kalpulli Tlateca of El Paso invited her to attend ceremonies at Hueco Tanks. The glyphs and pictographs resonate with Mesoamerican iconology familiar to them from other locations throughout Mexico and Central America. At their ceremonies, they pray to reunite their "families," the scattered progeny of tribal groups who have passed through Hueco Tanks for thousands of years.

The *antepasados*, the ancestors, they say, sing at night in the desert under the jaguar's protective presence, while the old knowledge, the old ways, wait to be recovered. At Hueco Tanks a "condensation of spiritual energy" exists that potentially everyone can feel, but to receive information requires spiritual attunement, a capacity for which human beings are genetically equipped. Tlakaelel and others *read* locations and shared with Kay the knowledge they acquired. The Tlalocs, masks and other icons, they told her, are not simply abstract figures that *stand for* something, like letters or words in Eurocentric sign systems. Catalysts or transformers of feeling, emotion, and energy, the figures both *signify* and *evoke* cosmic energy. One meaning of Quetzalcoatl thus accessible to Tlakaelel is *available energy in motion*. "The things I explain have a scientific foundation," he says. "They include the mathematics and history, and I could prove that it is true."

Tlakaelel endorses Kay's *Mecca* theory and offers an intriguing etymological analysis of the word, *hueco*. In Toltec, *hue* means far away and *co* means a big place or capitol (as in Mexi*co*, Xochimil*co*, etc.). *Hueco* means the far away capitol. From his readings at Hueco Tanks, Tlakaelel concludes that archaeologists will one day find evidence of four roads branching out in four directions from the site. All of the pueblos of the Americas were once elaborately connected with such roads, he contends. To facilitate travel, many of the glyphs convey mundane meanings referring to how many families live in an area or how much corn the people have planted and stored. Other figures contain astronomical information. One seems to be a calendar forecasting the visits of a comet in a 988-year cycle.

Along with Kay and Tlakaelel, Don Allehandro, the Quiche Mayan priest from Guatemala, visited Cave Kiva. There he saw a figure he recognized from sites in El Salvador. Like Tlakaelel, Don Allehandro is receptive to the energy of the place and received information from the glyphs. Some of the figures, he claims, tell about people who lived in caves or in some kind of protracted night for a long time. Possibly they traveled underground or in darkness to reach Hueco Tanks. The Tlalocs' white eyes speak to Don Allehandro of light in the minds of the people. They carried "a house" in their minds, he says, suggesting they carried within themselves the seeds of a new world.

Eduardo Diaz, who has studied Tlalocs throughout the Mesoamerican world, concurs. The word *Tlaloc*, he explains, derives from *Tlali* (land) and *okli* (drink), so it means a drink of the land. He told Kay he knew of a *pulque* or sacred drink, called *bebida de Tlaloc*, that "raises consciousness." Exploring Hueco Tanks, Diaz drew Kay's attention to some triangular patterns in the arrangement of Tlalocs. Later, when she asked Tlakaelel about the triangles, he said the pattern is part of a mathematical formula for "universal intelligence" that he, personally, can't explain, but like Tlakaelel, he insists there is "a science" to his way of knowing that can be learned.

Late in 2002, I came across F. David Peat's new book, *Black-foot Physics: A Journey into the Native American Universe.* Acknowl-edging "indigenous science," he writes, "as you sit with Native people, walk in nature, and spend time at sacred sites, an actual transformation of consciousness takes place." Among the Black-foot, Peat learned indigenous ways of understanding the universe, and he respects them enough to say that "at its deepest level, the dialogue between Western and Indigenous science will engen-der an increasing flexibility in human consciousness, an ability to [transcend] the boundaries of our own egos and worldview."

I read this, and I wanted to call Kay immediately. I wanted to drive straight to her house, run to her front door waving Peat's book over my head.

I would not be phoning her again. There could be no more shared coffee breaks between classes, no more waiting at restau-rants for her to show up late for lunch, no more afternoons enjoy-ing pie and coffee on her bright porch while her dogs snoozed at our feet. Earlier that year, the road Kay followed through this world had ended. First came breast cancer and chemotherapy, then acute myelogenous leukemia and more chemotherapy. The months ran on, and hope ran out.

Meanwhile, a flood in November 2001 destroyed her house. The waters rose nearly a foot inside it. One day I joined Kay to survey the damage. "Well," she said, pressing the cushions of a brand new couch that now both reeked and leaked, "we had just bought this." "Watter Hear," we joked. During the last two years of her life, Kay lost her lustrous, thick hair; much of her body weight; and then her home. She never lost her sense of humor, though, and she never stopped caring about Rain House or her ongoing con-versation with tribal people at Hueco Tanks. Close to death, Kay still radiated life. I saw a sunny, yellow color all around her then, and I still see it in my mind—a color like desert light, absorbed for years and slow to flow back to its source.

The desert was the place she chose to visit on her last vaca-tion. She and her husband, Jim McCulloch, traveled to one of her favorite rock art sites in northern Mexico. She sat alone for a while in a rock shelter, where she smoked a Native American pipe made especially for her and this occasion. I don't know what her thoughts were there, but I believe she found what she needed to face death. Collared by the jaguar so many years ago, she had come to know release from the material world, to let her spirit flow upward and outward with the smoke that vanishes into Mystery.

Under an earthly sun, our vision dims. The clear lines of our being wear away. Our bones sprout seeds of outlandish death. Perhaps beyond the tattering winds that beat us back into this world, a road unwinds among petroglyphs etched in light.

Photograph by Jim McCulloch

Kay Sutherland, 2001

The Tetris Effect

Cheryl Clements

The district attorney I debated wouldn't appreciate my pick-up-the-gun lecture, although I doubt he'd react as indignantly to it as he did to my claims this morning. I still contend that anyone with a nosy mother, an insistent child, or a lick of common sense would agree with me: the virtue of truth depends upon time and place. If the DA had expected me to lie when asked if I believed honesty is always best, he should've popped the question before I was sworn in.

Once again—despite the defense's best efforts—I have been ruled a person not of interest to our legal system, cut from the herd.

Now back at work, I speculate on my rejection with my colleague, Ann the Philosopher, whose office is beside mine at our community college. She's called for duty at least once a year and is always chosen, even served on a grand jury. If the court could see her office, though, they might judge her through different eyes. Ann's *The Birds* Barbie gets top billing beside her computer, but most of my vegan friend's dimly lit cave is decorated with snakes as she pays homage to them in photographs, plush toys, and etched glass.

Given that she has a plastic diamondback lying in wait beneath her desk, you'd think not much could rattle her. But last spring, Ann recoiled at a picture I shared from The Scene of the Crime. My husband, John, taught me to identify copperheads after we'd discovered one sunbathing on our front steps, and although my husband won't destroy most critters because they are "our friends," he educated me on the copperhead's shape—wider in the jaw than in the neck and narrower through the snout.

Usually, when I spot them in our development near the Brazos River, they are flatter than nature intended and are on the road. However, one morning when a lively fellow crossed my path, I pulled my Camry up beside it, snapped a picture with my camera phone, and zoomed in for inspection. To my surprise but as I later learned is in its nature, my prey froze awaiting my verdict: guilty.

I showed my *memento mori* to Ann and then to John, from whom I expected the praise a cat would enjoy for having nabbed a mouse. Because I wanted to know more about what I'd executed, I searched the Internet for copperhead trivia. Researchers have discovered their venom can retard the growth of some cancer cells, I reported to John. My husband's response was immediate: and you killed it.

I reminded him that they are not our friends.

Our subdivision is still under construction, with most of the homes and occupants too high-brow for John and me. When we were building, our electrician—who was never without coffee, having either a cup in hand or kept warm in a thermos—even said we weren't fit for our digs, particularly after he saw that my husband and I really did intend to paint our entire house by ourselves.

You don't belong here, our wired new friend claimed.

John laughed it off, but I felt the need to defend myself, so I answered, "I belong wherever I'm happy."

⊶⊷

Today as Ann tries explaining the error of my ways and why I was booted during *voir dire*, her tutorial is interrupted when a student—her two-year-old daughter in tow—shows up for Philosophy Central in our hallway. Little Miranda and her mother have come for help with logic. As professor, student, and punk kid settle at the help desk, I grab an expected chocolate kiss from the stash on top of my file cabinet and slip Miranda her fix. She and I established a special bond earlier this semester when she walked into my office and demanded that I lead her to "the other me." Miranda was adamant that we had a mission—to do something— and even grabbed my arm and coaxed me from my chair to help her hunt—for someone. Finally, her mother interpreted: the previous week Miranda had played with another logic student's daughter and was certain I'd know where to find her.

I'd rather savor chocolate with Miranda, but a young man

shows at my door and has a story to tell about why he missed our previous class meeting. His tale is pedestrian—car wouldn't start—but I give it three out of five stars on the bullshit scale. After all, he did season it with his missing work that day, too, and provided both the first and last names of those he called for a ride—even an ex-girlfriend, once a model and now an online porn star. Victim? Check. Sorrow? Check. Sex? Check, check.

I won't excuse his absence but take time to admire a picture of his former honey, fully clothed. Once my student leaves, I leave a voicemail for another English professor and tell her she's off the hook for subbing for my creative writing class today. I also pass on greetings from the gray-haired cowboy I sat beside in the court-room—Cowboy had known every third person who teaches at my college—and I tell her the mustachioed dude says to call him. This other potential juror had been friendly at first, even allowed me full rights to our shared armrest. For that kindness, I'd offered him my Miss Texas Smile.

Later though, a Panhandle-strength cold front hit. Cowboy hadn't appreciated my taking issue with the prosecution's ideas about honesty or my calling into question the State's remark that people intuitively know how to live a law-abiding existence—no matter how they were reared. Whatever my offense, by midway through *voir dire*, Cowboy was no longer interested in conversation with me. I didn't belong here, and he now knew my kind. He'd seen that my jaw was set, and I was venomous: I was not his friend.

Eventually, the defense attorney called roll and asked each of us a simple question to answer with yes or no: given what we'd heard today, could we give the accused a fair trial? Many in the jury of my peers answered to the negative, but *no* was not the *n-word* I heard.

In a last-ditch effort to keep me, the defense then asked if I could be persuaded to change the views I'd shared with them. I could see by his raised brow that he already knew the answer.

The young man on trial had brought his aunt with him. She sat with her back to the judge's bench and faced us. Rogue salt and pepper hairs stuck out from beneath her platinum wig, and her smile was a thin effort with just a slight tilt on each end. The defendant sat perpendicular to her and stared ahead, committed to his concentration on nothing.

I looked to the boy and wished he'd make eye contact—there's no weapon, not even the one he'd probably used when he broke into the houses, that cuts to the heart like direct eye contact. But he wouldn't let me enter.

Could I be persuaded to change the views I'd shared, those at least 49 others had been captive audience to hear? This was not the time or the place for a lie. I had my conviction to defend.

⸺◆⸺

At this point early in the semester, I usually tell my prose students my own true-life crime story, about when my handbag—passport included—was stolen in Cabo de Roca, Portugal. The little town is remembered by some tourists as the westernmost point of the continent, but I recall it as *The Armpit of Europe*.

As I was filling out paperwork in the police station and trying to translate dialogue from the reruns of *Batman* on their little black and white TV, an officer walked into the station, took off his belt and sidearm, and commenced yacking with his buddy. A cop put down his weapon on the counter, right in front of me, within reach. And he turned away.

He did not know that I had been robbed. He did not comprehend that I was still pissed. Most of all, he didn't appreciate that I'm from Texas.

Imagine what would have happened if I'd picked up the gun, I tell my students. Think of how my life would have changed. The person talking to you today wouldn't exist. I'd have landed in prison or might have killed someone, and then I'd have to live with all that. When characters come to a crossroads, sometimes you must make them pick up the gun.

As I discovered the first time I gave that advice, it resonates with students, perhaps too well. In workshop they even tell each other "pick up the gun." But I don't know that I can share this wisdom today, not after what happened in Connecticut this past

December and after the shooting at Lone Star College just two weeks ago.

Ann has asked me more than once when I will "pack heat," and she was amused that John gave my daughter Marlene a pink BB gun for Christmas. My husband insists that she learn to shoot—this from the same person who fussed at me for telling Marlene that Santa, whom we call The Big Man, is a big lie. Of course, John and I both told our daughter not to point her gun at anything she didn't intend to kill, but that's not what woke me in the middle of the night. What opened my eyes is that she'd thought her gun could protect her.

Christmas night isn't the only time my sleep has been interrupted by crossfire. It was 1991, the first year I taught for my college, the year of the shooting at Luby's restaurant in Killeen. It was the semester I could not make eye contact with a nice student, a good boy who'd done nothing wrong but appear in my dream after the Killeen tragedy. And he came to me night after night for more than a week, and he brought with him a gun.

My husband's best friend, Bradley, was in hypnotism school back then, before he got the calling to Buddhism. Although John and I had been teasing about why he didn't yet have a watch on the end of a chain, I decided that perhaps Bradley could help me find the source of my fear and put an end to my recurring nightmare. After all, Bradley had shared the theory he supported: we cannot dream of doing what we cannot imagine doing, and we are everyone in our dreams.

After he agreed to work his spell, I put our cat in the bedroom, turned off the stereo, and cut the lights. I assumed a comfortable position on the couch and closed my eyes. I can't recall details of how I was led into the dark. The sensation wasn't that of Alice's falling down the hole or of Jimmy Stewart's panic in *Vertigo*. Everything was focused on weightlessness and wandering. I was not falling but rising. And then my student—the boy I had no reason to believe was anything other than nice and good—enters the room where I'm teaching. He has a mission, and he has the gun.

"You are the teacher," Bradley said. "What are you thinking?"

I'm afraid. I don't know what to do.

"Now you are one of the students. What are you thinking?"

I don't understand what's happening. I look to everyone else for help, but they don't know what's happening, either.

"Now you are the gun. What are you thinking?"

I think I'm strong. I'm strong, and I don't feel afraid.

"Why don't you feel afraid?"

I don't feel afraid because I don't feel anything.

"Now you are the shooter. What are you thinking?"

I tried to answer Bradley. I also tried to open my eyes. I finally said that I wanted to run.

"What are you running toward?"

"I'm not running toward anything, just running away. I want to stop now."

"Why do you want to stop running?"

"No, I want to stop this. Now."

But my windows to the world wouldn't open on my command. They were beautiful windows, those the truck shattered when it drove into Luby's Cafeteria. They were beautiful windows on a beautiful day, and then that beautiful day turned into pitch because someone had picked up the gun.

———

My jury of one has returned with a verdict by the time I reach my creative writing class. This year I'll pass on my Portugal story, and as the campaign for right-to-carry on campus soldiers on, I'll continue hoping that when all is said and done, I'm still where I belong.

As I call roll, I take note of a young man on the back row. He's been absent the past two meetings, but that's not why I pause on his mug. From what I can see, he's a clean-cut student—nothing peculiar about him that would lead me to identify him in a lineup. But I know we all have it in us to pick up the gun—to shatter others' lives, drive our own down the path to pitch, and in a moment of panic become *The Other Me*.

The Awful Rowing Toward God

Betsy Berry

"Oh, she knew me!—she could twist me!
But I spent my life trying to be with her."
—Anne Sexton of her mother,
Mary Staples Harvey

On Christmas day in 2012, when high winds roared through the sparkling sunlight of a December Texas morning, I began to do what I had vowed never to do, and that was to write about my mother. She had been dead just over four years.

———◆———

We never called her mother or mommie. In our family, she became Mimi—an anecdote traced to my brother's first mangling of ma-ma. It was a story sounding so made up it just might have been true. We did have a mommie, my mother and I did. That's what I had come to call my maternal grandmother, my mother then following suit. My grandmother was Mommie to us both.

———◆———

My mother lived her life within the shell of a lovely vase with invisible cracks. She would seep water slow and steady.

———◆———

In a longer list of horrors on the death certificate, her final blow had been determined to be congestive heart failure. Meaning that she had died a lingering, terrible death, a wet suffocation, a drowning, really. Water, in its lack or overabundance, had been a constant symbol in her life.

———◆———

Our family home went through four major floods; one rushed through sandbagged doors to crest at nine feet. Only one of these did our mother not live to see. She and my father had taken root in their 50s on an island on "a hundred-year flood plain," as was the official claim. In my imagination, my mother was her own kind of island, anchored as near to the water as she could be. She was a superb fisherman, the arid Texas plain behind her. In life, her primary strategy was to dig in her heels and continue to "hold on tight." If I had a nickel for every time she told me to hold on tight, I'd be a rich 'un.

She could pretend she found you special, but the truth and my mother often were parted. There were times you could reach her, but mostly you watched her from a kind of distance as if she were a person of much interest, but not necessarily your mother. As much as anything else, that's probably how I made it through my life with her—up until her death, actually.

But there was no making it through that.

⟶•⟶

I don't have many childhood recollections, but all involve my mother. My father was an Air Force pilot, so we moved around a lot. Each time we did, I went ahead to the new place with my father so I could start school on time. She would be packing up our goods or overseeing the packing, and her absence was the kind of calm before the storm that made you jumpy. We had a privileged enough upbringing: my father, the most financially successful of his siblings and his parents before him; his wife the mystery girl from Mobile who had "married up," though plenty would guess it was the other way around; my brother, a Biff Loman type whose best times were in high school but who had developed an edgy sense of humor he'd have been sunk without. I was born at the northeastern edge of the island of Puerto Rico, a nervous, neurotic little girl who completed the nucleus.

Like the oldest family cliché, we looked good from the outside. Without question, we were tight, locked in a kind of death grip as soon as she'd given birth. For others, our parents were so flat-out fun to be around that friends clamored to do so. Their children paled in comparison, and our parents let us know it, too. I would like the luxury of viewing photographs at my leisure. But we were less a picture family than a portrait one. The portraits went down one by one in the floods, and the photos didn't do so well in the drink, either.

We had them once—photos. Boxes of them, like most families, and school annuals, art projects, cards exchanged, scrapbook stuff. Most all of it was gone by the second flood in 1996. Inexplicably, boxes had been taken from the attic and were under my mother's bed. When it was time to load the car and exit the island by bridge while we still could, only my mother knew the photos were there. Of course, she was in a panic, so who knows? (We *would* learn later that she liked to erase, or edit, history.) The Polaroids that hadn't perished looked like Andy Warhol portraits when you pulled them apart. In the very few I have, we look like strange water creatures. In one I'm an older teen with a fixed smile, dressed to go out, standing next to my mother, my brother far right. My head appears to have lost its mooring and floats freely. Part of my long dress appears to my left. My mother is seen from the waist up, a big bouffant of hair at the top. My brother's clothes are '70s style, his faced washed away completely.

I can remember a bit about being that age, about being anxious and a bit afraid, but not like feeling young. High school had been horrifying in the main, but no doubt I was fearful from the time I took my first step. A light and careful tread was the way to move within the fragile romance of my family, a feature written and directed from first to last by my mother.

—◆—

Early in 2008, in her 92nd year and worn out by life and caring for a bedridden husband, my mother fell, either accidentally or out of rage. She had fallen before and gotten up gamely, but this time she lay on her bedroom floor for hours. My father lay in his bed and talked to her, mostly about how impotent he felt—and was. Theirs was the kind of love/hate relationship that might be ended through murder but less often by divorce. Henry, the man who had worked for them for more than 25 years, drove from Seguin with his wife, a former nurse. He picked Mother up from the floor and put her in bed, where she wet herself through the night, unable to move and in what must have been great pain. That was the night when she went mute, in a sense of the word. Never again in her life did she move much—frantic, celebratory, or anxious movements, her stock in trade.

The next day, she went to the hospital in Seguin, where she would return several times in the next several months. She was operated on, flirting with doctors—maybe even contemplating a real comeback. Then she refused the rehab part of the deal, refused dramatically, as if rehab was something losers had to do. But the surgery had gone badly, anyway. She was a wreck in the hospital: hating me, my brother (my father was too frail to visit.) She snarled at her roommates, rolled her eyes at the nurses. All she wanted to do was come home, take the pain pills my father shared with her, and ... well, that was about it, as I think about it now. She'd no other real plans. She was in her last incarnation, a terrible thing to witness.

She became a little more of my father every day: sleep, worry, pain, pills. Brief euphoria, exhausted sleep. Waning interest, pills. Depression, day after day. She used my father's walker, for which he had no use now, and his potty seat, which was moved from each other's bed for only a short while until my father wore diapers. Now they were both helpless, moody kids, shut up in an overheated room with thick, dusty curtains. My mother, who had loved to read, could no longer do so. My father had enjoyed watching news, and sports, and weather, and movies, now seemed beyond that (just as well; my mother, who had bad hearing, complained about the incomprehensible noise that accompanied TV). When they talked, they hurled insults and recriminations. My mother often wished aloud, in the presence of the four of the family, that her kids had "made something of themselves," to which my father would agree. And then in another moment, she might just whack him in the arm with her water glass, if she felt like it. At times, of course, they seemed to enjoy their captivity, two stowaways in the dark hold of a ship.

On July 1, 2008, with my brother present and I having returned to Austin from my parents' just earlier that night, my mother made one of her last attempts to leave the bed and go into her kitchen. My brother went to her there and said she had better go back to her room. My father was dying. Two weeks before our father had refused his ubiquitous brandy, then his pills, then all food, and then liquids. Although he had been in full dementia, the unceasing babble that could make you laugh or cry had stopped. In its place was the death rattle. My mother went back and got under her covers, staring straight ahead of her and not in the direction of my father. Minutes later he died, torturously, of blood poisoning, tracking his eyes to my brother's face sitting nearby and saying his last words, "I'm sorry, Freddee," a deathbed confession.

My mother had been wheeled out in her chair, another of her husband's hand-me-downs, into a clear midnight sky where a rare summer breeze freshened the muggy air. Under those stars, she watched until the ambulance was out of sight, as he was driven to the morgue in Seguin, where he would be prepared for the second 40-mile drive to the Porter Loring funeral home in San Antonio. Then she was wheeled back to the room my father had just left, to live out her own days.

She napped most afternoons. Several weeks after Dad's funeral when I arrived to check on her, she was a sad silhouette in a shaft of late afternoon light. She was losing more and more of herself by the day, and she was sitting up against her pillows, looking blankly at her prized ficus trees on the back porch. A multi-green fence against the huge back windows, the trees blocked out the view of the lake from the living room, just as her heavy curtains blocked the water view from the bedroom. Just days before, she had had a long-lasting bout of dementia where she claimed to watch "a Mexican family" hacking away all the leaves from her trees. She had many details, including the clothes the cutters were wearing. They ignored her cries through the window. She worried obsessively about who would clean up the mess—though Henry had whitewashed the porch a month ago, and its surface was spotless beneath the gleaming green of the trees. That day I arrived, she had had no time to fix a face to greet me, and, instead, the one she turned toward my sound was in the process of shuffling away its earthly qualities. She pointed to my father's empty hospital bed beside hers, a torturous looking piece of connected iron that I had felt would be a bad thing to remain in her room, much less for her to make it her own bier. She nodded toward his bed and said, slowly, each word its own: "I know what happened over there."

Before I could get beyond the assault of these words—an assault to her as well—she swung her heavy head round from a neck stretched to its full. Then she gave me a straight look—lowered lids, a purse to the lips, probably the first straight look she gave me ever. There was a whiff there of true honesty, not the kind of scent given off much by my mother. It wafted in the air a bit as if waiting for the echo of her previous words to die completely. "I," she gasped. "I ... I." Three times, like that.

Then she lifted her eyes to mine, shading hers with a hand and, enunciating each word, she said, "I should have just left you in the ocean." As to what she meant, I haven't a clue. It wasn't to be offered as some kind of symbol, or reality, in a therapist's office.

It was more like a string of words and the essence of their sound together, some kind of chime she felt she needed to sound, that she had no doubt needed to sound for a very long time now.

But on this day, it was said, and sounded, and the effect of doing so brought her a temporary peace. She closed her eyes and stretched her arms in front of her. "If you have a drink, could I join you in one, too?" The idea of cocktails cheered us, and I went to fetch them for us.

In a way I can't explain, about a declaration from my mother I can't explain, residing in a place of memories I can't explain, my mother's watery salvo that day became, as strange as it sounds, a kind of gift to me. Confession, apology, outcry, joke, or just a reference to the wide gulf between us? She had wanted me both to know something and nothing at the same time, and this obfuscation she had used like a weapon would soon be part of her buried life, and then, later, of mine as well.

——◆——

My mother's caregivers were sleep-ins now, but their names had changed several times. Some stole from her and had to be told to shove off. Some got jobs with elderly much easier to work with. My mother became addicted to Xanax, and after her doctor cut her off, she plotted to send one of her children to Mexico in the hopes to procure more. Although she had complained for all of her life she could never sleep, she got better at it and sought its relief. She cried easily. She and the room smelled of urine and feces, and of my father's deathbed, on which she now slept, saying ominously of this, "Don't worry about me. I know what happened here." I didn't dare guess at her death, the time that would both free me, finally, and transport me to the other prison of whys and what ifs where I was to receive Life. I struggled to keep my other life as intact as I could, but as ever, she permeated my days and ways.

Then, early in the third week of October 2008, I drove again to her from Austin, that hour and a half of I-35 I'd traced so many times my tire treads must be grooved in the macadam. Her caretaker had called, saying that my mother was restless, wild-eyed, moaning, picking at "the bugs" on her coverlet with bony fingers. She was "in bad shape," like so many times before.

I let myself into her front door with my key, though with locks and balances so undone by the flooding, probably anyone could have gotten inside that door. I walked down the lighted front hall she loved calling "the gallery," into the dark of her room. The small bedside lamp threw a small circle onto her small body, bent into a circle on that narrow bed, and with room to spare.

"Mimi!" I called. "Mim, I'm here."

Later I would remember the whole event in vivid, slow motion detail. Her struggling up on one elbow, a soiled white T-shirt falling from a thin shoulder. Her hair, for so many years a shimmery, almost phosphorescent white pageboy that always evoked compliments, seemed to lack color of any kind. In the place of my mother's glorious hair were lank wisps of matted hair, oily mid-way down from the roots. And her face, the face I had tried to read millions of times before. Her eyes were wide, like the slightly hopeful and the horribly resigned. Here I had always thought she ruled the world with her fierce will, her carefully cultivated rituals. But all strategies had failed.

She reached up into the light, as if from a hole, faces of po-tential rescuers swimming above her near the light. I called an ambulance. Ambulances had come many times before to this house on the island, and now I was advised that, lacking signs of an emergency, I might have to pay for the service this time, and couldn't I, like, pour her into a car for the 15 minutes to Seguin? I looked again at her haunted face, beneath it a lump of flesh, dying like an animal. "I shall pay," I told the ambulance driver, sounding like something out of a Victorian novel to my ears. I hardly knew what was real and what wasn't. In all of the family romance that defined my life, I must have known the *denouement* when I saw it. On some level, I knew that for my mother, it would be a one-way trip.

As she was moved from the gurney into the ambulance, she made one more stab at it—life, I guess—wincing at the sunlight, ordering me to fetch her sunglasses, flirting with her handlers, and perhaps these were as good as any other buffers for the journey ahead. I saw her off, down the same road she had watched my fa-ther off. In the same silence that accompanied his journey, the am-bulance did not turn on its sirens. I called my brother in Houston, and because I was the only one in the house as I did so, one of the rare times within my family that I had felt so comfortably alone, I lingered some moments. Then I got a call from a hospital minister who implored me to okay the insertion of a feeding tube, a pos-sible measure to be called for. On her DNR document that I, as a Power-of-Attorney, had helped her draft, she, like her husband before her, had requested that she not be artificially resuscitated, and for her life not to be sustained by other artificial means. When

I phoned her doctor, he advised me, in a more persuasive argument than the ministers or even God, against it.

"If she lived then, what life?" he said. "I see this happen to families. Who makes the decision down the line to take away the tube then? That person has to live with it." Next, he gave me the usual business about her "wanting to be with her husband," and for the first time, he called me by my first name. Surely, somehow, by then I knew. Somehow, surely, I must have known by then.

She was admitted to a private room, where my brother and I stayed with her until late that night. We exchanged our usual good nights and sleep tights; I even told her to hold on tight! But she was miserable. By morning we found out that on several occasions she had not only tried to, but actually pulled the IV from her arm, the arm half again its size from the bruising. I thought of my neighbor, who on the night before he died had mounted his last physical effort in shedding his own clean T-shirt they had put on him at the last.

My mother was moved to a kind of intensive care but worse, I thought, 10 beds to the room, women and men together. Two nurses, one at a desk, were present all hours of the day and night. There my mother, barely opening her filmed-over eyes, motioned me to come closer.

"Did ... the doctor ... make me sick?" she asked me in a ragged breath, struggling not just with the words but their confusion. He was one of the few, this doctor, whom my mother had been completely unable to charm.

"No. You're sick, Mim," I said. "As sick as you've ever been. Freddee and I are here with you." About then they clapped an oxygen mask over her face, and in another moment, she was asleep or unconscious. Whichever one it was, I hope, relieved temporarily her fears and regrets.

I don't know if she had any idea she was with others who would die in this room, then be carted off to what Stephen Crane called that "different and sinister hospitality of the grave." That Friday the doctor talked to me about releasing her. The next Monday, October 29, was to be a major one for me.

It was planned that she be taken by ambulance to Austin, where she would live in a full-care facility near my home (arrangements I had made years before—and begged both her, and my father, to agree to back then). Either she was somewhat better, I supposed, or they were ready to let her go anyway. Finding a Bible in her bedside drawer, I asked if she'd like me to read from Ecclesiastes, the famous passage about time that had been so much in my mind for the last few days. "No!" she said, in a quiet way she'd always had that was better than shouting. I put the Bible away.

And on that Friday, my mother holding on, so they said, my brother decided to go home to Houston for the weekend. Because my husband was to speak at his high school reunion that weekend in Carrollton, Texas, I made the decision to accompany him because to go seemed to make as much sense as to stay. I went through the motions that I had known as leaving the hospital, returning home and packing, and then—a different direction on I-35 than I'd been in a while, to the city of my college years at SMU, a happy time. I think my parents had been happy enough then, too.

After meeting my husband's many high school friends for the first (or second) time, and losing a few of my worries in the process, we were back at our hotel, the once stately Melrose, on the corner of Oak Lawn and Lemmon. It was 10 p.m., and hotel and surrounds were fixing to erupt, full party mode. The week before Halloween, this heavily gay district in Dallas has a well known, campiest-of-the-camp celebration, which in my robot-like state, I had forgotten took place. The streets are cordoned off, French Quarter-style, and costumed revelers walk the streets drink in hand.

A man encased in a nude-colored banana peel and two balloons tied to his feet and wobbling as he walked by, giant penis and testicles that seemed as suitable a symbol as any to begin the bacchanalia. Although Don and I were anything but in a party mood, we'd decided to have a drink at the hotel bar, the Library. It had been a great bar in its day, and it just might be still.

We went up to the room to drop off my purse. The night had gone well, better than I could have expected, and I appreciated so much being with my husband. As the doors opened to the lobby after the elevator ride down, two figures stood in the lobby, seemingly looking straight at us. They were two drag queens—and formidable ones at that. One was at least six feet five inches in his stocking feet, but over seven feet tall in his over-the-top platforms. He was as thin as a rail, wearing a wig of long black hair, the white hose of a nurse, and French maid's costume. His companion was tall enough if not as tall, and far wider in the trunk, blossoming into a Mae West siren with a blonde wig and gold sequined, fish-tail dress. My jaw dropped instinctively at the sight. I must have looked so small in comparison! The French maid turned his eyes to my small, thin frame and long brown hair and approached me, his arms open for the dramatic hug. We were as in a soap opera, where estranged mother and daughter are reunited, and in the instant learn just how much they loved each other. For me it seemed like such a, I don't know, *perfect* moment for humor that I immediately shared in the joke, this funny family fantasy—and with a perfect stranger.

"Mommie!" he said, almost staggering with torture as he discovered his long lost mother, just a slip of a woman before him. "Mommie!"

"C'mere, you crazy kid," I said, wrapping my arms around him, where I came up to about his waist. We all had a laugh, a joyous laugh.

"You guys look fabulous, the both of you," I said, as they turned to exit and walk the streets in all their fabulous femaledom. "Enjoy your night!" we called after them, and turned toward the bar.

Then just after we were served our cocktails, I took two long sips of courage from mine and walked back out to the lobby to phone the hospital. I was put through to the nurse on duty, but it was too noisy on my end, so that I had to go outside the hotel and into the carnival of the cooling night.

"Ms. Berry?" the nurse said. "Mrs. Berry's daughter, yes? I was just saying what a hard night she's had, poor dear, a very hard night, I'm sorry to report to you."

And then it happened, "the moment," I call it, for it was to change everything that followed. Everything that was to come after for me would be changed.

The nurse told me my mother was tearing at the bedclothes, as if to throw them off her, and that she had several times succeeded in removing her oxygen mask to try to talk.

"She keeps saying, 'Mommie!'" said the nurse. "Mommie! Over and over, poor dear."

That is where the memory ends and the fallout begins. I've no idea what I said in return, if anything at all. I don't remember hanging up. I vaguely remember reentering the hotel and imagining the swell of hundreds of voices having fun. I saw the actions of talking and laughing and clinking glasses, but I heard nothing. When I got back to my husband, he told me that I looked like a ghost, or that I had seen one, anyway. I was weeping in silence, he said—and I do remember the sensation of my face being wet. It was all inside, the nurse's words, that would be her last words, though she was to live a while longer. Everything happening around me now was taking place in some other world, not my own.

I saw her, too, saw her as if on a screen, struggling up on one bony elbow and calling out—shouting out, probably, to her mind—calling out in the darkness of that cold dark quiet, the pulse of the hospital at night. Saying the words, too, in raspy, futile tones, maybe she didn't know she was saying them, her heart breaking that cold night and knowing that she could never be comforted, or saved, never again.

Mommie. Mommie.

I hear her saying it today.

That was Saturday. The following Monday, the doctor withdrew her release. She had "taken a turn," he said. Later that day, personnel came to move her to a "private" room. Four people in the room together would have to turn in unison. Her last room had no windows. You needed no explanation to understand that it was the last transition, a dying room. Time moved quickly there.

By now her hands and feet were blue, fingertip to wrist, toe to ankle. A dark blue, the kind you might expect after death but didn't want to encounter in life. I've no idea if she knew anyone with her, or if she'd a thought at all, and I hope it is true, that she was left then with only the instinct of waning life and the final *whoosh* of death, as I had thought before of it. At nine p.m., my brother went back to my mother's home to sleep. I can only imagine how frightened I was to have told him my own decision, to stay the night, in there with her and death hovering just outside.

Within an hour her breathing worsened, if that was even possible. Her eyes were shut. When I touched her hand, a layer came off like a purple onion. I hovered there, between her and everything around her. Hers was a face I'd never known and had known all along, one that had frustrated, scared, humiliated and tortured me—a face I do hope that had loved me. I knew her last breath when it came. I held my own breath, and then gasped when I had lingered too long. But there was no gasp from her.

And then my heart broke, damaged in the process already. Two nurses came with their stethoscopes, each to listen to her unmoving chest and assign the time of death. When neither nurse addressed my mother, I knew the jig was up.

My husband on the late night drive from Austin, my brother back in 15 minutes. When they told us we could have some time with her, we took it, each of us watching what we never in the world expected our mother to be, a body that had once housed the purest essence of vivacity I have ever known, the mind that died with secrets only the dead would know.

After a long while, we turned together toward the door, my brother flipping off lights that no longer shone down on our mother. There we left her to the dark, still waters of the unknown.

Note: My title is borrowed from Anne Sexton's posthumous collection of poems, *The Awful Rowing Toward God* (Houghton Mifflin, 1975), and is used with thanks.

Where There's a Will, There's a Way

Liz Bates

"You have breast cancer." Those are four words I never expected to hear. But on September 28, 2012, just seven months after my son Will was born, those words changed my family life forever. The diagnosis was devastating! How could this be happening? I was 32, in good health, and didn't have a family history of breast cancer. It didn't seem possible.

My first thoughts immediately turned to my son. In an instant, I went from looking forward to seeing my son take his first steps, starting school, and getting married, to hoping I'd be here to see it. And I feared he wouldn't know me. Those thoughts continue to cross my mind as I fight this terrible disease. So I continue to ask God to bless me with the chance to raise the most precious gift He's given me.

Photographs by Valerie Payne of Photerium, Austin, Texas

After some of the shock wore off, I started writing. Most of what I write is for my son. Whatever the outcome, he will know who I am and what he means to me and his dad. My entries are simple. They offer a snapshot of a day in our lives right now—and tiny little tidbits from my past. My first journal entry from late November 2012 is fairly typical.

> *Dear Will,*
>
> *We are currently sitting in bed, but you show no signs of slowing down. You're amped up. I imagine a variety of things got you going after we thought you were about to fall asleep—one being me tickling you. I know your dad would tell me not to, but I can't help it. I love to hear you laugh. Your laugh and smile are contagious. I could have the worst day, and then I see your smile, and I melt. My day immediately brightens.*
>
> *So it's no surprise that I love every moment I spend with you. Every minute is special. I pray you know the joy I have in my heart when you have children. I know children are born every day, but every child is a miracle. And that feeling—that you've experienced a miracle—doesn't subside. It grows as your child meets every milestone. Lately, we've felt as if we're experiencing a new miracle every day. You're nine-months-old now, but you have been on a roll! since you turned six months old. Since then, you've learned to sit on your own, pull up on furniture, and you're starting to crawl. I love it! And I love you! Muah!*
>
> *XOXO,*
> *Mom*

Journaling also helps me cope with my uncertain future so I can focus on my life's joys. For example, I try to write down what I'm thankful for each day. This simple act encourages me to reflect on what's most important in life and to savor every moment God gives me to be with my husband and son. Most of my journal entries relate to Will.

This symbolizes the importance he has in my life and the joy he brings to my life. One of my most memorable entries was from early January 2013. Will had just finished his bath. As we left the bathroom, I laughed and started talking to him in my best Dori (*Finding Nemo*) voice in the mirror. Will thought it was hilarious and started to laugh uncontrollably. For about five minutes, we exchanged laughs. I loved it!

And I find joy in things that might annoy most moms. For example, on January 1, 2013, Will peed all over me before I could stick him in the tub. Forget that I had just taken a shower. To me, it was just another part of being a mom—the best job in the world. Then, there's his birthday cupcake. I couldn't wait to see him make a mess. The messier, the better. And he didn't disappoint. He had cake all over his face. These lighthearted moments make my diagnosis easier to handle. And the seemingly endless number of things I need to do to care for Will ensures that there is no time to sit around and be sad. There are diapers to change, bottles to clean, and teeth to brush.

This reminds me of something one of my students wrote to me when she learned I had breast cancer. Her mom, also diagnosed with breast cancer at a young age, is still battling it 12 years later. When my student told her mom about me, she said "Thank God she has her son. And the fact that his name is Will is a *God thing*. Will is going to be her Will to get through this." My maiden name is Will, so we chose the name to honor my family. We had no idea how fitting his name would be. This shows me God knew I'd need a source of light during this otherwise dark time.

God also knew what He was doing when He led me to Evan. He is a supportive and caring husband who loves nothing more than taking care of his son. Evan was made to be a dad. All I have to do is watch Will's face light up when Evan comes home at night, and I feel calm. Having cancer has not been easy, but I sleep better at night knowing Will has a dad with a strong moral compass who's willing to stand up for what's right. I admire Evan's strong work ethic and ability to get things done. But most of all, I love his kind heart. It's one of the things that attracted me to Evan in the first place. His caring nature doesn't shine through more than when he's with Will. Will may not know it yet, but he's blessed to have Evan as his daddy.

And every time I look at them, I'm reminded that I'm blessed to have them. They give me the strength to fight and the courage to hope. I know that where there's a Will, there's a way.

Fruit of the Orchard
to the Keystone XL Pipeline

Tammy Cromer-Campbell

Winona, Texas, introduced me to the world of environmental activism. From photographing the very first photograph of Jeremy whose image haunted me until I asked Phyllis Glazer for the rest of the children's names that they believed were harmed by the hazardous waste injection well facility, Winona heightened my sense of my own responsibility as a photographer to go beyond mere documentation and presentation in order to embrace the more fundamental ethic of using my talents and skills to convey messages that need to be heard. With the help of other environmentalists, I realized that our lignite mines and power plants have the highest concentrations of mercury on the continent. With the burning of fossil fuels, extreme weather conditions occur. East Texas has been under drought for a few years now. Lake-o'-the-Pines is where Longview gets its water. It alarms me to see the deep end of a swimming area dry. I end back in Winona. This time with an image of the Keystone XL Pipeline that is being built in this tiny community of 550, we must move from fossil fuels to clean green energy such as wind.

Lost Love

Jeremy

Texas Hwy 322, lignite coal pit mine

Martin Lake Power Station

Islandview No. 1, Lake O' the Pines, Texas Drought Series

Islandview No. 2, Lake O' the Pines, Texas Drought Series

Hwy 16, near Winona, Texas,
the TransCanada Keystone XL Pipeline

Amarillo Wind

SONG

The Tapestry is Rich:
Women's Voices in Texas Music

Kathleen Hudson

I was sitting at the Kerrville Folk Festival, awaiting my third experience of a Mary Gautheir show May 2012. I first heard her name in a Ray Wylie Hubbard song. Then I chanced upon her at the Majestic Theatre in San Antonio as she sang the opening set for a John Prine show. I was walking across the lobby heading to my seat, heard her voice, and stopped in my tracks. Head turning like radar toward a signal, I searched stage. There she stood, in black leather pants, delivering stories that took courage to tell. I heard her in 2011 at the Kerrville Folk Festival, an event known around the world for showcasing the songwriter. As I listened to her in 2012, I became agitated, Something was missing for me. Later, I reported to friends, "Her music stirs up something in me. A longing to be that brave, perhaps? An urge to create out of my own experience of life."

One fine day, reading over an essay I had written on women in Texas music in the House of David, my writing cabin on the Dancing Star Ranchita out west of Kerrville, I was interested in the information I had collected but not at all interested in the essay I had written.

The material below is taken from that essay, and I have surrounded the information with some of my reflections at the end of June 2012. I have a music foundation celebrating 25 years of history (www.texasheritagemusic.org), a great-grandson 18 months old, a trip to the Kerrville Folk Festival with my daughter, Lisa, and three of her young daughters, Angel, Erin, and Maya, and a plaque saying I have taught at Schreiner University 25 years. All these threads in my life are part of this weaving as I reinvent the "essay" written in 2005.

The threads are beautiful: blue and green, silver and gold, red and purple. Each thread contributes to the pattern that emerges as the weaving begins. The tapestry of women's voices in the Texas music scene is rich and varied.

First, the emerging pattern. Rhythm, movement, and relatedness capture our eye here. Some edges seem gentle, while others zig and zag as they trace out distinct edges. The pattern grows, expanding and contracting before our very eyes. *I wonder at my attraction to moving patterns. The sky perhaps? We know the Maya were star-watchers, and I do visit San Miguel de Allende on a regular basis. The museum of Diego Rivera in Guanajuato contains his illustrations of the Mayan Popol Vu, and my "hermana," Marisela, in San Miguel is married to an archeologist who explored the pyramid site near San Miguel. My interests run wide!*

Looking through the spools of thread that await the weaving, we see the rich and tender life of Tish Hinojosa, the rowdy indulgence of Tanya Tucker, the wisdom of Carolyn Hester. Lydia Mendoza brings in the voice of a pioneer, joining with Cindy Walker, who has written for voices as diverse as Elvis Presley, Eddy Arnold and Bob Wills. The Dixie Chicks add a West Texas flavor through the voice of Natalie Maines, while Lee Ann Womack takes the music she studied in Levelland, Texas, to the world. Ruthie Foster has moved out of her East Texas home, taking her soulful songs to the world. Carolyn Wonderland rocks us with her songwriting and her performance, a favorite of Bob Dylan. *Today, as I worked in the House of David, May 29, I saw Bob Dylan given the Presidential Medal of Freedom by President Obama. Toni Morrison also was a proud recipient. Both of these people are part of my story about women. "She's got everything she needs. She's an artist. She don't look back." Dylan got that right!*

Terri Hendrix waited tables in San Marcos before she took to the road. Joe Ely says it best, "Terri Hendrix is an amazing performer and a great writer. Her storytelling has a certain kind of believability that is natural, and she can turn on a dime and twist it around to where it's as unexpected and funny as anything you could imagine. All combined, it's pretty amazing."

Lavelle White began playing the clubs in Houston in the 1950s with the Johnny Copeland Band. After a stint in Chicago, Ms. White returned to Texas and in 1994, recorded her first album on Antone's Records. Her smooth and seductive rendition of blues captivates every crowd who gathers for great music. No stranger to festivals and concerts, Lavelle White is a voice to be reckoned with. *When I interviewed Lavelle, she also invited me to her house in Austin for some of her food! Sharing stories creates family. Johnny "Texas Twister" Copeland was in my first book on Texas songwriters and was a founding board member of the Texas Music Heritage Foundation.*

Add Marcia Ball to the mix, a tall tornado of a Texas woman. In 1990, "Dreams Come True," a collaboration with Lou Ann and Marcia, became winner of the National Association of Independent Record Distributors' award for Best Blues Album. *Rolling Stone* said, "These three women—the first ladies of Austin, Texas, rhythm and blues scene—are not coy or cool. They attack this collaboration of venerable R&B tunes and originals full bore, throats wide open and wailing." *If I ever do decide to stand up and sing, I want to be sure I am wailing. My own Fort Worth stories include shows at The Hop on Berry Street when I was at TCU in the early '80s finishing a Ph.D. with Jim Corder and Gary Tate. Ann Gossman Ashworth was a mentor then who encouraged me to trust my own voice. Wail and have courage!*

Men on Women

Men have been writing about women for a long time. Guy Clark said, "She ain't goin' nowhere, she's just leavin'. She ain't goin' somewhere she can't breathe in. She ain't goin' home, and that's for sure." He knows something rare about women. James McMurtry described a woman who just left amid crazy winds and flashing yellow lights. Townes Van Zandt said, "She came and she touched me with hands made of heaven, reflection sent spinning through a face made of mist." And Billy Joe Shaver said, "Woman is the wonder of the world."

Why Women?

What is distinct about the voices of women in the world of Texas music? Subject matter? Style and approach? I have been documenting the stories of Texas music since 1986 when I attended the Memphis Blues Awards. The voices of women call out in many ways; the stories they tell are not the same stories men tell.

A study of mythology reveals a strong connection between the earth and woman. Perhaps the voices of women capture the Texas landscape in ways that reveal this deep connection to place. The earliest cave drawings of a supreme being carry the characteristics of a woman, fertility and growth often interpreted as female. Carl Jung explored the feminine and the masculine in a description of the energy we all manifest. Jungian psychologist James Hillman decreed that integration of these opposites is the goal of human development. But we live in a world that has repressed, confined, and submerged the female voice.

This essay is the beginning of a journey, a journey across the state of Texas listening to the voices of women. This essay is the beginning of an exploration; it is not a definitive statement.

The beginning could occur during the 19th century, when settlers gathered with fiddles and bows playing music to dance by. Belle Starr, the Prairie Amazon, enters the scene as an outrageous woman who played piano in a Dallas saloon. She is given credit for a song, cited in "Finding Her Voice," as "one of the most famous of all western songs, 'Bucking Bronco'/'My Love is a Rider.'" The beginning could be the woman who dares to step outside the lines, the woman who dares to defy convention. That thread is woven throughout time in this tapestry.

Belle was shot by an unknown sniper in 1889, but her story lives on today in myth and legend as the story of a complex woman who lived life exactly as she wanted. That description also applies to the women who became the pioneers in the field of Texas music in the early 20th century.

Reports on Women

Marijohn Wilkin, a schoolteacher born in Sanger, Texas, in 1918, wrote "Long Black Veil," "Waterloo," and "One Day at a Time." She moved to Nashville in 1958 and worked as a songwriter for Cedarwood Music, earning $50 a month. She hit the big time in 1959 with Stonewall Jackson's version of "Waterloo." By the end of 1963, her songs were being recorded weekly. She drank heavily, attempted suicide twice, and delved into spiritualism and the supernatural. In 1964 she started her own company, Buckhorn Music, which became a haven for the maverick left field of the songwriting community, notably the poetic Kris Kristofferson. Still troubled, Wilkin wrote "One Day at a Time" as a prayer for help. That opened a floodgate of creativity, and she entered the world of gospel music as a composer. In 1975, she was inducted into the Nashville Songwriters Hall of Fame.

Cindy Walker's name shows up in every book on country music and songwriting. She's the kind of Texas woman who traveled to Hollywood, saw a bus with the name Bob Wills, called all the hotels to find him, and within one week of meeting him, had five of her own tunes recorded. Now that's feisty! Cindy Walker went on to be the first female inductee into the Nashville Songwriters Hall of Fame, the first music video star in 1941 with "Seven Beers with the Wrong Man," and eventually wrote more than 50 Bob Wills classics. And that's just the start.

Reading the list of her hit songs becomes a Texas hit parade. Cindy calls her mother the wind beneath her wings. Until her mother died in 1991, she put the music to the words Cindy wrote. Often described as "gutsy," Cindy Walker is still considered one of the greatest songwriters living today. I often wonder why I am moved to tears each time I hear "You Don't Know Me." We all long to be known by others, and this touches a chord deep in my psyche. Nelson has a tribute album out honoring Cindy Walker. Listen to it for some real Texas soul.

Singing the Blues

Blues, a genre closely related to the development of country music, had its share of women performers during those beginning years. Although a written history of Texas music does not contain many women's voices, the women were there. Sippie Wallace (1898-1986) and Victoria Spivey (1906-1976) have influenced an entire generation of younger blues women. In *Nothing But the Blues,* edited by Lawrence Cohn, the chapter on gospel music contains more information on women than any other.

Texas-born blind pianist and singer Arizona Dranes was 21 when she made her first recording for Okeh in 1926. Author Mark A. Humphrey says, "It's easy to imagine the lineage from Dranes to late pentacostal-turned-rocker pianists such as Jerry Lee Lewis." Dranes was one of Okeh's more obscure but more appealing artists in the gospel tradition. Sippie saw no distinction between playing gospel and playing the blues. "In gospel, you say God; in the blues you say Daddy," was one of her explanations. One of her last gigs was played one rainy night at Manor Downs in Austin at a Celebrate Austin Music Festival. Rejoining Bonnie Raitt, these two women belted out "Women Be Wise" and "Mighty Tight Woman." Famous for the line, "Keep your mouth shut; don't advertise your man," Sippie became a hero to the independent strain of Texas woman.

As writers describe women in Texas music, the following words emerge: feisty, willful, trend-setter, innovator, challenging, gutsy, independent, bodacious, a force, passionate, rowdy and self-reliant. Of these are women who step outside of the lines, women who defy stereotyping. Tanya Tucker said, "It's a lonely business being ballsy." Most women were perceived as "swimming against the tide."

Jan Reid wrote *The Improbable Rise of Redneck Rock* in 1974. Janice Joplin is the lone female performer in the book, and she is mentioned in the chapter on Kenneth Threadgill. Yet her story holds a dramatic and central place in the history of women in Texas music. She is the only Texas woman in *Rock of Ages: The Rolling Stone History of Rock and Roll.* Women don't show up at all in the book until the chapter on the emergence of the singer/songwriter in the 1970s. Janis shows up first in the chapter titled "The Pros Turn Weird," and she is linked with Grace Slick as changing the face of music in the rock and roll coming out of

San Francisco.

Born in Port Arthur in 1943, Janis began to show signs of rebellion in junior high school, and by graduation from high school in 1960, according to Jan Reid, "her vocabulary of four-letter words, her outrageous clothes, and her reputation for sexual promiscuity and drunkenness (signs of alcoholism were already apparent) caused her classmates to call her a slut. Bereft of friends, without dates for school dances, ashamed of her acned face and overweight figure, Janis responded with contempt and insults to cover the rejection that scarred her for the rest of her life." I've never read the biography of a male performer that mentioned his skin and weight, but these issues are constantly part of the Janis Joplin story. The "rest of her life" was brief; she died of an overdose of heroin and alcohol in 1970. This short life produced one of the strong threads in the tapestry of Texas music.

After joining Big Brother and The Holding Company, Janis ended up doing a month of gigs in Chicago in August of 1966. In Myra Friedman's biography of Joplin, white blues boy Nick Gravenites recalled their engagement: "They were just too freaky! This chick had this hair hanging down, and she was dressed in this bedspread! And the jewelry! Chicken bones and Voodoo shit! And this patchouli perfume, reeking! Her complexion was a wipe-out. She had this sore throat, and she was screeching like a wounded owl! I didn't really like the sound, but I was impressed. They were aliens, and they were sticking it out." At the end of the month, the club owner told them they weren't even getting paid.

Groundbreaking Women

The Texana Dames know what it is like to break ground. Eclectic and diverse, they represent all the traditions that make up Texas music: from Mexican conjunto to western swing, from Cajun to blues and rock 'n' roll. Originally from Lubbock, The Dames incorporate their West Texas roots into all their music. Now based in Austin, the Dames have played in Mexico, Peru, and 15 European countries. The Texana Dames have become a standard part of the Austin music scene. Their beauty and harmony energize the music, and the music gets everyone up dancing. Stunning at their instruments, the Dames have harmony like only a family can. Traci seductively sings in Spanish while holding her accordion close. Conni sits in front of a pedal steel guitar, inviting everyone to get out on the dance floor. Charlene, the proud mother who looks like another sister, stands behind keyboards and belies her 50-plus years of recording experience. She did begin recording at Norman Petty's Clovis, New Mexico, studio. Sonny Curtis, former Crickets member and songwriter, cited Charlene and her husband, Tommy Hancock, as "a strong influence on Buddy (Holly) and us all."

Traci's music will break your heart with soulful Spanish songs accompanied by her own accordion licks. Conni will tear out your heart with her flashy smile as she strokes a steel guitar. And ... Charlene will keep you hoppin' as she lifts the notes right off the keyboard.

Pioneers usually break ground, and Lydia Mendoza is known as the first lady of Texas-Mexican music. Born in Houston in 1916 and known as the "Lark of the Border," she moved around in this country and Mexico until she settled in San Antonio in 1927. Her first recordings were on the Okeh label. Also known as the first Texas-Mexican recording star, she continued performing until she suffered a stroke in 1988. She received the National Medal of Arts from President Clinton in 1999.

Her mother, Lenora, orchestrated the success of the family troupe called La Familia Mendoza. They originally worked in restaurants and barber shops in the Rio Grande Valley for tips. Calling themselves Cuarteto Carta Blanca, they became part of the fabric of Texas music.

As this part of the journey through the women's voices comes to an end, I want to end with a story about one of the most energetic, positive, and lit-up young women out there today, Terri Hendrix. Anyone who has spent time around Terri comes under the influence of her radiating light. Lloyd Maines, her producer and performing partner says, "I consider *Wilory Farm* to be one of the top albums I've ever produced. Positive energy follows Terri wherever she goes, especially into the recording studio. The musicians understood, the engineer understood, we all understood that Terri Henrix's music is straight from the heart, to the heart. Very inspiring...."

Terri visited English classes at Schreiner University several times, telling her stories and singing her songs. She participated in the monthly coffeehouse. Since then she has toured the world, made more albums and led successful songwriting workshops. She was featured with Lloyd Maines at the 25th anniversary celebration of the Texas Heritage Music Foundation in September 2012 held at Schreiner University. Her music has been described by Joe Nick Patoski in *Texas Monthly* as "Visualize Sheryl Crow in overalls or Ani DeFranco with a down-home Texas perspective: That's Terri Hendrix, the singer-songwriter-entrepreneur-czarina, in a nutshell.... "It's a Given" and "Places in Between"—tunes simultaneously intimate and universal—telling stories that hold the listener...."

Terri's latest creative project in 2012 is a rare book that includes tips for the business, stories about the art, songs, personal memoir, photography and other forms of personal documentation. "Cry Till You Laugh: The Part That Ain't Art" is her manifesto, and she is leading the way in uncharted fields with this format. David Shields has been a mentor for me, since he wrote "Reality Hunger" in a way that broke down lines of genres. This essay is a big nod toward David. My own creative mentor, Gabriele Rico, gave me the Shields book when she discovered I was teaching a creativity course. Terri's book also is the "text" for a freshman composition course at Schreiner University. .

Terri Hendrix has become the voice of independence in the Texas music scene. Her professional website gives reviewers and fans all the information they need to understand her approach to music. She not only includes a description of each album and a listing of all the band members, she also includes "Ditties," bits and pieces about each song. She comments that "Hole in my Pocket" was "written on the way back from Terlingua, Texas, while watching the sunrise of the Texas hill country. It was written as a prayer." About "Joy or Sorrow," she says, "The idea came from a conversation I had about fear.

I believe fear is like a weed in the garden of dreams." About "Two Dollar Shoes:" "I think of it as a kind of signature song now. What does it mean? I wrote it about people who always stay on the bench and criticize the players on the field ... or ... I wrote it about cheap shoes. You get to decide."

She also runs her own business, in a tradition established by women before her. Barbara Mandrell, after her accident in 1984, said, "There's a strong side of me that I'm only still discovering, the kind of business and military instincts we call 'masculine.'" Terri has those same instincts. Wilory Records was formed in 1998 with the release of *Wilory Farm,* her first album. She says, "My business had grown to a point where most labels could not do any better for me than what seemed to happen naturally by me going about my business independently. I say 'me' loosely. I work with great people that help keep this business running."

As I did the research for my book, *Voices of Women in Texas Music,* I talked with Rosie Flores again after seeing her rock the tent at the Songwriters Festival in Frutigen. She also became the voice on the Texas Music Heritage Foundation's Peabody-award-winning radio series produced by Lex Gillespie.

She is carrying the rockabilly banner forward. *I went to New York to accept that Peabody with her, staying at the Chelsea Hotel and having a Dylan/Leonard Cohen experience as I walked to Greenwich Village, where I was serenaded by Avi Colon and ran into an old creative mentor, David Amram. I was still chasing Dylan by leaving a letter in the office of Jeff Rosen. Don't remember where I found the address. Walked right up and left a package on Texas Music Heritage Foundation, with an invitation to come to Kerrville and sing some Jimmie Rodgers.*

No one was omitted from this essay deliberately. Time and space constrict. As T.S. Eliot says in "Little Giddings," "At the end of all our exploration, we shall arrive at where we started and know the place for the first time." Let the journey begin. *And I, too, begin again with a night of women's voices in my head from the 2012 Kerrville Folk Festival, a gift from Susan Gibson when she said to me, "I will come help whenever you call me." We both need those wide open spaces. My non-profit, delivering free educational programming using stories and songs, is celebrating 25 years, a Silver Jubilee. Terri Hendrix and Lloyd Maines are giving a songwriting workshop. I am teaching a Texas music class at Schreiner for freshmen, and our provost is dreaming with me of an MFA degree with a focus in songwriting. I carry the stories of all these women with me, along with my mother, Annabel Lee, and my sister, Carolyn Pillow, my daughter, Lisa Marie, and four granddaughters: Jessica, Angel, Erin and Maya.*

Wings of War

Christine Albert

As a child, I loved our family slide show night. My dad would get the carousel out, unfurl the white screen, draw the curtains, and we'd all settle in. We kids would squeal with delight at the images of cutting down Christmas trees, '50s looking New Year's Eve parties, romping at the beach as toddlers and lining up in matching Easter outfits. Even though most of the pictures were only 10 years old, they already seemed like a bygone era.

There was one slide that always brought a hush to the room … thousands of white crosses stood in perfect alignment on a carpet of green grass, and my uncle's name—Richard A. Albert—was etched into the marble of one of them. I was slightly confused by this; although I knew that my father's brother had died in the war, I didn't understand where this place was and why he was buried there instead of close to us.

A world away from his home in Niagara Falls, my uncle fell from the sky in a Republic Thunderbolt P-47 on February 5, 1944. He took his last breath in a pastoral field in the center of a small village a few kilometers from the coast of the North Sea in Suffolk County in England. As was the custom, fallen soldiers were buried in the country where they died, so Uncle Dick was interred at the Cambridge American Cemetery.

I couldn't conceive of the loss my grandparents and father had experienced; I was too young and innocent and a lifetime away from their grief. Over time, my uncle's life became condensed into a few sentences for me, always with that slide as the accompanying visual in my mind. "He died in a WWII plane crash while stationed in England. He was 22. He is buried in Cambridge."

If I hadn't become a songwriter and moved to Austin, Texas, those three sentences are probably where Uncle Dick's story would have ended—for me anyway. But fate, or synchronicity, or perhaps Uncle Dick himself had something else in mind. This is the continuation of his story—rich and complete—as it unfolded more than 60 years after his death.

Friendships in Austin are formed and forged around music, collaborations, songs and gigs. Slaid Cleaves is a songwriter I have always admired and respected, and we played occasional shows together. In 2006, Slaid and his wife, Karen, invited my husband/partner Chris Gage and me (aka "Albert and Gage") to be part of Slaid's fall tour of the UK. We played 14 shows in 16 days; the company and the gigs were great, and I was energized by the kindness of the people we met along the way. From Buckingham to Nottingham, Bristol to London, we sang and ate our way across England.

When we pulled in to Hitchin, we found that perfect combination of venue, meal and accommodations all in one. The next day we were off, so we'd get to stay here for two nights, do laundry and enjoy walking around this quiet village. I was definitely ready for some downtime.

While bonding with a young couple at the hotel pub after the show, I mentioned that my uncle is buried at The Cambridge American Cemetery and that if our tour took us close enough, I hoped to visit his grave. Before our glasses were empty, Andy and Sophy had informed me that we were only 50 kilometers away, and a plan was struck for them to spend the night at the hotel, escort us there the next morning and put us on a train back to Hitchin in time to do our laundry.

I almost wimped out when the alarm went off, tempted to roll over and go back to sleep. But the image of my grandmother came crashing into my heart. I could feel her all around me, and I began to weep. I knew that I had to get up and make this trip for her, because she was never able to travel to Cambridge and stand at her youngest son's grave. My music had led me to this moment, and I was not going to turn my back on it.

When we arrived at the Visitor's Building at the cemetery, we were greeted by Arthur Brookes, a genteel British fellow who took charge and with great enthusiasm led us through a ritual for family members of the fallen, filled with reverence and respect.

As we walked outside, Arthur motioned for us to stop, and we stood facing the reflecting pool that leads to the memorial chapel. He asked us to observe a moment of silence in honor of my uncle, pressed a button, and "Taps" began to play from loudspeakers, filling the 30 emerald acres with its sad and evocative melody. Once we found his headstone, to better see my uncle's name, Arthur rubbed the letters with sand from the beach at Normandy and planted small British and American flags.

Standing in front of the white marble cross from the slide show created a profound shift in me, and I experienced an unexpected blow to my heart. In that moment, my tears and the chills that were racing up and down my spine made my uncle, his death and our family's sacrifice painfully real. I am the mother of a son, and my grandmother's loss was unthinkable to me; my brother shares my uncle's name, and seeing it there brought home the deep grief that my father must have felt upon losing his only brother.

I suddenly understood the quiet sadness that was always present when my grandmother played piano and why she climbed the stairs to her bedroom on the anniversary of Uncle Dick's death every year, grieving in private in her darkened room. On Feb. 5, 1965—21 years after my uncle died—she didn't emerge from her afternoon's seclusion. My grandfather found her peacefully lying on her bed; under her pillow, wrapped in blue tissue paper and gold ribbon and worn thin from reading and rereading, was every letter my father and uncle wrote to her during the war. She quite literally died of a broken heart.

As we were leaving the cemetery, just in case his spirit was within earshot, I told my uncle that I would carry him with me now and honor him by writing a song. Almost as confirmation that I was on the right track ,a nut from the towering oaks above us hit me on the head, hard! "OK, Uncle Dick! I get it! I'm supposed to do something with this!"

When I returned to Austin, I was pulled in other directions, and the song for my uncle was put on the back burner. But I knew it was a promise I needed to keep, and two years after that October afternoon in England I began work on the song, hoping to have it done in time for my dad's 90th birthday on October 31, 2008. After circling around it for several incarnations, Chris, our co-writer, Steve Brooks and I eventually landed on "Wings of War," and we recorded it in time for my dad's birthday celebration in Florida.

All families have myths—some based in fact, some stories that are so deep and complex that it is hard to know the truth from a subconscious fabrication. One of our family stories is that Uncle Dick was the outgoing, popular one, the charismatic, charming and fun-filled mother's favorite. My father, on the other hand, was shy and had a bad eye that strayed and made him self-conscious. He was the introspective artist who felt that he never measured up to his younger brother's confident lust for life.

Dad was stateside completing his own military training when he received the telegram from my grandfather stating, "Dick killed in plane crash in England. Come if you can. Mother needs you for a few days." However, his commanding officer refused to allow him to take leave and return home to comfort his family and grieve for his brother. My father carried regret for the rest of his life that he didn't have the "courage" to go AWOL and hop a train to Niagara Falls that night. He always said that "Dick would have done that—that's why he was my mother's favorite. He was that kind of guy." I tried to assure my dad that his parents wouldn't have wanted him to break the law, but he held on to that regret for a lifetime.

Even as children, we learned to tread lightly around talk of Dick, knowing that my dad had mixed feelings about him. It was obviously very painful to lose his brother, but then there was the lingering competition between them—even though Dick was gone—and my father's insecurity.

I had been profoundly touched by visiting Dick's grave and was proud to have put his story into a song for my dad. But at that birthday gathering, I could feel the uneasiness in the room at making him listen to a song that calls his brother a hero. We were all very practiced at avoiding talk of Dick. There was a concern that I was rubbing salt in the wound, although I'm not convinced my father experienced it that way. I know he appreciated the gesture and the gift, and I had fulfilled my promise.

The compelling force I felt that day at the cemetery was still at work. My uncle's story was not complete and apparently I was chosen to be the vehicle through which it would be told. At least that's how it felt as the next two years unfolded.

In November 2009 I received an email from a music lover who had been checking out our website. He noticed the inscription on the cross marking my uncle's grave, which included "The 56th Fighter Group." His father had served with the group and was stationed at the same base in England during the war.

In truth, Austin filmmaker David Grosvenor had more than just a passing interest in or knowledge about "The 56th." He had produced a PBS film—"The Last Best Hope: A True Story of Escape, Evasion and Remembrance"—about his father's experiences during the war. Together they retraced his steps from the moment his plane crashed in a field in Belgium through his release from a German prison when the war ended. David had relationships with the curators of the Halesworth Airfield Museum and access to information about the soldiers who were stationed there, including my uncle.

One morning, David emailed me a picture of my uncle that I had never seen before. That afternoon, he sent a scan of the actual, handwritten accident report written by the East Suffolk Police and put me in touch with a woman who had witnessed it firsthand. The true story of Dick's last day was coming into focus.

It was a cold February morning when a group of pilots took to the skies over the village of Wangford, England to train for an upcoming mission. When a snow squall broke out, they lost visibility and my uncle's plane collided with one being flown by 2nd Lieutenant Roger Phillips from South Dakota. Lieutenant Phillips' plane came down outside of the village in a fiery explosion. Uncle Dick's plane was sliced in two, and the front half landed in a field in the center of Wangford, just across from the general store.

Joan Hunting was 18 years old and working at her family's store at the time of the crash. She ran to the site, but it was too late; Uncle Dick was gone. She said that he appeared unharmed, as if he was sleeping peacefully in the cockpit with a slight smile on his lips. When the authorities arrived, Joan returned to the store and went into the back room, understandably shaken by what she had witnessed. She cried for my uncle, lit a candle and said a prayer for him.

Too many parents in 1944 received a simple telegram with just the facts. "Report received states that he was killed 5 February in England as result of an airplane collision." There was no time for research, no Internet to facilitate it, and a war was raging. My grandparents couldn't easily get on a plane to visit the village where their son had died.

It brought me comfort to know that a candle had been lit for Dick, that he had a peaceful expression on his face, and that a prayer had been whispered for him. I can't help but think my grandmother would have taken comfort in that as well, and I am grateful that my father lived long enough to hear those small details.

We also learned that a group of local citizens had recently been successful in their decades-long quest to create an official memorial to Richard A. Albert and Roger A. Phillips—to commemorate their sacrifice. It was their way of honoring all the airmen who were stationed there and those who lost their lives protecting England and her people. The plaque had just been completed and was in a temporary location, to be dedicated at a later date.

One day we knew nothing of Uncle Dick's death, and by the end of the week, we were reading the accident report, the words of the first responders, and learned that he had recently been memorialized. The words "We will remember them" on the plaque reinforced what I felt that day as we left his grave. I was determined to keep his memory alive; I didn't realize that it was not my responsibility alone.

Six months later, my sister and I were immersed in the task of moving my parents from their home in St. Petersburg, Florida. Boxes were unearthed from under the beds, and we discovered one simply marked "Dick." We thought we had rummaged through all of our family archives over the years, but here were things none of us had ever seen ... that painful part of my father's past that had been kept locked away. Something told us it was time to gently lift the lid with Dad by our side. I'm glad we did.

Chris was back in Austin working on a video of "Wings of War" and here was a treasure trove of memorabilia—the actual telegram from Washington, the letters my grandmother had kept under her pillow, an interment letter sent from the Department of War describing where and when Dick was buried. His story was coming to life not only in song but with visuals. I noticed that my grandmother kept the letters written to her by my uncle as well as my dad. In letters she had written to them, she offered her motherly love—in equal measure.

Her diary was filled with love for both her sons. We also found a poem entitled "To Dick," written for my grandmother in December 1946 by John Aranyos. John was my uncle's best friend and they were stationed together at Halesworth. The poem speaks to their shared love of flying and brings hope and beauty to Dick's final flight. What a sweet Christmas gift for my grandmother. Here is an excerpt from the poem "To Dick" by John Aranyos, 1946:

> I remember well that cold bleak day
> On England's Eastern shore
> The "Great Commander" took you away
> From all the hate and war.
>
> Perhaps He saw the silvery sheen
> Of your wings as you did fly
> He was thrilled to see a soul so clean
> Cavorting through the sky.

There was a telegram announcing the arrival of my uncle's namesake—John Richard Aranyos—in December 1945. My sister Linda immediately got online and began a search for John Aranyos—senior and junior. Within an hour, I had them on the phone and I felt privileged to share with the elder Mr. Aranyos the news that Wangford had created a memorial dedicated to Dick and Roger, and more importantly, to all the men who had served there. How odd it must have been to be reminded of words he wrote 63 years earlier.

An opportunity to share his poem arose on October 9, 2010, when we took part in the official dedication of the memorial in Wangford—coincidentally, four years to the day after we visited Cambridge. Dignitaries, Mrs. Hunting, the guys from the museum, and dozens of locals—we all gathered on that chilly, damp morning on a triangle of land at the crossroads of the two main thoroughfares that wind through Wangford. "Wings of War" had truly come full circle from the moment of its conception at the military cemetery, to its birth in Austin, to being sung a stone's throw from the spot where the plane came down.

My sister Susan read Mr. Aranyos' poem, and while she recited his words, a P-51 Mustang did a flyover—an auspicious sign, as we later learned that Mr. Aranyos, who had gone on to fly P-51's throughout the war, died that very day in Pennsylvania, knowing that his poem was being read at the dedication in England. I can't think of a better tribute for a man who had carried on a lifetime love affair with flying.

When that acorn hit me in the head, I knew that it was a wake-up call to somehow bring my uncle home to our family. His body had been left on a foreign shore and in some ways his memory as well. The more our family learned about Dick's death, the more he came to life for us. The outpouring of genuine love and respect from the Wangford community made us realize that although we are one family, we represent thousands and thousands of families who were impacted by the war.

I sat at the kitchen table with my dad the day he watched the video of "Wings of War" for the first time. He was leaning into the laptop screen, watching the images of his mother, father, brother, beloved Niagara Falls, the telegram, Cambridge ... float and fade in and out. He died one year later. I am hopeful that by shining a light on his brother, we rekindled the connection with his entire family and he died knowing that he was loved unconditionally, not just by his wife and children, but by his family awaiting him in the great beyond.

Wings of War

Christine Albert, Chris Gage, Steve Brooks

The fifth of February 1944
An airman's plane came crashing
It shook the ocean floor
Upon the plains of England
He sleeps beneath his name
He never saw the falls
Of the Niagara again

His father worked the city desk
Each day he read the list
He'd print for all the families
Of the boys who would be missed
He read one name a second time
Then walked 10 blocks alone
To tell his wife her baby boy
Would not be coming home

  Rest your head fallen hero
  Over on that foreign shore
  May you wear the wings of angels
  As you wore the wings of war

The 9th day of October 60 years have passed
A fleet of marble crosses
Floats on a sea of grass
I've come to find my uncle
His name is hard to see

Till we rub it with some sand
From the beach at Normandy
I wish that my grandparents
Were standing by my side
They never came to Cambridge
The water was too wide
Our name will rest forever
Upon this field of stone
But in my heart my uncle
Is finally coming home

  Rest your head fallen hero
  Over on that foreign shore
  May you wear the wings of angels
  As you wore the wings of war
  May you wear the wings of angels
  As you wore the wings of war

Written in honor of Richard A. Albert
and for John L. Albert
on his 90th — October 31, 2008

Mama Said

Ruthie Foster

Mama said, "Girl, you better learn how to pray
You've got a soul to save
Child, you've been looking for an education
You'd better fall on your knees before you fall
    in the wrong direction

Through many of trials I have known
Trying to give my children a happy home
Through times of trouble and tears from worry
I tried to keep my head held high
Teach my feet not to be in such a hurry"

Mama said, "Girl, you better learn how to pray
You've got a soul to save
Child, you've been looking for an education
You'd better fall on your knees before you fall
    in the wrong direction

It was a cold February morn
East Texas baby girl was born
I prayed for her soul to sing a righteous song
And when my head grows cold, Lord, keep her
    in a light that's warm"

Mama said, "Girl, you better learn how to pray
You've got a soul to save
Child, you've been looking for an education
You'd better fall on your knees before you fall
    in the wrong direction"

I rode the Greyhound bus from Waco, Texas, to Hearne, Texas, every weekend during my first semester of college at McLennan Community College while studying voice in the Commercial Music program. My brother, Michael, would pick me up at the Hearne bus depot, and we'd ride in his Chevy Impala and catch up for another 15 minutes to my hometown, Gause, where he, my younger sister, Rosland, and my mother lived. I always looked forward to both the bus ride and the home visits.

The bus would travel 100 miles over three counties, blurring past Live Oak trees and old pickup trucks while making frequent small-town stops to let local folks get on and off for what usually would take two hours on a normal car ride. But I didn't mind; I really loved the opportunity to cue up my new portable cassette player with a new favorite artist which I'd picked out just for the trip.

My mama liked hearing all about my bus trip and my many adventures at the music school. We'd sit and drink coffee together at the kitchen table while chatting into the late night about how much I was learning and what instrument I wanted to try next. (I'd come home with a different instrument every couple of weeks— saxophone, bass guitar, even a banjo. Papa got a real kick out of that choice!)

One particular night, I'd proudly boasted to my mother about how all of this education would help me become famous one day. She put her coffee cup down and stopped me, then said that becoming famous was not why I was there. She explained I was there for an education and reminded me of how far I had already come. I used to be a little girl who was so shy that, when spoken to or asked a question, would stammer and sometime stutter. Now, she said, I was singing like a little bird. She told me about how many nights she'd sit and pray for that same little girl to live her life by example—as the shining star she already was. Then, she'd be more than just famous someday. By sharing and baring her own true soul, she'd be saving other people's souls at the same time.

Remembering my mother, Shirley Jean Johnson (1943–1996)

Joaquin

Tish Hinojosa

Joaquin shed a tear for the treason,
But who'd hear his desperate cry?
He learned to speak English from tourists
And reading by kerosene light.

He couldn't afford education,
But something was burning inside.
He heard things were good in America,
An that's what had been on his mind.

I met him, when I was travelin'
Through Mexico one summer day.
Eyes twice as old as the young man,
Who taught me a lesson in faith.

Fate made him poor, but he knew there was more.
Though I never did see him again,
I know, somewhere in America
Joaquin must've found him a place.

(chorus)
Joaquin loves his homeland,
But it can't give him enough.
He wants a good life, a job, and a wife,
And some children with dreams that come true.

Moonless night crossing the badlands,
(echo) Ayuda me Dios *(Help me God)*
Sign of the cross o'er his chest,
(echo) Mi vida, mi fe *(My life, my faith)*

Pounding heart racing till sunrise,
Mile after mile without rest.

Back at the border there's papers,
But politics get in the way.
It may not be right, but they take through the night
Some pay for the dream with their lives.

A Lesson Learned: The Story of Joaquin

Tish Hinojosa

When I was 17, my sisters and I took my mother on a trip to Mexico to visit her homeland in northern Mexico. My father had died the previous year, and our mom was suffering from a deep depression. We decided to make the trip in spring, when the weather is pleasant and desert flowers are blooming, and we also decided that we would go as tourists. Instead of staying with relatives and doing only family visits, we booked a hotel and made plans to visit local points of interest and eat at restaurants.

The trip from San Antonio, Texas, USA, to Sabinas, Coahuila, Mexico, is about five to six hours by car. My mother's mood lightened, as the trip got closer, then became quite cheerful once we got on our way. She was excited, and so were we. This was a place in Mexico we had visited often as children, but now as young adults, we planned and looked forward to enjoying it as tourists. We were happy above all that our mom seemed to really enjoy our idea.

This town, Sabinas, is not a tourist mecca, but it does have a cathedral and Mexican Revolution history and points of interest. We stayed at a decent classy old hotel right on the plaza. After we checked in and were wondering where to go and were asking the front desk about interesting places to visit, a young man came up and introduced himself to us. His name was Joaquin. He was well spoken in Spanish and even spoke impressive English. He said that for a certain sum, not much, and some food and drink on the way, he would be happy to be our guide for the few days. He was so friendly, willing, and sincere that we took to him right away. He jumped into our family car and told us stories and took us to all kinds of cool sights and shopping markets, on and off the beaten path. In the evenings when we returned to our hotel, he would sit and talk with us in the hotel lobby. Because he was around my age, we seemed to have more to talk about. He was inquisitive and curious to know about my school, about American music and teen culture and about my dreams for the future.

I would graduate from high school in one year and was already singing and playing guitar. Although the idea of college interested me, I was a product of American pop culture and was too impatient for college. I was anxious to go out there and conquer the world with my music. I had lofty ideas. Joaquin shared with me that his big dream was to go to college in the U.S., then to work and marry and have children. I responded that it is a great idea. After all, he was bright and spoke good English, which I learned that he had taught himself by hanging around at the hotel and talking with tourists. He said he would never be able to live his dream because he had to take care of his parents who had been older when he was born, and he was their only child. His mother was not in good health, and his father was blind. However, his belief and success in self-learning was obvious. He took me to his house so I could see his book collections. I was saddened by the condition of where they lived. Their home had dirt floors and was lit by kerosene lamps. However, it was clean and cozy. He had an extensive book collection that he had gathered through making friends with Americans and other foreign travelers who would promise to send him books. It seems that most of them kept their promise. He didn't have a great shot at life. He knew that pretty much was the way things would be for him. He had a great attitude about it though, and thinking of his dream made him happy.

His story touched me, and it taught me a lesson on fortune. This is something that I had never thought of in that way, not at 17. I didn't think it was any big deal to be a middle-class American. I was lucky that my parents went to America before I was born. Had I been born in Mexico like Joaquin was and with my mom's history of hardship, I might have been stuck just where he was. I was lucky. I knew I was lucky to have been born in the U.S. and to have had better opportunities. I knew I had more choices ahead in my life. We stayed in touch for a while. Then I lost touch with him. He was supposed to have tried to get a visa so he could visit us in San Antonio. All of my family had become fond of him and wanted to help. We never did hear from him again. I have always hoped that he was able to find a way into the U.S. and go to school and get his job and find a nice wife and raise a family— achieve the American Dream.

We considered our trip to Mexico a success because it had lifted our mom's spirits and we had had a good time. I felt that I got something extra special in having encountered Joaquin and the wonderful lesson he taught me. I pursued my music dream. I became a singer-songwriter. I recorded albums and CDs and toured around the world. One song in my repertoire tells the story of Joaquin. The song is simply titled "Joaquin." It is the opening song on my first internationally released album called *Homeland*. It is often requested, and I also included it in my concert for the Clintons at the White House in 1996. I think Joaquin would be pretty happy about what I learned from him and where his story has taken me. I will never forget him.

Four Songs

Amanda Pearcy

Better On My Own

Chilly Valentine morning
Left me cold to the bone
A broken heart sign warning
When a red tail hawk flies alone

Too far a drive for an old friend
Too many miles to cover
Twelve hours west on the I-10
Is even too far for a lover

That silver moon has done cast its spell
And pulled you away from our happy home
Baby I guess it's just as well
I do better when I'm on my own

Stay gone, stay gone, stay gone then
While I lay back and moan
I'll bed down like we did back when
But I won't be beddin' down alone

That silver moon has done cast its spell
And pulled you away from our happy home
Baby I guess it's just as well
I do better when I'm on my own

This song was born from one of the separations from my ex-husband. It started not in the way separations sometimes start, with a fight that has gone on too long, or a love that has lost its fire, but just as a thing. He wanted to go live and play music on the Florida/Alabama Gulf Coast. Maybe it was his way of dealing with the grief of losing our beautiful Austin home we had remodeled together. We didn't just design and decide on fixtures—he not only basically rebuilt the house, but laid custom tile designs, built the kitchen bar from hundred-year-old barn wood from Iowa, and replaned and resurfaced the aged wood from the outside of the house to become gorgeous wainscoting in the dining room and the ceiling of my son's room. That was 2009, and not only had the real estate market tanked, I had lost my day job and was in debt for a huge loan to try to get my son out of trouble. So we sold the house ... at a loss. And he wanted to go 700 miles away.

I stayed in a rent house on the southwest edge of Austin, and he left on Valentine morning. It was supposed to be that I'd go, too, eventually, but a few months turned into a year and then into over a year and a half when a misunderstanding occurred, and we didn't connect for three months. I wrote this song in the midst of that separation.

He had discovered that pocket of the country—known as the Redneck Riviera—by way of a songwriters' festival he'd been attending for a few years. There's a big ass bar that sits right on the state line of the two states called the FloraBama. Up until recently, there was a package store (liquor store)/live music venue across the street from it. (It looks like just a street to me, but it's called the Gulf Coast Highway). The combo venue/liquor store was more of a listening room venue. Surprising, huh, that they'd have that sort of place down there where you'd expect everyone would want to hear "real" songs like "Sweet Home Alabama"? Anyway, the place was called the Silver Moon. So when I say "that silver moon has done cast its spell," I'm talking about a live music venue with a liquor store in the back, where a songwriter can get his fix by actually being heard for his own songs, not just for background music or for "real" songs. Yeah, so it's *that* Silver

Moon doing the spell casting in the song, not the voodoo one up in the Louisiana sky.

As a woman, and as a wife, I resentfully made the case that he loved performing for an appreciative audience more than performing for an appreciative wife, so to speak. All the while having an internal struggle with myself because I, too, knew the high from getting to do those kinds of gigs, the ones where people are actually really listening to the songs you wrote and loving them—not asking you if you could play "Bobby McGee" or whatever. I also knew he wanted me to go there and live that life with him, but I wasn't ready to let go and leave my life in Austin.

So it was a chilly Valentine morning when he pulled out from the old house on the hill in an area mixed with mobile homes from the '70s called High Valley in far southwest Austin. There may have been a red tail hawk that morning, I don't recall for sure, but they were common out there. I didn't feel broken-hearted when he left, since I knew I'd be seeing him again, but I didn't foresee the summer split of no speaking for three months and, potentially, the end of our marriage—so I guess there could've/should've been a "broken heart sign warning" that I missed from a random red tail hawk flying alone somewhere that day.

One of the ingredients of the breakdown of the relationship was that he hardly ever wanted to make the drive to Austin ... he always had a gig he'd need to turn right around to get back for, so I felt like I wasn't worth the trouble and not worth the drive. I felt like I was the one being burdened with juggling my schedule to make the drive to him—a drive that can take eleven hours on I-10 per the Internet route maps, and is possible to make in eleven, but always seems to end up more like twelve. Besides, twelve sounded better in the song than eleven. In the song, the line is "twelve hours west on the I-10, too far a drive for an old friend." This isn't the only song of mine where I make reference to "old friend." This comes up in the title track of my CD, *Royal Street,* too, because one of his best loved and most requested songs (and title track of his second record) is "Old Friend." Tragically funny enough, he had written about us during another time we spent months not speaking—during one of our breakups in our years of on again/off again "dating" prior to our marriage.

So after all the hurts and resentments and frustrations, I had just had enough. The music to this song has that kind of ballsy, weary, coming down-off-a-fix feeling to it. And I wrote that "I do better when I'm on my own." And I did. Kinda. I mean I did fine, as I had after I'd been widowed, and as I had after a short marriage to an ex-con heroin addict ended. I liked being sorta single. I mean I didn't date anyone else, but it was nice having the freedom of not telling anyone what I was doing, or when, or why, or why not.

And I got in my groove. And I flirted. And I wanted to have a crush on someone, so the lines telling him to "stay gone, stay gone while I lay back and moan" didn't mean by way of my own hand, but with someone else the way we used to. "I'll bed down like we did back when, but I won't be beddin' down alone." It just felt real good and naughty to say that. I think that's what's so freaking fabulous to do in song, to just go on and say it. It's like you're allowed to push the envelope cuz it's just a song after all, and the icing on the cake is you get to say it every time you play it at a show or someone listens to the recording of it.

So after two years and nine months of a long distance marriage, I did eventually go there to live with him. I'd been there eight months when I pulled out of that Alabama driveway and headed home to Texas. I've not been back since.

Indian Summers

She carries her bags down to the station
Pale bra strap keeps slipping down her fair shoulder
No such thing as a summer vacation
When you spend your youth just getting older
She carries her secrets in her wide hips
Tulsa girl's leaving for Ponca City
She buries the truth behind her red lips

She won't ask for your dimes or your pity
And the ways of my grandmothers
Have all but been lost to me
Days of Indian summers just like they used to be
Leaving corn crops scorched
Mares' tails wispy in the late day sky
Recliners on front porches
Old men sippin' whisky as the train goes by
Baby girl born in an old blacksmith shop
She carries on hoping that he'll do his part
Tears won't be cried because her momma was taught
Their trail of tears and hers are worlds apart
And the ways of my grandmothers
Have all but been lost to me
Days of Indian summers just like they used to be
Leaving corn crops scorched
Mares' tails wispy in the late day sky
Recliners on front porches
Old men sippin' whisky as the train goes by
She carries her bags down to the station
Pale bra strap keeps slipping down her fair shoulder
No such thing as a summer vacation
When you spend your youth just getting older
When you spend your youth just getting older

    I learned from my mother that the wisps of clouds in the early fall are called mares' tails. She was born in a house in the old part of Tulsa, Oklahoma, a house whose original structure was a blacksmith's shop. Her mother, of Cherokee descent, died in 1932 of "a sleeping sickness from a horse fly that had also killed the mule," when my mother was only six years old. Today we'd call it encephalitis or West Nile virus. Her father moved her and her brother to a farm in Haskell in Muskogee County to pick cotton. The three shared a chest of drawers, the size of what today may be in the bedroom of a small child.

Other than having been born in an old blacksmith shop, the girl in the song is fictional and was born out of memories of both my mother's and mine. My mother never knew her mother's father. They said no one ever knew what happened to him. Maybe he ran off, so that's why there's the line about hoping he'll do his part. I have one old photo of him. I see the Cherokee in his high cheekbones. But maybe I'm imagining that because his facial features are not clear—the picture is of his slender frame next to a mule in the middle of a field. The first verse is repeated at the end of the song to represent the family cycles that get repeated. Maybe the baby girl grew up to go through the same things her young mother had.

My mother used to talk about Ponca City with fondness. I don't recall the context, but there was a differentness about her when she spoke of it. Recently, while looking through a photo album after my brother's funeral, I found several photos of a huge statue called the Pioneer Woman. Guess where it was taken? Yep, Ponca City. It's a bronze monument that was dedicated in 1930. So, unbeknownst to me at the time I wrote the song, it's fitting that the girl is going off on her own, headed to Ponca City, leaving childhood behind, headed into the strength and bravery of childbirth and motherhood that could include the hardships of single parenting. So she, too, is a Pioneer Woman.

The song includes a reference to the Trail of Tears, as a way to honor my Cherokee blood on my mother's side. But the line in the song also refers to how it was growing up in the "quit yer crying, or I'll give ya something to cry about" mentality of past generations. When you're told that, you only cry harder while trying not to cry at all and slurping snot mixed with salty tears, trying to hold it all in. Maybe that mentality came from their experience that there ain't nothing to cry about that compares to things like removing a population of people from their homeland and the genocide along the way.

The ways of my grandmothers have all but been lost to me. Yeah, I used to make a good pot roast and the gravy to go with it, and a good ol' meatloaf. To save money, I'd even buy a whole chicken to cut up for frying instead of buying it cut already. But the wisdom and true skills of my grandmothers have been completely lost to me. My mother was a fabulous seamstress, and it's all I can do to replace a button. But this line really makes reference to humanity's universal indigenous grandmothers and how their ways have been lost to us.

Even with two older sisters, I feel like I didn't learn a lot about being a woman (maybe because my mother grew up without her mother). Like the line in the song about how the bra strap keeps slipping down her shoulder, I have a vivid memory—or a collection of memories—of walking home from school with the uncomfortable feeling of my bra strap slipping off my shoulder. I put up with that into recent adulthood before I realized I could just adjust the damn straps, and when I finally advanced from layaway at Walmart, I found out you can even get fitted appropriately at a department store.

We took a couple of family summer vacations. And I've seen yellowed old photos from one or two that were taken before I, the last born, came into the picture. I really only recall two road trip vacations, and my oldest sister wasn't around for either of those. Growing up in such a turbulent home with a raging alcoholic father, my sisters moved out early. At age 17, both used marriage as their way to get out of my parents' house. Although I didn't follow that same route, I lost my virginity way too young and moved out on my own before graduating high school. Spending our youths just getting older....

"Old men sippin' whisky in recliners on front porches...." Back when I was raising my son in Smithville, Texas, as you drove into town from the south, the closer you got to downtown, the more rundown the homes became. One quintessential house is imprinted in my memory. A rundown Craftsman next to the tracks, with a raggedy old couch and equally ratted out and lopsided La-Z-Boy style recliner on the front porch. A collection of old black men passed a bagged fifth of liquor. Literally, as you crossed the tracks, the scenery "improved," but I am fond of the imagery the old house and the old men provided.

Maybe some of the ingredients in this song come from ideas for another song I intend to write. In looking through an old cigar box of photos from my mother's side of the family, I found a newspaper clipping about the death of a young "Indian" woman. She had been shot to death and was with child. I don't know if she was family, but everything else in that cigar box was about family. I'm not gonna say any more about it, though, since I don't want anyone else to beat me to writing the song.

Make Me a Pallet on the Floor

Mama prepare, prepare a room for me
Mama make me a pallet on the floor to sleep
I'm comin' home to you
I'm comin' home to you
I ain't gonna go on like this no more

Papa bring your mean, bring your mean on me
Papa ain't no mean I ain't known or seen
I'm comin' home to you
I'm comin' home to you
Like the prodigal son, I'm comin' home

We will run like we can't walk
We won't float when we can swim
We'll go on and on and never stop
And we will never all fall down again

Mama prepare, prepare a room for me
Mama make me a pallet on the floor to sleep
I'm comin' home to you
I'm comin' home to you
I ain't gonna go on like this no more

"Make Me a Pallet on the Floor" (an earlier title was "Never All Fall Down Again") was written in the fourteenth month of a dry spell where only three songs came out of the 12 months prior. It was written two days after my brother died. My brother, Kevin, was born in June '53 in Hawaii where my parents met (Dad Navy, Mom WAVES). He had severe cerebral palsy. Cross-eyed as a boy, he lost his vision in one eye in young adulthood. As a child, he walked with crutches and those brown leg braces (like the child Forrest Gump character), then metal canes. He spent his last years in a wheel chair. He was passionate about politics and loved the Houston Astros. I took him to a few baseball games when I could. One time my son and I took him with a friend of his. They were so sweet and funny together—how excited they got at the game.

The day after he died, my sister shared on her Facebook page a post saying, "Kevin, I know Mama has prepared a room for you." From that, I wrote down the first line of the song and the line about Dad being mean, and then I left the words, thinking I wouldn't come back to them—as had become the norm for other lines that I had jotted down during my dry spell. I didn't see an end to the dry spell and had been in it for so long that I simply assumed the song wouldn't get finished, or for that matter, wouldn't even get finished at being started. So I just left the words on the paper and let them be, as I had become accustomed to doing. I took a shower the next night, and afterwards, with the towel still wrapped around me, I couldn't get to the paper quick enough to finish the song. The rest of the words, to go with the two lines from only the day before, came pouring out as if they had just been rinsed off of me. As I picked up my guitar and added the bluesy, gospel-y sounding music to the lyrics, the words didn't change except for one line.

My mother, who passed 10 years prior, almost to the same date of my brother, could prepare a most comfortable room, or if no room, a nice pallet on the floor. When we'd get sick with a stomach virus (which seemed to happen to me a lot), we always felt better on the pallet on the floor she had prepared in the living room in front of the TV than in bed. We got a steady serving of peppermints and 7-Up or Ginger Ale, along with re-run episodes of *Leave it to Beaver*, *I Love Lucy*, *Bewitched*, and *I Dream of Jeannie*. All was well by 9 or 10 at night when Dad was finally ready to eat supper after his drinks. The sick one would get a soothing baked potato. Late at night after everyone had gone to bed, when the house was quiet and dark, and with just the street light spilling in through the window, the midnight freight train would find its way into our dreams, or its boxcars rumbling over the tracks would sweetly lull us back to sleep after awakening us with its horn. Of course, it was the same a few feet away in the bedroom, but I always remember the "midnight" train from the perspective of the pallet on the living room floor.

My dad was mean. A raging, functioning alcoholic, he was only sweet and endearing around the time he was finally ready to eat supper, after the alcohol had mellowed him out and made us all forget the rage of earlier that morning and the uptight impatience that he brought home from work with him. His rage's arrival was announced every evening with the sound of the car pulling into the driveway. In regard to my brother, I know my dad loved him, but it was obvious my dad wished to have a non-handicapped son. In a cruel twist he was given three daughters instead—and not good girls, but wild childs he was ashamed of. We all left home as soon as we could, but my brother was not so fortunate and carried the brunt of my father's rage right up until my father's passing three years after my mom. Those must have been the hardest years for my brother, without even my mother for comfort and understanding. Of course, I'm sure my brother wished he could run, not just figuratively, but literally, but no one ever mentioned that out loud.

I lived at the neighborhood swimming pool in the summers. My two best girlfriends and I would walk home in the dark after the pool closed, walking in the streets instead of on the sidewalks with their unevenness that often stubbed our toes. And as we walked, we assumed the bumps under our bare feet were the rounded dried dollops of black tar that was used to patch the pothole-ridden Houston streets. Our minds just didn't acknowledge that some of what our bare feet were stepping on was actually any number of the huge flattened toads that covered the streets as intermittently and as commonly as the tar patches, their skins dried from baking on the pavement in the humid summer heat. (I have since found out that my sister and her friend used the toad skins in love potions. I, too, made love potions, but chose to use the lantana flowers that grew abundantly around our house. I think it's brilliant that they chose the dried toad skins.) A highlight for me once or twice a summer was when my dad brought my brother to the pool. I forgive my dad for not bringing him more often, since this was the era prior to the Americans with Disabilities Act, and the pool was built on a hill, so that there could be a deep end of the swimming pool for a diving board. My memory recalls it seeming like there were a hundred steps up to the pool entrance, like the pyramids of the sun and the moon at Teotihuacan. But really it was *only* 25 or 30 steps. It must have been quite the challenge to carry a young man (my brother was 13 years older than me) up all those steps.

So, Dad, I understand now why you didn't bring him more often. The times you did bring him made me so proud. And I would think, in regards to the other kids at the pool with their dads there: "Yeah, that's my brother, my crippled brother, and yeah, that's my dad holding him, helping him float. Your dad may come to the pool with you, and lift you up fast out of the water by your feet and toss you back in, or maybe you climb on his shoulders to dive back in, but my dad holds my brother so he can float." I would have died if all I could do was float, and then only twice a year at that. I couldn't get to sleep at night on the last day of school anticipating the opening of the pool for the summer and swimming under that cool water again with my eyes open like I was flying. I knew my eyes would be burning from the chlorine the next night while I fell asleep, but still, I couldn't wait.

And there were the falls. Kevin would walk with metal canes through my childhood. He would slip, often it seemed in the kitchen, and he would fall hard, calling out, "Oh! Oh! Oh! ... Darn...." It truly seemed like he fell harder than anyone else. Which makes sense of course since people without physical disabilities can change something in their muscles to cushion the fall or change how they land. Kevin couldn't do that. But now he will "never all fall down again."

The Story of My Heart

The story of my heart
Is so much more than a photo in a locket
Shot of whiskey,
Pool stick chalk,
Eight ball in the corner pocket
The smell of cash money,
Spilt liquor, and stale beer
Your lips as sweet as honey
Baby
Take me anywhere
The story of my heart
Is so much more than a photo in a locket
Shot of whiskey,
Pool stick chalk,
Eight ball in the corner pocket
Once I had a diamond
I used to like to wear
Spin me one more time and
Baby
Take me anywhere
All night diner coffee,
"What'll it be dear?"
I ain't where I oughta be

Baby
Take me anywhere
The story of my heart
Is so much more than a photo in a locket

OK—caution—the story of this song is not for those quick to judge. And this may be real short … it basically boils down to being a party doll out of the necessity of trying to fill the hole left by not getting the kind of lovin' you were 'sposed to from your daddy growin' up. Really. I think there's a comedian that said it right, something to the effect of "Fathers, if your daughters grow up to be strippers … you messed up." My girlfriend auditioned to be a stripper. They didn't hire her. So she was a party doll instead.

A "Party Doll" gets dressed up, draws attention to herself, is the girl all the guys wanna go home with. All of them. Gets drunk. Dances sensually. Maybe she goes out for 2:30 a.m. breakfast at an all-night diner after the bar closes—if she hasn't been able to seal the deal with the guy she picked that night. All the while ignoring the remorse she knows she's gonna feel the next day. It'll be different this time, cuz he's THE ONE.

Or in between the going-out clubbin', she works at a live music venue near downtown Houston. We counted our money at the end of the night while finally getting to really tie it on after only sipping at beer during the shift. And there were the after parties for the employees after the sound guy said through the speakers, "Time to go. You don't gotta go home, but you gotta leave here"—or something to that effect. So the smell of cash money, spilt liquor, and stale beer … and sex with the cute blonde dread-locked bartender on the pool table. She had her pride after all, and she says she never slept with any of the band members that stayed in the house we shared behind the bar for cheap when they came through, but she did sleep with most of the bartenders. And the sound guy.

But the take away: she always felt the essence of some self-loathing the next day. If you get a chance to hear the music that

goes with these lyrics, and you listen to the end, it gets slow and
sad. Party dolls pay.

Tie Me to an Angel

Emy Taylor

Television is rarely worth watching at 4 a.m. As I sat in a dazed state known only to catatonics and couch potatoes, the stations flipped by, and a soft syncopated rhythm of clicking kept time. Somewhere between the fancy rotisseries and the aluminum can-cutting knives, I landed on the Weather Channel. Other than minute-by-minute forecasts of ever-changing Texas weather, I had known no other benefit to the station. On this occasion, how-ever, a documentary had me completely consumed. Unfortunately, when the Hollywood-types finance a weather-related documen-tary, it does not involve a sunny day at the beach.

On September 8, 1900, a hurricane devastated Galves-ton, Texas. What we see today—a seawall protecting resorts and vacation homes—is a testament to a community that rebuilt itself following a storm that drowned what was the most prosperous city in Texas. The day when the ocean met the bay, Galveston Island temporarily became the lost City of Atlantis, and 6,000 people lost their lives.

What struck me most were the children of the St. Mary's Orphan Asylum and the Sisters of Charity of the Incarnate Word who cared for them. As the storm surged, the nuns ushered all the children into the girls' dormitory. The children watched in horror as the water washed away the boys' dorm, attempting to comfort themselves by singing the French hymn *Queen of the Waves*. Before long the girls' dorm was ripped from its foundations. The sand dunes between the orphanage and the sea were no protection from what remains the worst natural disaster in our nation's history.

When the water finally subsided, a child was found buried in the sand with a rope around his waist. At the other end of the rope rested one of the Incarnate Word sisters. As workers continued to dig, six to eight other children were found tied to her in the same manner. All the nuns did the same: with clothesline rope, they tied several children to the cinctures they wore around their waists as the water began to reach the upper floor of the children's dormitory. Even as far away as the mainland, one sister was found dead clutching two children, keeping her promise to never let them go.

What I witnessed that night forever changed my thoughts about love, devotion and family. Afterward, I grabbed a pen, and on a paper towel scratched out the words to the following song, which is a tribute to the Sisters of Charity of the Incarnate Word for their heroism and sacrifice:

Tie Me to an Angel

Six years old in a house on the shore
Five years earlier dropped at the door
They took me in with 30 or more
To raise us all in the name of the Lord

It all went down in September that year
We all thought the skies would clear
But as the sea grew near
They unleashed a reign of fear

Tie me to an angel so I can go home
You were the only family I had ever known
Tie me to an angel so I can go home
You always made sure I was never alone

Breakers tore away the dunes of sand
The only protection that we had
We sang hymns and the sisters prayed like mad
The storm surge took over the land

None of us made it out alive
No matter how hard those sisters tried

With ropes around our waists they tied
As man and water collide

Tie me to an angel so I can go home
You were the only family I had ever known
Tie me to an angel so I can go home
You always made sure I was never alone

The bells rang like crazy that day
With all those angels being made
Next day's sky was perfect they say
Angels pushed all the clouds away

Tie me to an angel so I can go home
You were the only family I had ever known

A Small Story of the Universe

karla k. morton

While studying journalism at Texas A&M University, Texas Poet Laureate karla k. morton fell in love with photography—the creative process that comes not only in the darkroom, but in the lens as well. She finds poetry in shape and movement, line and texture—each photo telling a small story of the universe. Morton, nominated for the Texas 2-Dimensional State Artist, has had several photography exhibits, and has co-authored *No End of Vision: Texas as Seen by Two Laureates*—a book and traveling photography/poetry exhibit with fellow Texas Poet Laureate Alan Birkelbach.

Night Crawlers

My New Boots

Eola Schoolhouse

Our Old Friends

Retirement

POETRY

Rosemary Catacalos

Picture Postcard from a Painter

for R. Anguiano

Slick tourist photo, umbrellas and sling chairs in dazed royal blue.
Everyone faces the sea but one lone man, unsheltered, thrown down
between water's edge and flowers rioting foreground.

One lone man daring the blaze to burn more than it already has,
 looking it
in the eye. Lost in masses of flowers, echoes of umbrellas blown
inside out by coastal wind. Thin-skinned, hot pink with screaming

red throats. Morning-glory shaped, but it's high noon. Can you see it?
Vines, all right, but hugging the ground, no place to climb, spilling
across dunes, froth on a dry ocean. He can deal with contradictions.

Up close, the leaves are fat and succulent, seem gentle.
The man's story. *Moiré air outside Cotulla that day, full of heat
waves, air that made you see things, promised water, love, safety,*

*when there was nothing but brush country. I didn't know to say
 "moiré" then,
didn't think it was fancy air, just hell. Americanos said
"hotter'n spit on a griddle." We said, "más calor qu'el quinto infierno,"*

*Dante's fifth circle. Didn't know Dante either, that's just
what we always called it. Cotulla is an hour from the sea.
The rare curve in the flat-out road took him by surprise. He wasn't*

from around there. My mother made a red star in the windshield.
He died too. I've tried to paint a big '57 Olds gone soft as a seaside
flower, fat, lushly turned and seeming gentle. Can you see it?

He'd touched me in the wrong places, alcohol, his own childhood,
my real father long gone. I never told because she would sing
when this one came around, sing and paint her face. I remember.

Closest I've come to her is a painting I did from a snapshot
my grandfather took, cheap rayon dress, flower in her hair. An old tire
slanting in the background. The runt dog must have barked.

I glued blue and green sequins around her, floated it all
in dark tropical leaves, nothing like Cotulla. Can you see it?
Then that day at San Fernando, Día de los muertos,

everybody with marigolds and kids, oval portraits of the dead
set in headstones, I thought we'd never find her,
all those years without seeing the grave. Since I was four.

The blue umbrellas side by side, the people looking away.
Dotted line of horizon, separating heaven from what he keeps
trying to make out. *I've done everything without her.*

Can you see it? Are you there? Let me know if you come to Texas.

La Casa

The house by the *acequia*,
its front porch dark and
cool with begonias,
an old house, always there,
always of the same adobe,
always full of the same lessons.
We would like to stop.
We know we belonged there once.
Our mothers are inside.
All the mothers are inside,
lighting candles, swaying
back and forth on their knees,
begging the Virgin's forgiveness
for having reeled us out
on such very weak string.
They are afraid for us.
They know we will not stop.
We will only wave as we pass by.
They will go on praying
that we might be simple again.

Homesteaders

for the Edwards Aquifer

They came for the water,
came to its sleeping place
here in the bed of an old sea,
the dream of the water.
They sank hand and tool into
soil where the bubble of springs
gave off hope, fresh and long,
the song of the water.
Babies and crops ripened
where they settled,
where they married their sweat
in the ancient wedding,
the blessing of the water.
They made houses of limestone
and adobe, locked together blocks
descended from shells and coral,
houses of the bones of the water,
shelter of the water.
And they swallowed the life
of the lime in the water,
sucked its mineral up
into their own bones
which grew strong as the water,
the gift of the water.

All along the counties they lay,
mouth to mouth with the water,
fattened in the smile of the water,
the light of the water,

water flushed pure through the
spine and ribs of the birth of life,
the old ocean,
the stone,
the home of the water.

Swallow Wings

*for Maya Angelou, with profound
respect and gratitude*

I been to church, folks.
I'm an East Side Meskin Greek and
I been to church. I'm here to say
I grew up hearin' folks sing over hard
times in the key of, *Uh, uh, girl. It ain't nothin'*
'bout lettin' go a this life.
I grew up in a 'hood where every day at noon
black girls at Ralph Waldo Emerson Junior High School
made a sacred drum of the corner mailbox, beatin'
on it to raise the dead. And make them dance.
I grew up readin' in the George Washington Carver
Library, and marvelin' at the white
lightnin' gloves that Top Ladies of Distinction
use for church. I grew up where grits is *indeed*
groceries, and a hale mountain of a woman passed
my house daily, always sayin' the same thing:
Your name Rosemary? My name Rosemary, too.
I grew up, folks, and I been down 'til I couldn't
get no more down in me. And now a preacher lady
come to town and caused me to paint my face and
put on some good clothes and go to church.
And I'm here to say I have a right
to take this tone, 'cause it ain't nothin'
'bout lettin' go a this life.
Swallows keep makin' their wings
out to be commas on the sky.
World keep sayin' and, and, and, and,
and.

karla k. morton

Valentine Outlaws

Party at the Watsons' House

We slept through church,
the party running into the night;
another year checked off our body calendars—
catching up on children and siblings,
adventures and jobs.

New friends from Ireland and Russia,
with new mottos:
no stoppers on the vodka, the wine;
good luck comes in the free flow.

The authorities called in;
the policeman sweetly apologetic—
it could be *his* parents in there—shoes off,
classic rock blasting at 2:30 in the morning,
grooving on rusty hips
and knees
that will limp and snivel tomorrow.

And we wake up, randy and smiling;
knowing *we still got it,*
even if it's just one night a year.

A little gray in our rebellion;
a smirk of outlaw with our olives
in the noon-time Bloody Mary.

karla k. morton

Six Bottles of Red

A woman once told me
after her husband's funeral,
that she just doesn't *get* this
Texas tradition of bringing food
to the bereaved.

She said every person
who came to her door
brought something to eat,
and that she'd *never be caught dead*
eating gravy on biscuits,
and *who in the hell*
would ever put chicken
in spaghetti?

Perhaps that woman
never came back exhausted
from the cemetery,
knowing she *should* eat;

breaking down in front of
the poor teenager at the deli
because he was out of fried chicken.
Not one freaking piece of chicken.

Perhaps she never
wandered the grocery aisles
with heavy legs,
leaning on a basket
of avocados,
eye cream,
and six bottles of red.

Destiny

> *It is the destiny of mint to be crushed.*
> –Waverley Lewis Root

Cicadas burst and sing and mate and die;
grackles weave silent circles—
beaks open and panting;
mornings are hushed and still.

It's just me and the trees
and this unfaltering mint—
donning green armor
against summer's bully sulking around us.

Late August in Texas, Fall is a myth.

Yet we wait for him
like left loves
in our verdant dresses;

worried we won't remember
what he looks like,
or the color of his eyes;
or his musk of rain.

I watch the horizon for his wind-swept gait;
believing he will return—

cool hands against my heat;
tussling my hair; my skirt;

mint, crushed and ready
on my tongue.

Shine Shine Shine

I have a crow-like affinity to anything that shines.

Secrets of the Ya Ya Sisterhood
Gathering stones from the river,
I watch them unmask—
the glamour drying
to the plain glory of themselves;

remembering grandmother's house,
finding box after box of unused
nightgowns, pajamas, and robes
we had given her each Christmas

to replace that thinning housecoat
she wore every night.

My Grandmother—
that beautiful rock
who never stepped one foot
into the river of vanity,

yet made me dresses of cotton
and silk, with rhinestone buttons
and matching earrings,

that I may be glossed and eyed;
that I may rise from her waters
and shine shine shine.

Sarah Cortez

Waste

We'd run plenty
of calls there
before the final
night.
        She had to know
        she was killing
        herself.

Look here at the
crime scene
photos.
        Nude W/F. Sitting
        on toilet. DOA.

You see, the liquor
ate her up inside.
        Look at the bed. Huge,
        bloody hunks of her
        innards, melting
        on beige sheets.

She didn't care no more. Lived
in an inherited house. Stayed
naked; stayed drunk.
        Can't even tell which parts
        of herself she pushed out
        before she died. Look
        in the bowl.

        What a mess.

K-9

Dog handlers are weird.
Female dog handlers
are weirder.

           Think about it.

Eat with the dog. Sleep
with the dog. Cart
dog around on family
outings. Train dog
daily.
Dope-finding
dogs, accelerant dogs,
bomb dogs, bloodhounds,
ag dogs, money dogs,
search-and-rescue dogs,
cadaver dogs.

           You'd be weird too.

Moist, black nose. Liquid
brown eyes. Thick, muscled
neck. Implicit threat
in saliva'd jaws and teeth
that will save your life
one night on cold concrete.

           Ask any K-9 handler.

Frances Hatfield

Espadrilles

Okay, I bought the shoes
though really I had no business;
they aren't in the post-divorce budget,
the happy weather they're made for
is cooling to grey, calling for boots.
It was the color I needed more than food,
an earthy apricot, it made me think
of Bosnia that summer
a few years after the war, how on every
street of every city people would gather
at the storefronts selling shoes, standing
between the bomb-eaten walls of stone
looking intently and only at shoes,
debating their merits in a tongue swollen
with history, as if strolling in fine leather
down the avenue at dusk could remember
them to beauty,
as if to coax their feet
to stand them up again
to step out of the door
or the absence
of a door

Waiting for Rain

Ribbon of road unwinding
with El Paso at the end. Bare sky
and brown shrubs rooted in long empty wind.
The thrill of gathering speed lifts the furrow in your brow,

as you talk about your friend who couldn't win
because he couldn't drive by the seat of his pants.
Leaving the city, your shoulders loosen, forget
to stay vigilant for the next heavy blow. I still see

the invisible "S" inscribed on your chest,
the ghost of the towel cape you loved to wear.
I am too much like you to know who you are.
When we were kids, I made shoebox altars

and preached to you about God & all the saints.
I think now of the miracles we never learned to name,
the peculiar speech of the lizards you heard,
the time I flew to the top of the old pine

while still standing on the ground looking up.
I want to tell you
how slowly the soul wakes,
that you'll be all right.

We fly through hills crowned with tall stones
like a crowd of ancient men all standing together.
From their view, maybe we are shadows, or bats
or faint pearls of light. To me, brother, you look

like the lone tree left standing
on the arroyo's dry floor, tough
from bitter winters, waiting for rain
and miracles, for the morning star to rise

out of the coldest of nights. We fold down
into the green and red and dark of the closer slopes.
You remember your lover, turn the dial on the radio, listen
for voices.

Sherry Craven

Pickups and Love

Girls, when your mother asks you
if you're a virgin,
don't tell her
about the time you saw heaven
from the seat of a bright white pickup,
your hands lovingly wrapped
around a gun rack,
or the time you met ecstasy
in the summerdark
climbing to a rapture
not mentioned in the Bible
on extra-long limbs that
reached into the
hot Texas night out the
rolled-down window.

No, better tell her that
you and the boy from
Sunday school, the one
in law school with the
crisp khakis, cool countenance,
fell in love, tumbled into passion,
for your first time.
Better tell her what she
needs to know—love—
like table manners,
has to sit straight up,
have its proper place,
be clothed in serious starch,
durable fabric, nothing

gossamer and sheer that
floats on hope, uncatchable.

Girls, hang onto dreams of pickups,
snap-button shirts, starched Wranglers,
and warm, clear nights that waltz you
to sleep and fill you like a field of
Texas wildflowers.

Don't let memories slip into years
until you no longer recall love
lingering, with a drawl, at all.

Coleman, Texas, and Us

Farm to Market Road 2230
winds into the night,
like a scar cutting pasture
from plowed field, slicing
the past from now.

To the south, through winter cold,
the dirt road to the green shingled world
of your old farmhouse on the small hill,
holds forth like an old woman who is
secure in the knowledge that
she is worth more than beauty.

The silvered barn hosts the owl family,
while craggy oaks bend and sigh
in wind's rhythm, branches calypsoing
with the splintering porch swing.
A birdhouse sways to its
own song, no one listening.

The distance from FM 2230
down the dusty road to your old place
is too far to travel, riding on old memories,
navigating with faded photographs, crossing
over from then to now.

I can't reach that far back, to us,
but merely drive through the Texas day,
the windows down, the fragrance of cedars
a soft moment in the present.

Magnolias

The magnolias are in full regalia here in deep East Texas.
They are so blatant, bear no shame, dancing a sort of
16th century promenade at the end of their branches,

proud yet supplicant, wanting to seduce, knowing they
can, reminding us it's all right, acceptable, to display our
best efforts, wear our gossamer silk shirts, go to excess

and fling our arms in the air and sway our heart at passersby,
at strangers. And why not be like the creamy, soft magnolia
who spreads her petals and shows no shame for being in full bloom.

The magnolias in deep East Texas light up the forest and peek through
the dark and take a chance for beauty. There is always something—fungus,
red ants, aphids—that attacks the tender flowers, but then, that's the
        way it is:

to live in spite of. We have a lot to learn from the deep East Texas
magnolias. We have a lot to learn about
lighting up the darkness.

I Sit Here Knitting

My sister has cancer and
I sit here knitting, trying to
put things together, make
a pattern, tie up loose ends,
stitch her back together

like the dolls we used to play with,
sewing the crooked seams and
putting the ragged cotton
arm back on the flowered dress.

My sister has cancer and
I sit here working balls of yarn
because I don't know what else to do as
I am not a doctor, or God

and can't knit and purl a perfect piece, so with each
stitch I will her into my heart, attempting to knit
strength into her body, to rip out the invasive

tangles the tumors weave in her body. I flash my
metal needles like knives or scalpels
against an army of cells marching like
Genghis Khan across her breast.

I sit here knitting, and with each
loop of yarn I pattern her into whole
once again and loop my love across her
body, rolling and raveling her into

sister love, into wishes for my sister,
who at 3 years old had silky, golden
curls like buttercups and eyes of the summer skies,

and I envied her beauty but
today I sit here knitting
looking for just the right stitch.

Naomi Shihab Nye

Farming

When I worked on Mueller's organic farm, the rows knowing
my step, I plucked berries gently, never bruising.
Filled small pint boxes—all my life has had
that light, square shape. Such sunstruck pride
in the farmer named Al, who loved his mounds of squash,
his sacks of beans, with fierce intensity.
His okra had an essence of perfection, his corn
whispered inside its perfect sheaves, its drifty web of hair.
You are here, it said. *You will always be here.*
I wish I could harvest that patience from fifty years away.
Al long dead, his wife dead, their farm still a farm though—
    one victory.
I wish I could tell him how right he was about slowness,
the path of sunlight through leaves, birdcalls beyond,
how no tomato was ever better than the one he held in his hand.

Room for You Here

The Palestinians got to heaven and there were no beds.
Someone said, just imagine the beds,
and they said, we know how to do that.

A heavenly tree was wilting, but they
knew how to haul buckets of water from
small springs far away. *We will help the tree.*

Even in heaven there were problems.
But not as bad as before.

Everyone who couldn't see them when they were on earth
now could see them. They were dressed in radiant silk
and softest cottons and nubbiest linens,

their pockets filled with grapes which they
offered to anyone, same way they did on earth,
no reason to feel surprised.

The only thing that had changed was, there was no land
to feel sad about. All that scuffling and seizing had vanished.
There weren't any houses. Everyone floated.
No one was unchosen.

Sorrow took wing.
No one could remember how it ever
seemed so heavy.

Song Book

Tiny keyboard bearing the massive reverie of the past—
press one button, we're carried away on a country road,
marching with saints, leaving the Red River Valley ...
it's almost too much to bear.
Here is every holiday you hated, every hard time,
each steamy summer wish. You closed your eyes
in the wooden stairwell, leaning your head against the wall,
knowing a bigger world loomed. It's still out there,
and it's here tucked in this keyboard too,
now we are an organ, now we are an oboe,
now we are young or ancient,
now we are smelling wallpaper in the house
our grandfather sold with every cabinet,
table and doily included,
but we are still adrift, floating,
thrum-full of longing layers of sound.

Loving Working

We clean to give space for Art.
— Micaela Miranda, Freedom Theatre, Palestine

Work was a shining refuge when wind sank its tooth
into my mind. Everything you love is going away,
drifting—but you could sweep this stretch of floor,
this patio or porch, gather white stones in a bucket,
rake the patch for future planting, mop the counter
with a rag. Lovely wet gray rag, squeeze it hard
it does so much. Clear the yard of blowing bits of plastic.
The glory in the doing. The breath of the doing.
Sometimes the simplest move kept fear from
fragmenting into no energy at all, or sorrow from
multiplying, or sorrow from being the only person
living in the house.

Este Recuerdo

Kathy Vargas

Most of my work deals with time, and with a reflection on the cycle of life, death, resurrection and remembrance. "Este Recuerdo" is a re-photographing of images of my immediate family as a way of preserving their memory. Except for me, they are all gone now, so I have re-contextualized them within the textures of gravestone and earth (for where they are now), but also hearts and flowers (to denote that they are still beloved). This new context places them at a physical distance, within frames and behind veils. However, the overlapping double-exposures imply that moments can co-exist; occupying the same space in time, thus making time simultaneous and allowing someone who has died to find a way back into our lives through an ongoing pentimento of past into present.

All of my images are hand-colored, selenium-toned, black-and-white darkroom prints. They are double exposures done in-camera, not in the darkroom or computer. And even though they are photographic prints, each is unique due to the chemical toning and hand-coloring applied after printing.

Innocent Age: First Communion

*Este Recuerdo: My grandmother, Marina Soriano Salcedo,
with my mother, Jesusita (Susie) Salcedo and my uncle, Mike Salcedo*

Este Recuerdo: My mother walking

Deborah Parédez

The Gulf, 1987

The day upturned, flooded with sunlight, not
a single cloud. I squint into the glare,
cautious even then of bright emptiness.
We sit under shade, Tía Lucia
showing me how white folks dine, *the high life.*
I am about to try my first oyster,
Tía spending her winnings from the slots
on a whole dozen, the glistening valves
wet and private as a cheek's other side,
broken open before us. *Don't be shy.*
Take it all in at once. Flesh and sea grit,
sweet meat and brine, a taste I must acquire.
In every split shell, the coast's silhouette:
bodies floating in what was once their home.

Tía Lucia Enters the Nursing Home

All morning my daughter pleading, outside
outside. By noon I kneel to button her
coat, tie the scarf to keep her hood in place.
This is her first snow so she strains against
the ritual, spooked silent then whining,
restless under each buffeting layer,
uncertain how to settle into this
leashing. I manage at last to tunnel
her hands into mittens and she barks and
won't stop barking, her hands suddenly paws.
She is reduced to another being,
barking, barking all day in these restraints.
For days after, she howls into her hands,
the only way she tells me she wants out.

Bustillo Drive Grocery

On the corner of Bustillo Drive
in the years before the campaign
to widen the street so cars veered off
Roosevelt Avenue right into mailboxes
right into stray dogs and second cousins,
in the years before we found the cockroach
floating inside a bottle of R.C. Cola
and swore off sodas forever
our righteous boycotts lasting
only halfway through Lent,
in the years before the thieves
tore through the screen doors and cracked
open the cash registers and Abuelito's head
with the butts of their guns, in the years
before I turned sour as chamoy
coarse and tough as stale chicharón,
I was in charge of los dulces.
In those years, Abuelita harnessed
me with my first job, setting me on a stool
behind the counter, setting me
like chocolate poured—quick—into the
candy mold before it hardens.
In the afternoons I fulfilled my duties
with a reverence for the expansive variations,
the countless shapes of sweetness:
aligning cylinders of Life Savers by flavor,
the Milky Ways near the 3 Musketeers,
the dainty swirled straws of Pixy Sticks near
the prized plastic heads of Pez dispensers,
the packets of Pop Rocks in grape, cherry, and orange.
I sat tall on my stool, a big girl. I was in charge
of los dulces. In the shelves above my reach

jars of Spanish olives, bottles of Bayer aspirin,
rolls of Charmin stood at attention,
awaiting their orders, but I could not be bothered
by the weight of such practical inventory.
I cared only for saccharine indulgence
so when on Friday nights the regular crowd
of relatives arrived for the gossip and the gambling,
I descended from my dulce throne
leaned coyly against the domino table
until Uncle Louis finished off his Falstaff
slapped his last domino down and with the same
triumphant hand, grabbed hold of me, swooped me up,
the fringes of my crocheted poncho fanning out in radiant plume.
He would lower me into the cavernous
depths of the oldtime soda water cooler
that ran the length of the front wall, the length of a coffin
and twice as deep, my body plunged head first
into the cool humming darkness, arms outstretched,
hands grabbing hold of a slender bottleneck
and just then—catch complete—my plumed body
in pelican dive—I went soaring again—
Uncle Louis pulling me out from the depths,
poncho fringes fluttering, giggles spouting
from my mouth, syrupy bubbles erupting
from the opened bottle of my shaken Orange Crush.
In those years, my unwavering devotion to los dulces,
my faith in the choreography of return spurred
every harrowing descent, brought me back
every time—flushed and dizzy and eager for more.

Hermine Pinson

Four Sisters and the Dance

1

It's morning, it's evening or afternoon.
Sweat glistens the tips of our noses.
I two-step to some old-school.
Barefoot in her nightgown,
one sister waltzes alone to music that moves her.
One kneels. One listens.
Umm Kulthum sings,
We outran our own shadows

2

We outran our own shadows
The song's breath bears traces of the sub-Saharan moan,
the gospel holler. We grip our lives in our hands,
sure of that much. Joy, like anger, runs deep as memories
we carry like scars or diamonds,
or like the potbound onion grass we tend or neglect.

Our rounded shoulders, passed down from Louisiana
on our father's side, have ministered to others,
our flaired nostrils hint of Spanish, hint of Italian,
hint of Choctaw, and the rest belongs to Africa.

3

One day is a door to open or a window, and
even if, after all, we have to shut the window
against the rain, or take off our hats to
catch the kiss of a snowflake, we remember

the dance that binds us in the trail
of letters, cards, phone calls, emails.

Our deep regard or frostbitten gaze
holds us fast on this shrinking globe where
the mothers of New Orleans see the images
of waters rising over Iwate and bless the daughters
of Miyagi, Fukushima, Ibaraki, and Tokyo.

Beggaring hyperbole,
we run, we weary, we sit down in the grass
on the side of the mountain, we soothe our children,
comfort our husbands, we wail or hum or watch.
We shape our days, our days shape us.

4

Here's a photo of us
as four coppery-brown pigtailed girls
holding hands. What did we know then?
What did we believe?

5

African violets for the eldest,
blackthorn roses for the middle sister,
bird of paradise for the youngest,
whose robe is the color of the boronia.

We hold hands to bridge the distance
between faith and fallibility.
We pass on the dance.
We pass the dance on.

Dove

I

I've watched mourning doves perch
on the telephone wire
that runs across my backyard

And wondered if someday a god
would again send them as a
sign of truce

I've watched doves rise straight up past a haloed moon
toward the blue-seamed promise of heaven
clutching in their beaks weedseed, or buckwheat,
or plain grit.

II.

Once, a lone dove sat on the line for half an hour.
Did it ponder my kind
while I reclined against the sun porch
puffing a cigarette?

Tobacco smoke assailed the air,
reaching up to the black bordered tip of its tail wing.
I like to think it disapproved,
this traveler, this singer whose song means lament
in the language of those who treasure or hunt it.

III.

Dove notes piece together
another evening. I listen for this grace.

from one music lover to another

when you turn up the bass too loud
the door vibrates
neighbors know you're
inside
trying your best
to get off
to everybody from
brubeck to basie to bonnie raitt

the door vibrates
and your heart
beats for the good note
the one that will somehow last
beyond your concrete steps
with the geranium plants
that you have not watered since
the last rain
tears won't do—
salty and too few
must have clean water not
soiled by
the deadly seven
must have clean water
if not from you then
wherever the idea
of god has taken up residence

up there in the sky somewhere
birds flap their wings
at so many somethings per second
music alone cannot suffice
must have something else
since you abandoned camus

Hermine Pinson

and sex
you are alive still
in a universe
where celie could not even reach god
to tell him she was good

Melissa Morphew

A Short History of the Cold War

I wanted to tell you the art
of eating chocolate was lost
in the "heady" days of Marie Antoinette
when Spanish oranges were spiced with cloves
and women tucked lavender sachets
between the talcum-dusted moons
of their breasts,
                  but as usual
you cut me off with that not-again-
twitch of your left brow,
and now we sit here, each alone
in the granite-topped-coolness of our
February kitchen, glancing out windows
at the jittery birds. *What's that?*
        Yes, I suppose you're right, even my anger
tends toward the poetic, the calculated
metaphor that lets me assume meaning exists somewhere in our
haphazard bric-a-brac.
        Do you think we might start over? Agree
to read the same books, listen
to the same bleak piano plink out
a Satie soundtrack to our silent walks,
make love at 4 o'clock
every Wednesday afternoon.
        Very funny, and how do you know
I won't forget to pencil *you* in,
to mark off the edges of a calendar
which seems more and more a parallel universe.
        I thought you wanted a poem, a painting
colored out in words, an endless conversation

that swirled into nebulas
and never grew old, but then like everyone
we ever knew, those fathers, mothers
with their happy hour martinis, garnished
with pearl onions and the chill of endless bickering,
we've settled into a routine,
moving through rooms as if in pantomime,
a couple in a silent movie, indelible
in grainy hues of black and white.
Oh, so that's your answer—just leave, just pretend
the last 15 years are someone else's story,
a documentary which could only play
in an art house theatre downtown because the plot
is nonexistent, *it's just life, just life.*
      And what am I supposed to do *now*? Forget
I love you, or is that too cliché, after all
we live in a postmodern world, and love
isn't the point. Where do you propose we go?
How do we end this? And where should I place
those years that still pulse through my dreams—
the summers at the beach, the way the sun
lit the room with blues, bleached whites,
and you kissed me and your kisses tasted
of wine, apples, the decadence of honeyed-brie.
      Tell me, how do I forget this life, comfortable
even in its bitterness?
      Tell me, how do I close this house for winter?

Dallas, 1959

Our house, this museum of summer's
voluptuous heliotrope—boundaries
of flower boxes delinquent with spent amaryllis—

we lounge beside the pool, nameless
travelers tempted to exchanges of soliloquy,
the indolent blah-blah of weathered postcards.

I want to tell you how, once, the sky unfolded
mantis-green, dissolving into a reverberation of storm,
and I let the screen door slam behind me,

rushed outside, the silver maples an incomprehensible
panic of limbs and leaves invented
between camera-flashes of lightning.

The same way you invented me with the economy
of your kisses, those resinous hours
trapped inside the persistent architecture

of glass-front buildings, chrome-gilded Cadillacs,
tea parties backdropped by purple orchids
and talk of money. Our marriage

a science of country air and lakefront property,
traces of birdsong settling the trees, the simplest
moments clothed in autumn lanes, perspicacious bishops.

Compotes and comfits—the currency of pleasantries. And my
recurring dream, a woman in a blue skirt making her way
through an endless field of cornflower, arms spread wide.

As if Our Lives Starred Joanne Woodward
& Paul Newman in a Script by Carson McCullers

       Nacogdoches June, the heat a steady pulse
like static on the radio, an AM station
siphoning Tejano music hundreds of miles from Mexico,
a spare love of spent heels and Lucky Strikes,
pinball machines and night-blooming jasmine,
a pink cotton dress forgotten on the clothesline,
sawdust settling on our skin.

We found Grandpa's Victrola in the attic,
filled the kitchen with the simmering crackle of Bob Wills
and the Texas Playboys at 78 rpms—records
with the heft of dinner plates.

What happened?

He bought me a Hershey bar, a cherry Coke;
we snuck into the movies to see *Splendor in the Grass.*

You wouldn't understand.

       A boy moved piles of dirt at the public
playground. He was 7 or 8, wearing
a red and white striped T-shirt. One of his eyes
always seemed to be looking away, cocked
toward the western horizon.

You live in lala land girl. Got it—lala land.

What if I told you, we made love underneath
a rundown house—surrounded by Juicy Fruit wrappers,
the skeletons of mice and baby birds—

his hands like sandpaper, and I
      was something hewn.

What if I told you, I ripped
out the carpets, painted
the walls blue, thankful
        it only took one summer.

Sandra Cisneros

Las Girlfriends

Tip the barmaid in tight jeans.
She's my friend.
Been to hell and back again.
I've been there too.

Girlfriend, I believe in Gandhi.
But some nights nothing says it
quite precise like a Lone Star
cracked on someone's head.

Last week in this same bar,
kicked a cowboy in the butt
who made a grab for Terry's ass.
How do I explain, it was all
of Texas I was kicking,
and all our asses on the line.

At Tacoland, Cat flamencoing crazy
circles round the pool
player with the furry tongue.
A warpath of sorts for every
wrong ever wronged us.

And Terry here has her own history.
A bar down the street she can't
go in, and one downtown. Me,
a French café in Austin
where they don't say—*entrez-vous.*

Little Rose of San Antone
is the queen bee of kick-*nalga*.
When you go out with her,
don't wear your good clothes.

But the best story is la Bárbara
who runs for the biggest kitchen knife
in the house every bad-ass domestic quarrel.
Points it towards her own heart
like some Aztec priestess gone *loca*.
¡ME MATO!

I tell you, nights like these,
something bubbles from
the tips of our pointy boots
to the top of our coyote yowl.

Y'all wicked mean, a voice at the bar
claims. Naw, not mean. Shit!
Been to hell and back again.
Girl, me too.

Original Sin

Before Mexicana flight #729
en route to Mexico City departs
from San Antonio International Airport
I buy a 69¢ disposable razor at
the gift shop because I forgot
in Mexico they don't like hair
under your arms only on
your legs and plan to

shave before landing but
the stewardess handing out declaration
forms has given me the wrong
one assuming I'm Mexican but I am!
and I have to run up the aisle and ask
for a U.S. citizen form instead because
I'm well how do I explain?

except before you know it we're
already crossing the volcanoes and
descending into the valley of Mexico City
and I have to rush to the back
while the plane drops too quickly as
if the pilot's in a hurry to get home

and into the little airplane bathroom where
lots of couples want to coitus fantisizus but
I only want to get rid of my underarm hair
quick before the plane touches down in
the land of *los nopales* disregarding
lights blinking kindly return to your
seat and fasten your seatbelt all
in Spanish of course just in time

for flight #729 to deposit me finally
into the arms of awaiting Mexican kin
on my father's side of the family where
I open my arms wide armpits clean
as a newborn's soul without original
sin and embrace them like the good
girl my father would have
them believe I am.

Bienvenido Poem for Sophie

This morning that would've meant
a field of crumpled snow if we
were in Vermont, brought only
a crumpled sky to Texas,

and you and Alba for breakfast
tacos at Torres Taco Haven
where you admired my table
next to the jukebox and
said, Good place to write.

You promised we could come back
and have tacos together and sit
here with coffee and our writer's
notebooks whenever we want.
And nobody would have to talk
if we didn't want to. Next time

you come by my house, I want
to take you up to the roof.
At sunset the grackles
make a wonderful racket.
You can come whenever you want.
And nobody will have to talk
if we don't want to.

Carmen Tafolla

Mechanics and Menopause
(A mechanic's daughter discusses menopause)

Interesting things happen when you start steering
through menopause. Especially when
you're a mechanic's daughter.
Now if you were a physician's daughter,
you could say it was, biochemically, like adolescence backwards.
If you were the daughter of two attorneys, you could say it was,
contractually, like redefining the terms.
If you were a carpenter's daughter, or a contractor's even,
you could say it was leveling the foundation
and reconfiguring the structure.

But for me—other phrases come to the tongue, like
"I need W-D 40!"
"My thermostat's broke!"
"Engine's overheating, radiator hose blocked."
"The timing is off, too fast, out of synch—
Missing.
Pistons are rubbing, low on oil.
Sweating beads of moisture from the engine block at night,
and there seem to be sudden and unexplained lurches
from the transmission, after running it for long hours."

Good thing this car has always had
a good wheel on its shoulders
and very reliable power steering,
even down strange roads
and in very
difficult
conditions.

You Can Tell We're Related

You can tell we're related
I can see it in your thunder and your rumble
your voracious appetite for sweet newness, for bold beauty
the *Esperanza* flowers you weave into your hair
the red seeds you hang from your neck
the wanting, the dreaming, the power in your belly

You can see it in the way I'm always building something new
yearning for something more
changing the way things are
Guts aching to open waterfalls, tear down walls
plant trees in unexpected places
press saved *cositas* to my heart

I can see it in your bright dawning arms, stretching wide with welcome
Sunrays clear as cornsilk slip an extra plate onto the table
always room, always room
Shield the shivering under your mantel, fold them into growth
In the crisp of autumn's chill, toast them at your hearthfire
Celebrate breath, *hierba buena, anise, maíz, canela*, cycles

You can see it in the way I quiver, dream, want, grow
My hardheaded *terquedad* determined to stand strong, free
always building mountains from the crater of my center
erupting revolutions passions transformations
the solid rock of my core the same taste as your soil
I expand. I discard. I recycle
Everything
As do you

You can tell we're related, *Madre*
I wrap the shroud around my dead
to warm them, care for them, memorize them

see them in each feature of the newborn's yawn
And know you will wrap me too some sun-filled day
as you envelop me
hold me
in the brown earth
of your heart

Feeding You

I have slipped *chile* under your skin
     secretly wrapped in each enchilada
     hot and soothing
     carefully cut into bitefuls for you as a toddler
     increasing in power and intensity as you grew
     until it could burn
     forever

     silently spiced into the rice
     soaked into the bean *caldo*
     smoothed into the avocado

     I have slipped *chile* under your skin
     drop by fiery drop
     until it ignited
     the sunaltar fire
     in your blood

I have squeezed *cilantro* into the breast milk
     made sure you were nurtured with
     the clean taste of corn stalks
     with the wildness of thick leaves
     of untamed *monte*
     of unscheduled growth

I have ground the earth of these *Américas* in my *molcajete*
     until it became a fine and piquant spice
     sprinkled it surely into each spoonful of food
     that would have to expand to fit your soul

Mijo, Dear Son
Dear Corn *Chile Cilantro* Son

This
is your *herencia*
This
is what is yours
This
is what your mother fed you
to keep you
    alive

Monte — unmanicured wild country, either jungle or brush country, but uncivilized, natural growth.
Molcajete — a mortar and pestle made of volcanic rock and used in traditional Mexican food to grind spices.
Herencia — inheritance.

Survival Instructions:
Summer, a Hundred and Three

Feel yourself sizzle on the streets
Sizzle on the streets
Sashay sassy as salsa
Slip survival into sunglare like a native
Toughen up the soles
Strengthen the heart muscle
Reinforce mind with steel and sunrise
Drink more water
Bless the air conditioner
Fry your *huevos rancheros* on the sidewalk
Attend the wake
Give a dollar to the homeless man on the corner
Holding his bright blue windshield-cleaner-spraybottle
wiping circles in the empty air
Hoping for a yes
some coins
a bed
Lasso the chaos of your collapsing life like a lost steer
wrangle it with this well-worn rope
made to survive the torrid heat
the chaparral of baked dirt
the creeping cancer of years peeled to bone
Feel yourself sizzle on the streets
Sizzle on the streets
sashay sassy as salsa

Susie Kelly Flatau

Amid the Storm She Dances

The sensual stroke
Of sun's reflection—
Like a silver swath atop the cresting surf—
Sweeps the pebble-skinned floor.
Waves of wind through open windows
Wash velvet fingers across the sea of bent necks.

Pencils and pens and pens and pencils
Swell
And glide
Then surge—
Crashing down upon mica-slick pages.

Yet strangely, amid billowing life-stories,
All is calm
As the circle of women
Write on ...

... within that circle, one woman receives the fire of her creative belly as she stares into upturned hands that cradle the smoldering life-energy. Lifting her eyes, she stares into the ocean green that surrounds her and listens to the blades of grass singing her desire. Delight arrives upon hummingbird wings, keeping tempo with her breath. Then, in a place where voices cease and silence reigns, nature's siren sings, "Let go. Let us go." This woman, once frozen amid life-storms, celebrates as raindrops echo her stories. Laughs as lightning scribbles her message. Laughs—then pauses to embrace the release. Wrapping the ancestral shawl about her shoulder, this woman kneels at the altar of joy and glimpses the future etched into the fleshy canyons of her communion palms.

Heading to Hell By Choice

Seeking salvation
reaching for redemption
begging for blessings—
the days have been long as of late.

A little bit of 'dis—a little bit of 'dat.

Not resisting the temptation
of original sin,
He whispers sweet nothings in his new friend's ear.

With permission
he begins to play,
heading to hell by choice.

Late February Snowflakes

Late February snowflakes,
like dragonfly dancers in downy satin,
swirl and sweep in downward spirals.
Their icy hips sway, arms circle—
luring me with sultry whispers,
beckoning me to place my hand in theirs,
tempting me to dance to my deepest longings.

In that moment
when my flesh touches the crystalline satin,
laser sharp reflections of car lights fracture
the snow-dune contours of the earth's floor,
explode the ballet of beauty,
splinter the dance of dreams.

Rebecca Balcárcel

Wish In the Penney's Parking Lot

Mom and I surf an escalator wave to the store's second floor where
shammed pillows poof themselves on bedtops like sunning sea lions,

where we squint in fluorescent bouncing off floor squares,
and inside I'm Pop Rocks, zoings, and zippy flips

because my new room, freshly painted, calls for new bedding,
this trip to Tyler, and a smile ride with Mom.

I can't ask for tasseled satin or custard-thick thread counts,
but pocketcost cottons, yes, and when I choose pastel panels,

cornflower fairy veils, to hang behind blossomed curtains,
I'm almost afraid I can't live up to light blue, to the stretch of Caspian

hanging in my window, to the princess vibes on my warts.
I make a wish right there, on the shopping bag handles, one, two,

on the dime and nickel I saw in the parking garage,
on the seat belt click and the car door latch,

to be a yellow worthy of her room's blue, to be canary-colored
strands in the blue-tinted light, a strip of glitter spangling sky.

I promise the blue gauze gods to walk into that room, opening.
To rise out of roller-printed flowers, shining.

Behind the Piano

When the evening crumbles into grown-ups shouting, or
no's roadblock every trail I want to take,
I crawl between pianoback and living room wall.

I press my cheek against wood struts, add my
half-pound stresses to eighteen-ton tension held firm,
until my wobbling thoughts straighten,

my breath slows, and quiet rings like a final chord.
I'm not sad thinking every tune ends here.
That songs pierce through silence to trill into being,

breaking quiet's surface to leap like dolphins into air,
only to disappear into its depths, where I meet them now
in the afterring, in the one sound that follows every sound.

I feel myself hush-hugged, tuned to the first pitch
and the last, of all songs, here
on a shelf of Sitka spruce.

Swings

What Saturdays are made for. Stomach-slung flying,
stand-up swaying, leg-pumped sailing. Chad swings high,
and I swing higher. At the top of the arc, we can
nearly tap a green apple, small and hard, dangling
from a twig tip on a branch bending toward us.
I think it will ring like a bell when we reach it.

Then Ronnie shows up.
Two swings, three kids. Somebody waiting.
Ronnie's never played with us before,
and I heard his brother stole a car.
His house needs paint, and his here-and-there hair
wouldn't pass my mother's inspection.

I can swing anytime—they're mine—so I say,
"Here, go ahead," and he grabs the chains,
pumps hard, and I can see he's happy in the air,
defying gravity. He spies that apple too
and says, "Bet I can bite that from here."
He's challenging Chad, but looking at me,

and it's the first time I can remember
feeling like a girl in that yard. I thought
we were all just kids, not boys and girl,
but he's saying, "Chomp!" to make me laugh,
and I laugh every time he nears the apple.
"Chomp!" makes me laugh so hard I'm tearing up.

Every "Chomp!" lifts a metal clasp off my worry.
Each "Chomp!" is Ronnie leaning forward, straining
toward the branch, biting into the air, and soon
the light spots in the dappled shade make my head

feel floaty, and he's laughing at my laughing,
which makes me laugh more.

When he leaves that day, I want him to stay.
I'm bored of the sandbox, my Holly Hobby bike.
I watch Chad's hair as we take turns on his skateboard.
The neat, layered cut swinging tamely when he jumps off.
I look across to the paint-peeling house,
imagine a bit of trouble behind the door,

and Ronnie, a decent boy defying
his home's gravity, one hand in a hoodie pocket,
one spinning a yo-yo. "Your turn," says Chad,
and nothing could be easier than skating away
from his straight-cut bangs, down the hill
toward my own darkness.

I'm ashamed of the girl I might turn into—
her sarcasm, her coiled snake tattoo,
her stride toward forbidden sparklers,
and I'm afraid, so much that I can't sleep,
of liking her.

Ysabel de la Rosa

Each into One

Second-grade young, with a pinwheel in my hand, I clutched
the stem, blew north into its pink and turquoise center.
The pointed colored parts became one soft round shape
my eyes believed to be still and my heart knew to be moving.
I learned then I could see fast or slow,
could see the pieces or the whole or both—I could choose.

I could choose how to see.

I walk alone now, after raising the child
whom I made sure had his share of pinwheels.
Windmills punctuate the line where land meets sky
in a sentence nearly infinite to my eye. Space is, and
I am small in it, in awe of it.

Weathered grey blades divide the sunset,
make pie charts of magenta-tangerine clouds.
The wind blows north into their centers, turns each into one
soft shape spinning in front of the sunset blazing as it fades,
light on its way to night, first with clouds on fire, and then
with one cornflower-blue haze.

And still, I can choose what I see:
the blaze, the fading,
the one soft shape, the separate moving parts,
what I see with my eyes, what I see in my heart.

En el estado de no estar

Tengo miedo de escuchar
la música de aquel lugar
de donde vengo,
en donde no vivo,
en donde nací,
de donde salí
hace tiempo ya.

Si aprieto el botón con flecha
ahí mi corazón se me va a transportar
aunque yo no puedo regresar,
y otra vez más por dentro se va a crear
esa distancia dolorosa e imposible de cruzar:
la nostalgia.

La nostalgia: el estado en que es posible,
demasiado posible, sentirse ahí sin estar ahí
en aquel abandonado país que
siempre era mi hogar.

Si aprieto el botón con cuadro
a ninguna parte se me va a transportar
y así no tendré que tratar de abarcar por dentro
esa distancia dolorosa e imposible de cruzar.

¿Que hago? Lo que no puedo
hacer es olvidar ni cortar
el pasado sin sacrificar
las memorias que construyeron esta vida,
ni está en mi poder cambiar
el presente exigente que requiere que me quede
aquí en este extraño lugar.

Lo que hago es mirar
estos pequeños botones y pensar
una vez más en lo mucho que no quiero llorar
ni permitir que me entre el dolor que me entra siempre
por sentir que estoy en aquel estado en donde no podré más estar.

Family Tree / Árbol de familia

Treasure the seed, her father said,
It is the beginning and the source.

Revere the root, her mother told her,
It is our anchor and our strength.

Touch the trunk, said her sister,
and you cannot be lonely.

Make your home beneath the branches,
her brother advised.
They will give you shelter.

And dream your way to the highest
heart-shaped leaf, she told her son
when the time came.

———✦———

Venera la semilla, dijo mi padre,
es el principio y la fuente de la vida.

Valora la raíz, dijo mi madre,
es el ancla de nuestra fuerza.

Toca el tronco, dijo mi hermana,
y ya nunca te sentirás sola.

Establece tu hogar debajo de las ramas,
aconsejó mi hermano, y siempre tendrás cobijo.

Y, cuando llegó el momento, a mi hijo le dije:
Lleva tus sueños hacia la hoja más alta,
aquella hoja en forma de corazón.

Anne McCrady

Camp Song

In the pale light
of a canvas tent dawn,
cicadas kazoo
the last verses of their camp song,
that tinnitus of summer.
Hidden in beds of thin grass,
crickets whistle
their own tinny hymn,
and out by the pond,
amorous tree frogs blurt
wet advances too late now
for evening love.
In the dim air,
dashes of new sun backlight
leftover brown bats catching
the last slow mosquitoes,
and mockingbirds breaking
their full moon fast
fly from feeder
to field to feeder.
A redwing cries;
a woodpecker tattoos
the trunk of a water oak.
Hummingbirds buzz
the butterfly bush.
Jays puncture the air,
and in the oldest pecan tree,
two squirrels run
spiraled wind sprints,
risking the attention

of the new puppy
sleeping at the feet
of a woman who sings
to meet the morning.

Dusk

> *... both dark and light are true.*
> —Kathleen Peirce

Evening deepens to deceive us.
In the autumn orchard, trees darken
sweet green to aging gray to blue-black,
as newly set apples ripen into sunset.
Roses, extravagant rusted buttons,
fade to remain only as the memory-laden scent
of your grandmother's dusting powder.
At the edge of the yard, verdigris
wind chimes disappear into chime.
The dog, collar and all, dissolves
into the rope of his nose-up howl
at the empty bowl of the moon.
Inside the house, curtains close
to hide water oaks and pines.
Drapes darken. Rooms cool.
Clocks lose track of minute hands,
but keep tick-tick-ticking
the clicks of inevitable time.
At this hour, no one knows
the final form of things.
Even the small child in his quilted bed
becomes a mysterious changeling:
one moment a tearful tyrant;
the next, a sleeping cherub,
the apple of your eye.

Dove Season

There is something troubling
about the turned acres
of the farm this September—
the fields, empty, time-tired.
Carrying the inheritance
of shotguns across tucked elbows,
we feel it but do not say so.
As we bend to climb through
barbed wire, boot-stepping
the strands into rough clods
of matted black earth
spiked with dry cornstalk shreds,
we still do not speak of it,
just as we do not mention
the time you forgot to unload
your 410 or the day I lost my way
back to the house as a boy.
As our spindly shadows
stretch and pull in liquid ripples
across the tiered rows and turns.
we step off the same stories we love
to tell every year about dogs and guns.
At dusk, we check the pastel horizon
for flights of doves heavy with seeds
of the head-high sunflowers that face us
nodding like worried parents
who know the truth before they hear it.
Stopping to rest in the shade
of a low cloud, I finally say I remember
the last time we were here. It was spring,
the corn a waist-deep wonderland
of pale green streamers fluttering

like May Day ribbons. The mourning doves,
no different then, from sparrows or killdeers;
our mother, still a Texas songbird,
so much summer left to live.

Marilyn Robitaille

A Fine Blue Stone

Not by design, but quite by accident, I am here
Little more than a stone's throw
From Hoa Lò Prison, Hanoi Hilton
Time heaped upon time for suffering
More than brick and mortar all entombed
The whispers in all languages of the men
Whose wings were clipped, whose souls sucked dry
Pleas to heaven and the sun, evermore a memory
In this dark, demon-place time turns in upon itself
With cold walls and shadows smelling of the grave
I withstand the moment with the touch of stone
A smooth, blue rock made perfect by a hand
Who knows so well the moments of this country
The smell of fear, gun-metal green, break of day
Across the fields whose smoke-filled haze
Ignites the glow and brings it all together
All that he is beyond this place, he fashions out a perfect jewel
I wear it as a talisman to keep me safe, a token peace
Around my neck, one perfect, blissful blue stone
All that it means so clear now that the burn has cleared
In reverence to the ghosts, a fine blue stone
Beauty defined and defended
In Hanoi

For My Aunt Flossie (Winona) and Summer, 1957

Your light burned hard and long, Winona Bowen.
You pushed through poverty and pain to
        make us sweet, uneasy poetry
In stone-carved manuscripts. You always looked for more,
        the next best thing to take our breath away.

Of all the memories to keep, I like the first one best.
Still keen across time, the picture well-defined.
It was the summer of 1957.
Rabbit-ears adjusted on the black and white TV,
I ate Cheerios, watched Captain Kangaroo
Made mud-pies, played dolls, sang to August wind.
I was five years old, nearly six when you arrived.

In the haze of summer sun, I watched you
Tall, lean, and beautiful, sleek and promising silk
Arriving in a white Cadillac, you and your man
Waltzed right up our stone steps with a brand new baby.

Fresh in from the road, all the way from Phoenix
You smelled of some sweet scent I didn't know
You breezed in, lit up a cigarette, and sat that baby on a quilt
So I could get a better look up close.
You smiled at me, touched my hair, held my hand
And introduced my one and only cousin
Your one and only baby, perfumed from your presence.

You didn't stay the night, only one August afternoon
The visit punctuated with strong iced tea and sandwiches
Then hugs, kisses all around as we said our goodbyes.
I stood on the front porch, truly all amazed
By your coming to the country, to the farm

Your city radiance beaming glamour and glory
      like it was the second-coming, not the first.

In the final moments, brilliant Uncle Johnny
      your shining knight, pushed a magic button
And the hard top of that white Caddy
Unfolded, slowly into the trunk like it was Harry Houdini's,
Now you see it now you don't.
You laughed and flashed that Hollywood smile,
The light on your dark hair and rhinestone-studded glasses
Adding to the glow that lit us up
My cow and chicken, mud-pie life now forever changed
Because from here on out, I had hope and drama.
I had Aunt Flossie whose gifts gave me
      my one and only cousin and real-life drama,
Precious gifts that only you could give.

A Frank Sinatra Sighting in New York City: Winter 1991

It rained that cold afternoon in New York City
Gun gray skies met gloomy sidewalks
Landscapes washed away the city's color.
In a blur of steel leaves, damp and dripping
We walked through Central Park

Bundled you in your black coat, me cocooned in white
We looked like companion penguins
Wobbling down the street against the wind
It's a damp cold, you'd said, and I agreed.
We need a strong drink—Irish whiskey, you'd said
          And I agreed again.

Rosie O'Grady's bar the sign alleged, so
          We went in, shelter against the cold
Both inside and out.
We started toward a table, then gave pause
The bar looked more New York
Polished gravity against the years where all
Those Irish whiskeys turned saints into sinners
          Or maybe, sometimes, the other way around.

We settled in, hoping to hide our tourist otherness
          meaning business, ordering two shots
Downing them like they were our last
Because maybe they were we thought
          gasping against the burn

Precisely then, just then the door opened wide
And we saw him standing there, Old blue eyes
Mr. Frank Sinatra and his entourage
Advancing in tuxedo regiment to Rosie's back room.

He smiled and waved like the Queen of England
As they marshaled through the bar

You stood up, smiled, said hi, Frank, like old friends.
I seized pen, then napkin for an autograph
Thrusting them with my best Texas smile
and he looked at us
          Bluely
Then he was gone, all gone and the back door closed.

He might as well have been
          A stranger in the night for all it's worth.
The door to Rat Pack heaven closed to us
Since we weren't canonized.
Frankly speaking, I hollered out, thanks for nothin', Frank.
Then we rallied up our strength to meet
New York City's damp, gray cold now
To the depths of our good Irish whiskey

Betsy Berry

Fourth of July

To my father on his second Fourth of July, the first coming too soon
Too soon after you left us, babbling like a child, your face beatific
Do you remember saying "I'm sorry, *I am*" to your son, last words
All those years, war vet, browbeaten lover, deserter, dead man?
One blazing July Fourth in the days when I was still your Miss Annie
We lay side by side, sneezing, then laughing at the dandelion's dance
Did someone put us there, or was it like our lives together, a dream
Where we watched fat clouds speeding over us in time-lapse film?

On your back, the source of your deformity, the locus that the family bore
Of your endless dying, when you began the process of leaving at last
In a Crown Royal bag in a box, a flurry of small checks your jet trail
We declined to take the scaffolding of your spine from the crematorium
Titanium rods that wouldn't burn, so that they remained on the gurney
Like a cage. Remember when they wrapped you in wire for 16 hours?
Toward the end, they plopped your head on top and you never forgave
It was precious metal, costly, taking up residence in you, its country
Until in anticipation of what was coming it began to unravel, clanking
It pushed out of your skin like a front line advancing, bolt and screws,
Screws and bolts that had unincorporated in the corpse you were to be
Not all the metal in China could fasten down the trouble your body reared.

And your mind, what was once your funny, funny mind lighting the sun!
It cranked and whirred even when your eyes were ringed like a sad hound
Other times, your temper torching, spraying like the scald of a hot gasket
Remember that fourth when you drank and danced, the life of the party?
You the purveyor of mirth, the one who never, really, never really grew up
Foretelling that the cloud forms of my own imaginative declinations
Would never, in the whole of their convictions, be enough to save me
To learn the final truth, that no one sees truly in the same way as another

And there is no lasting bond, just what was once you, drifting by in lacy jags
I thought of this yesterday when under the sear of a cold blue sky
I watched paint peel from the deck on the lake, your version of a den
I try to read the paint blots and wonder if they are messages from the dead
What shapes do you see now? What messages would you send? You,
Who will never again do anything, anything you had prayed for in the dark
The ball turret gunner, forth flies the squadron into the boundless beyond!

In this only, with you at the helm, dropping the full weight of U.S. steel
In those moments you were lifted from that which would gather you intact
To the swell of ground, to the fields coming to greet you as you journeyed back
In this you were free from sins and omissions, from family strife, free from
Soil's stain, floating through air caves and icy reaches, curving round the globe.

In pieces I have remembered you on other days, in earth and in sky
Here and there I imagine you in the spaces you inhabited, or inhabit
Remembering, I suppose, for the planning of my life and time after you
Still holding out hope of finding the space that only I see, that is mine alone
A place that is anchored, and unanchored, a place of no memories, a place
I fear that you do not know, nor will ever know, that no one may know
Where I am still you haunt, in all the predictable ways, on predictable days.

June Zaner

the song he sang ...

my father sang love songs about her,
creating from thin air a woman I had never known
one who hummed continuously and
walked in the blue haze of monthly migraines,
wrapped her children in gauze and black salve,
made them eat liver and drink cod liver oil and
guarded them from the white slavers who lay
in wait for the young, the innocent.

I didn't see in her snapping black eyes
the woman he sang about, a bawdy tune sometimes
and other times a kind of dirge that sighed and sobbed
making the mornings clammy and hot and the
evenings full of terror and curses
and then, as quickly as it started, it was over
and love lay like an empty bird's nest, scattered.

Senior Prom Redux ...

If I could do it all over again, maybe I would
choose the lavender tulle gown and forgo
the dusty rose lace with the mermaid bottom,
which left me looking mother-of-the-bride
instead of prom queen, not the me I was at sixteen,
when being sixteen and having long brown hair
and dangling earrings was the best thing in the world.

That night, prom night, if I'd been young, acted young,
and dated a boy who danced instead of holding
his Baptist principles to his chest, and not me,
wearing my long white gloves with the little pearl buttons
and the pale pink roses beribboned at my wrist.

Or ... maybe I should have worn pale blue tulle,
pinched and gathered in tiny ruffles to the floor, strapless
and boned and soft to the touch, sighing softly
as I sat with my silver slippers tucked under the skirts,
not moving with grace, not moving with my hands
clasped behind his freshly barbered neck ...
gliding on the polished wood of the Rice Hotel ballroom.

I had dreamed of this night all year.
This night, this magic night, this incredible
once-in-a-lifetime night, which we had been aiming
toward as surely as an arrow shot from a bow.
I never thought my dusty rose lace would, all these years later,
remind me, not of that night, but all the others, when the
right choice was so obvious, and I made the wrong one.
I looked 30, maybe his teacher, maybe an older sister ...
and he looked like a young Paul Anka, only frozen in stone, as he
stared with a hunger he could not quite conceal at the
blonde blue-eyed teen in the lavender tulle ball gown, who

swirled away from her date and then back into his arms with
the ease of one so sure of her footing that she floated on the
waxed glittering floor of the rented ballroom ... as sparkling as the
mirrored globe she danced beneath ... one step ahead
of me, and me, glamorous it's true, but not even part of the race.

at the nursing home

Melora's Origami

Today I found love notes folded into elaborate shapes ...
the origami of little girls, blue-lined notebook paper
shaped into swans and teapots and sailing ships.
They'd been pressed and folded, handled much,
lovingly protecting the secrets written inside with
newly learned cursive loops and scrolls and circled periods.

Our little girl, learning how to be seductive already ...
with her x's and o's signed at the bottom of the notes,
had put them all away one day in a shoebox tucked in a trunk,
moved with each cross-country trip we made to new homes,
protected, closed with many wide rubber bands that snapped
and held the whole intact and safe until now, her middle age.

It was a shame for me to open the box, to finger the notes, but
how resist admiring the frailty of this treasure from
forty years ago, our child in first bloom ... but I could not,
did not open even one to read, not even the butterfly-shaped note
that seemed to hold special importance, for it had glitter on
the folded wings, and dots of blue in crayon for the eyes.

They are all locked away now, awaiting a visit from our child
to pick up little treasures we have stored ... the dusty corsages,
now brown and flowerless, the Christmas ornaments she made,
her yearbooks, diplomas, photographs, and surely the box of
lovely origami notes.

I might slip just one out, to keep, to hold against my heart,
unopened and smelling of her perfume, as a fond remembrance,
after she has gone away ... I especially like the butterfly....

Insomnia is no promised land ...

There were trails of blue veins on her hands,
laid like the iridescence a snail leaves
on the morning porch
they seem so frail, almost able to be
lifted and fingered like a silver chain
but these pumped life, pumped magic.

Turned hair to silver and opened up
the dragon's nest where sleep was kept,
where young men asked for dances,
stroking her arms and waiting for golden sun
to open her brown, brown eyes
and make the day begin.

In some promised land
there would be scarlet skirts and
lacy shirts and dreams that
didn't shudder, scatter, shatter
but, not now, now is the never time
the time between wanted-to-be and was
the time that night brings down on us
with each dream's death.

Charlotte Renk

"Rugged and Common as Stone"
(Tao Te Ching, #39)

Not opal full of green and fire light,
nor rich as ruby red, nor diamond dazzling:
certainly not mock-gemmed and gaudy-dangling
rhinestoning some starlet's ambitious breast,
this truth is plain, "common as stone."

Once mountain, she eroded unremarkable,
modest as any rock along the road—
flat-hued, dull-rust, pale-coral, gray-tar,
jagged-edged, flat-faced, round-bubbled,
thumb-stubbed ... humble.

That is, until she weathered, fragmenting
so small, she granulated into sand—
tones varied sugary tan to Belizean black.
And the Way she lay along salt-coasts
or fresh-river banks, people gathered there

to rest nearer their Mothery-source.
She fed life to all, spilling rich silt
to corn, cacti, rice, suffering men bent
in fields, alleys, holy temples, and even over
executive desks charting China's high rise.

Seeing such possibility, men ground her
into service, blasted her into glass
where she windowed
and mirrored the world's
sad knowing eyes.

Once, a brave boy lifted a common stone
to slay a giant who kept coming on.
Where's that boy? Where's the rock?
Look down. Look down. The Way lives
small, yet floors and cradles us fragile all.

Rocking from the Irrawaddy* to Walmart

From the comfort of her rocker, gift after 42
years of teaching, *Ellie* nibbled toast and sipped
black coffee watching the play of sun and shade
as breezes stirred leaves beyond her window.
Woman of golden years mused as a chickadee
fixed its hold upon the feeder despite the bold
scarlet cardinal who jolted the trough, taking
most black seed into his thick-arced beak.

Meanwhile, one mother among the homeless
millions in Myanmar, survivor of Cyclone Nargis,
begs a man, masked against odors of floating
prone bodies, to take her in his boat of blanket-
driven sails, cutting salty Irrawaddy waters,
to take her to where the market once stood,
to take her to where she'd sent her boy
to buy rice and seed to plant this season.

Ellie remembers something about crab Rangoon,
but reluctant to ponder Burma's deep suffering,
she shifts then nuzzles feet into plush slippers,
puzzling instead how to spend this day ... alone.
Yet film clips ravage her peace of mind,
for she is quite sensitive and basically kind.
Cyclonic thoughts howl; her stomach sinks as
deeds of the dead modify the guts of the living.

Another mother, weak-kneed, heart aching,
stumbles amid rubble, halting startled as she
spies the splayed fingers of a bloated hand
grabbing at the sky from a quake of earth.

Desperate, determined, she steps toward school
where a teacher had covered one child's body,
but both had broken and died. Yet she insisted
"One lived 100 hours. 100 hours!" she cried.

Walls of a world crumble from fault-laden cracks,
pulling in and falling back to an unthinkable *"If"*
So clutching her birdlike perch upon the line,
she dialed her daughter frantic for time ...
a cup of coffee, a slice of pie, a drive to the
country, maybe past the school, Liang's stir-fry,
the mother-heart seizing, a shopping spree for ...
for ... *Earth Shoes and seeds at Walmart?*

---

* *The Irrawaddy (or Ayeyarwady) River in Myanmar (formerly Burma) is*
1,350 miles long. Its lower third is a highly polluted commercial waterway.

Hurricane Reverie: Persimmoned Memory

Breezes crinkle lake waves rough as broom skirt,
blowing hair back, gauze-light beneath this pier,
sending me back to spending nights at Vickie's
house, its fireplace popping corn, the Mulligan
stew, our whispering and giggling till daylight
when we foraged for chinquapins and persimmons.
Then my best friend tested out of Okaloosa
Elementary to attend honors classes uptown.

(I missed her more than Ishmael missed
the motion of the mast in port.)

Sun reddens the nape of my neck as remnants
of Hurricane Lydia's wrath stir softly here
to cool the burn. Musk of a moccasin wakes me
from my reverie where I press persimmoned memory,
drawing to my palate tastes of algae and venom
as I recoil from here. I want to go back,
to skip across this corrugated lake to the past.

My beloved breathes quick hot breath onto my neck
just above my collar bone. I am his.
He nuzzles and nips and licks, cooling the stings
with his tongue and breath. He sucks my life
with his kiss. He gives me life with his breath.
I am the lake, musk of no moccasin—liquid,
yielding to the current, rising and falling with
the wind, his wish, piscenian scent, born
of tremor and gaping need to be filled,
to be held, to be loved, to be....

There in that bedroom in November—small, red-
glow warm—incubating two hearts world-worn,
wearied by withdrawn love. I became his "other";
he became my only.

And then the nightmare: his wife who never cared
would not let me see him as he lay dying.
Then the slide and slam fact of the door,
her smirk reverberating from behind the glass;
he lifts his hand motioning me to his side,
then drops it to her will instead.

(I miss my beloved more than Ishmael
missed the sway of the mast in port.)

November is a wild hog, rooting and grunting
through this wooded muddy slough.
My neck burns and wind blows me away to other
wheres. This is the way now. Lydia drowns
New Orleans; the levee will break ... will fall.
And when these waters subside,
West Nile hovers backwaters ... waiting for all.

Frances Treviño Santos

She, the Owl

For Francesca de la Luz

She calls every bird in the sky an owl.

At dusk when hundreds of blackbirds
gather along the lines of telephone wires,
she says, "Owl, owl, owl?"
And sometimes makes the
Hoo, hoo, hoo sound.

And I look across an apocalyptic evening
of orange and pink and blue
and see all the owls that ever were
flying silent in the sky—
hovering, serpentining, over the dead city.
They rest and watch from buildings, wires,
locked houses, and desperate city trees.

They watch this child who stepped out
of bright light and into the flight of owls.
And if I were to turn away for the slightest moment,
they would carry her off, infant car seat and all,
and take her to a homeland of owls,
and she would speak
like the spotted,
like the barn,
like the desert,
like the snow.

She would know the thoughts of owls,
begin to live at night
and become a great and glorious owl.

And when Athena takes notice of this
half-owl, half-girl messiah, she will call her,
fall deeply in love and rename her as
Goddess of Fire and Light
and I will be her mother no more
(if that were ever true!)
and this creature made from volcano
and prickly pear, will glide over new worlds.
She will fly through the bodies of new races
and leave tiny fires inside.

Once Awake

In the black and white photograph
she falls into his body, her arms
around him like lace,
the last kiss is caught before
the months that will follow.

She will clean out cluttered drawers,
attempt the unfinished manuscripts,
poems started and left unstrung,
tiny words turned to ash.

She will wake from a light
sleep because she dreamed that her
plans had changed, that she was
falling, that she heard a poet's voice
during the blood moon eclipse
whispering to her about ochre
and zinc oxides from lost caves
of what was once their Iberian home.

She will remember the dark
theater, how he laughed when
lightning struck as ribbons of
rain came down, in the months
that follow she will remember
lightning and laughter.

In the black and white photograph
it is as if lips were opposed to goodbye,
as if eyes shut tight made leaving
impossible, as if she could feed
forever on skin and breath and bones.

Jan Seale

Walking Straight

My father was disappointed
in one of my childhood heels,
and the rest of me, attached.

If I would only *think* when I stepped,
Watch out for twisting, pounding.
Only horses need reshodding.

It took some years, but he came
to a lift on the lefts of all
his fine leather shoes. Years more,

to forgive the childish hurt,
see neither of us as heels,
to know the told-you-so course

we walk: the heel coming first,
errant and pounding,
victor for a nanosecond

before the toes of love catch up,
spring us forward
by lying down ahead.

Power

Now that I drive
we're on a different journey.
Time was, I rode shotgun,
handing peppermints and threats
to a back seat writhing with boys.
Your eyes focused
the destination in your man-brain,
your hands caressed the wheel.
Now I'm awash in traffic and gasoline.
You sit beside me,
wary, propped in your pain
and mostly yearning for our driveway.
I try to imagine what it was like
to have controlled almost everything
for years and years.
For sure, I remember how I trusted,
took a catnap to the hum of the road
or your music CD.
Now you're the one saying "Watch it!"
as you brace your hand on the dash
and make that breath-sucking "sleeee!"
that you asked me for decades to desist from.
Now, if I don't talk,
try to entertain you as in old times,
I can often turn at the right place,
remember the order of our errands.
On a dark night, arriving home, and
having forgotten to turn on the porch light,
I may command,
"Get out the flashlight"—
after all, you're now
closest to the "glove department,"
as one child christened it.

Yes, the flashlight—
power after I've killed the engine,
after you've labored out of your seat.
We go in, the light steady at our feet,
hanging on to a little power.

Hypomimia (forced laughing)

In the literature, which is much,
and claims a section in our file cabinet,
the Parkinsonians are smiling greedily,
even laughing, their heads tossed back,
teeth gleaming, dimples showing.
They wade the surf with grandchildren,
or lean to lovers on the decks of cruise ships,
ready to go inside and dance the night away.
They are quilting, playing Santa, woodworking,
grooming dogs, baking cakes, and sailing.
A whole subset lies in the grass, head
in the lap of the other. Always sun and wind
treat them well, and their dentures are holding.
In fact, they are so happy you would think the world
would be a better place if everyone had Parkinson's.

Haiku Cycle on Pills

"Medications" sounds
more Greek than "pills" can muster,
more ... medicinal

The compartments wink
open/shut like a wall of
post office boxes

The mass is ready:
Morning, Noon, Evening, Bedtime—
you pray the stations.

Capsules and tablets
descend, then climb the steep wall
to your waiting brain

This first-aid candy
convinces your feet to walk
and your mouth to talk.

Little prison cells
hold secrets for your escape
'til the next arrest.

Small chunks of potions
each with its saving graces
our graceless saving

It's levadopa-
carbodopa time again:
twins in the belfry.

Pillows, bullets, chips
all there to do the magic
for a few more hours.

Throw them in your mouth
Be ruthless, angry, resigned.
Miss? Now hunt them down!

Advice to a Caregiver
First will be bewilderment,
then anger, and finally, grief.
Despair will knock. Don't answer.

Learn the new language.
Your pronouns will be plural:
directives with "Let's,"
suggestions: "If I were you,"
difficulties: "We *have* to talk."

Assign silly names:
The disease is Sparkie.
The walker is Rolanda.
Dyskinesia is The Disser.
Take every good memory
as invitation to smile.

You will lead a double life.
"Have we taken our meds?"
"We've a doctor's appointment."
"We can't go there."

Understand that
the frown is not for you.
The worried stare
is the brain in cement shoes.'

Jan Seale

The silence is all
that can be managed.

Your life will carry you forward
like a disobedient ocean wave.
Knowing that nothing can improve
the Golden Rule as mantra,
nights you lie wide-eyed,
thinking how it must feel
to be living in that ragged body,
a thunderbolt of fate to the brain.

Now pray the release of sleep,
for you and for the other.

Loretta Diane Walker

How to Fight Like a Girl

To fight like a girl
you must first become an ocean
to hold the crush of tears
pooling beneath the ducts.

You must learn to walk
through the day with a fish of fear
floating through
the coral of your belly.

At the sound of battle,
you must paint your nails
the boldest blood shade of red
and use them like shark teeth
to maim and masticate
those piranha emotions
gnawing at your strength.

You must get off your knees
after the tentacles of cancer and chemo,
nausea and fatigue, pain and weakness
grasp your body and feed on all things woman.

You must remember you are a woman
when lavas of sweat roll from your bald head
and flank your face, and your lips crack and flake
like a dried beach.

You must stand straight, wash yourself in softness,
tattoo stars on your fists and sing praises
for the half-moons in the sky of your breasts.

Loretta Diane Walker

The Help's Daughter

*What does it feel like to raise a white child when your own child's
at home being looked after by someone else?*
                    – Kathryn Stockett, from "The Help"

Feelings were commodities sealed in dented cans,
sold in ten for a dollar baskets at "Safeway."
Too extravagant for a husbandless woman
with seven mouths to feed.
Had she taken the time to open them,
each of us would have died
from poverty's rusted toxins.
Sitters were luxuries afforded to those with incomes
above government cheese and powdered milk.
We guarded each other with the ferocity of a Doberman.

Before leaving to clean other people's houses
and wipe the little boss's feet,
she divvied up chores as though they were an inheritance
and instructed, Don't leave the yard.
But each child stepped off the sidewalk,
crossed the muddied lines of disobedience and adventure,
left to move about in the world.

At times, we half swept the floors, sloshed Pine Sol
scented water while mopping, left Comet streaks
on the back of the toilet bowl.
We folded the towels but stuffed underwear in the drawers,
fought over whose turn it was to do the dishes,
take clothes off the line and who ate the last cookie.
No one ever tattled and our prepared speeches for absolution
were cleaning rags we never used.

Now, without debate, we use her rags to wipe dust
she can no longer see, mop floors with the precision
of a Swiss watchmaker, wash dishes and fold her laundry
as though this was our design in life—to tidy up her illness.

This evening when darkness comes out of retirement,
I hear my brothers talking to my sister on the cell phone,
moving through the house as though motion is a cure.

Mom sits on the towel-covered toilet seat and says,
Diane, you'll have to go faster than this. I'm cold,
as I smooth cream over her frail body.
I will my hands to move faster, but caution creeps
in my fingers, causes me to slow once again.
Before slipping the lilac cotton gown over her thin body,
I examine the testament of scars on her stomach
stretched into the lives of six children.
Her wrinkled veined skin conceals seventy-eight years of living.
My eyes are glued to her back as though it is a magnet
pulling me through amazement.
There is no evidence of aging, diabetes, dialysis, decline,
and the desperate blows of survival.
It's smooth and clear, transparent as the moment she began
teaching us to live without her.

Loretta Diane Walker

Abundance

After seeing Michael Nye's "About Hunger" Exhibition

When life is fissured
like a ripe yellow melon,
and woeful circumstances eat from it
until the soul is a rind of shame,
hunger festers,
becomes a deep brooding wound.

If hunger is darkness, what of light?
Is it like a layer of skin love can put on?
And who can fit such skin,
give a bowl of soup, fist of bread.

I fast to know such darkness.
My tongue is wet with choices.
How can I say I know how it feels
to exchange pride for a cookie?

You with begging eyes, cracked skin,
dried mouth, empty hands—
hands now diving in dumpsters, swimming
through a sea of discard,
catching chicken bones—fear.
Forgive me.

I sat down with my full stomach to write
about the sky's generosity last night,
how it opened banks of clouds,
washed the city in relief and when I woke,
my mood rhymed with the color of morning.

I wish my words were seeds.
You could eat them to fill your emptiness

Celeste Guzmán Mendoza

Buffet

While I choose a cherry
tomato from the shallow
bucket of the buffet
maze, you ask, Did
I ever beat you?

You cradle a baby
carrot in the ladle
of your palm.

I steal crisp skins,
lettuce held tight
in tongs.

I don't remember
it, you say, then
bite quick into the thick
of a cucumber.

A mushroom laid flat
onto the hollow
of my plate.

No, no, I
never touched you, I
never hit you, I
never laid a hand on you.

The olive popped
into the concave

of your mouth bobs up
and down like a capsized ship.

Why do you write
about it, you ask, it
never happened, and
why do you lie

about it, it
never happened, and
why do you remember
it; it

Happened, I say.
grab a hard
boiled egg, thin
shell, broken bits
of porcelain.

It happened, I repeat,
as I reach
for the warmth
of bread.

La Pisca

Rows of cotton
    like lines of braided
        string, la tierra
            strand tras strand tras strand
                as far as the eye can see

a thousand fibers
    rolled tightly in
        an orb   a fist
            volando
                flies made of flour
                    rising off their backs

flat hats
    shield them from the downpour
        of rays
            uno   dos
                uno   dos
                las manos trabajando
                    in pairs

lips count
    cuarenta y siete
        cuarenta y ocho
            cuarenta y nueve
            rags ripped
                knotted around knuckles
                    nothing to remember
                    to protect

a nick   a gash
     centimeters deep
       dirt dusted off with a sigh
         cuarent ay   que?
           bag filled with white
             weighs the back
                55°   45°   35°
                  breath an incense
                     for the brambles
                       fists of sticks

clenching cotton close
    How many bolas make a shirt
    How many bushes a bag
      How many rows today's
        Frijoles   Tomorrow's
          Llénalos   Llénalos
           we are so close
             to finishing the day
               Llénalos   Llénalos
                we are so far away
                 from today.

Marriage: Hunger

Oil droplets gather around the edges of the chicken strips, fries
the meat to a golden brown. Vero's hand flings the chicken over,
the pale skin of her face reddening from the smoking oil. Five
hours and 37 minutes ago she unlocked the restaurant door,
turned on the grill's pilot light and tied Alex's apron around her
neck then waist. She has no papers to prove she is his wife. No
papers to show the restaurant is also hers—half half, he'd said
nine months ago over a Tecate and a fajita taco. No papers to le-
gitimize their children—a ten- and five-year-old, one born in the
United States the other here in Mexico, one in an odd numbered
year the other in an even. No papers to the house they rent or the
car she drives. But Vero doesn't believe in papers or the power of
the pen. She wakes up at 5 a.m., washes her face with hand soap,
brushes her teeth; then ties her hair back with a rubber band,
pulls on one of Alex's old t-shirts, her one good pair of jeans, and
the flip flops she bought from Doña Jovita for 75 cents. By noon
the booths are full of her neighbors wanting salads and enchila-
das suizas to go. No time to ask for a signature when the whole
world's mouth is open, hungry and waiting.

The Little Helens

Helen Kwiatkowski

For many years I have kept in my studio a photograph of my sisters and me. In 1998, following the death of my father, I did a painting from that photo entitled, "I Build a Lighted House." It was not intended to be shown, but rather, it was my way of dealing with my loss and channeling my grief. That painting quickly led to another, and eventually into the series called The Little Helens.

The initial paintings in this series were all based on family photographs and reflected my personal experiences and recollections as a child. Over time, this series has steadily evolved to include a broad range of narrative scenarios that give voice to things that are on my mind and help me make sense of things—both large and small.

I am often inspired by words and phrases I hear in a poem or song, but since I rarely work from sketches, making a painting is, ultimately, a leap a faith. By working this way, the paintings allow a story to unfold rather than illustrating a pre-determined narrative.

We Become What We Never Were

Looking Back Moving Forward

Finding Your Place

I Am Here, Where Are You?

Queen of Hearts

I Build a Lighted House

FICTION

Outsiders

LaToya Watkins

I'm trying to understand why Ayira wanted me to drive out so close to the university to meet her. Lord know I ain't got no gas, but I ain't want to say that when she called me and asked me to come. Thought it must be important cause she don't hardly call us. She don't never want to come to the east side either. She think she too good for what's over there. But all Africans think they better than us—get here fore somebody say something to me—something fancy—and I don't know what to say back. Plus, I don't know what kind of rules they got for places like this. They might tell me I got to leave cause I ain't ordered nothing to eat. I walked up to the line and asked for a cup of free water, and the lady handed me the cup like she ain't want to—like I was stealing or something. I ain't got no money to buy nothing from a place this fancy. They got lemon slices at they drink station. Packs of sugar, too. I got about ten lemon slices and six packs of sugar and took them to the table to mix my own cup of lemonade. They got chairs and tables outside with big umbrellas and stuff. We ain't got this kind of stuff on the east side of town.

We barely just got our first donut shop. It's called the Sweet Tooth. Some Korean folks own, but they let black folks to work there. Probably can't get nobody else to work there no way. Everybody on the east side think the Sweet Tooth got the best donuts in the world. Still don't know how to show preciation. Sweet Tooth been robbed three times since it opened.

I see her, my brother's wife, walk through the door and twist her neck looking for me. I don't want her to think I been sitting here waiting on her. Don't want her to feel like her time better than mine. Plus, the characters on her scrubs look crisp and new, like they worth something, like they more important than the faded out characters on mine, like her job being a doctor student more important than the one I got as an attendant for people born that ain't right in the head, like I'll never be who she is so easy.

"Hello, Miesha," she say, and I look up and try to act surprised she done made it. She got a messenger bag wrapped around her and it make her look like she important and got something to do all the time. "Have you been waiting long?" she ask, and I can't help but want her words—the Africa she put on them. It make her sound like she from somewhere different, like even if she ain't have no money, she got something special in her voice. A land. Her hair lay perfect against her scalp. It's short like a boy's, but I bet she don't never get accused of being a dyke or nothing like that. When my hair was cut short, I did. But her face softer than mine. Darker. African darker, but still softer. She look like a woman.

I shake my head and squeeze my big flea market purse against my stomach, hoping she don't see my scrubs. "Nuh, uh. I ain't been waiting too long. Just got here. It ain't been too long."

"Good," she say, smiling like I said something pretty. "Are you going to eat something? I'm hungry. I have not eaten since last night," she say, pointing to where Mexican ladies in hats and hair nets scooping food for folks. "I'm going to get something and then we'll chat, eh?"

I swallow hard. I don't want to talk to her—don't know how to. She got education and I ain't even got my G.E.D. I wish I didn't come. "Uhm, ain't never been here," I say. "How much it cost?"

Her eyes look light and she kind of laugh. "I invited you, Miesha. I'm buying, silly."

I throw my hand up real quick, like some kind of stop sign. Her face change and get serious. "I don't need no handouts, Ayira. I can pay my own way," I say to her.

Ayira smile again and look over her shoulder at the line forming at the serving bar. "I know you can, Miesha. I was just thinking that since I called you here ... you know. It's the hospitable thing to do. In my country, it's what we do."

"Hump," I grunt. I don't want to let her know I'm hungry too. I ain't ate since last night either. I surely don't want to let her know that I'm kind of wondering what the food in here taste like. I look around at all the folks talking so free and easy with each other. That make me nervous. I know me and Ayira ain't gone do that.

"Uhm, okay," I say, "just get me what you get." I smile at her without really opening my mouth cause her teeth so white and I know mine ain't. Her smile real pretty. Her lips is pretty, pink hearts and mine is big, black rubber tubes.

Something bout her hair make me feel little too. I pull my hand up to the top of my own head to make sure my lace-front sitting right. Ayira's eyes widen and her smile disappear. "Good gracious, Miesha," she say, sliding into the chair across from me. "What happened to your hand, eh?"

I want to cuss out loud. I meant to hide my hand the whole time, but I done slipped. I look from her shocked face to my finger. It's wrapped up in what look like a cast. I think about my patient, Vic, and what happened with him yesterday. I kind of wish I could be honest and tell her about how that fool acted when it was time to leave the community pool yesterday.

As company policy, Light in August don't allow us attendants to handle no more than three patients at a time. My three is usually Vic, Theresa, and Tabby. Ain't none of them never really been violent. I always been thankful for that—well that and that ain't none of them real messed up. Just all from rich white families that don't want to deal with grown mens and womens that's Downs Syndrome and stuff like that. In the three years I been at Light in August, ain't a one of them gave me no problem. They like my family. I done even took to bringing them round my boys.

Fore yesterday, I thought I had the best three patients in the world. I decided to treat my patients to a day at the East Side Community Pool. I ain't really supposed to be hauling my boys around while I'm on the clock. My job is mainly to drive my patients to the doctor and sit with them at the apartment community—keep them company cause they ain't normal like they families. But sometimes I get them out and take them around town. Yesterday I decided I was gone take them swimming and ain't no way in the world I was gone take them three to the pool and leave my boys stuck up in my momma's house. I hate living there and I done moved out a few times, but the money I make always send me back. My boys hate being there just as much as I hate them being there cause my momma a junkie. Her habit make me real nervous bout living in her house. I always have flashbacks of men touching me and my brother. Rubbing me and my brother. Splitting us in two and paying her. I'm always knowing it's just a matter of time for she let somebody take they axe to my boys. I get my boys out of there as much as I can. That's all I was doing yesterday. Getting them out for the day.

But when it came time to leave the pool, Vic's old, tall, goofy-looking self wanted to act silly. I had to keep telling him to get out that kiddie pool and come on. He finally looked at me with them big buck teeth and yelled at me as loud and as slow as he could, "No." He dragged that word out in slow motion, and I swear fore God it embarrassed the shit out of me.

I walked right up to the edge of that pool and bent down where all them babies and his big ass was splashing. My boys and Tabby and Theresa was standing behind me. They was waiting cause we all thought I had it under control. They always look at me like I got stuff under control cause I usually do. I was thinking bout that when I stuck my finger right in his face and gritted my teeth real hard. "Get out that pool," I commanded him.

That fool opened his mouth like he was bout to say something and closed it around my finger as hard as he could. He wouldn't let go either. Tabby and Theresa was yelling at him. My boys was yelling at him, and I was praying to God to spare my finger. A lifeguard started blowing his whistle, and I guess that got him cause he don't like sharp sounds. He let go, but I couldn't call nobody for help. Had to hide and act like it wasn't that bad. Had to go through the rest of the day acting like it ain't hurt fore I could even go to the hospital. I would've lost my job if Light in August had found out where we was when Vic attacked me. I didn't feel like making up no lie, so I didn't say nothing. I didn't report Vic to nobody, but he ain't never gone be like my family no more.

"I slammed it in my car door," I say. And her face look like she really care.

"Oh my God, Miesha," she say, making a big deal out of it. "Is it fractured? What did they do? Who did you see?" she talking real fast. Africa all in her voice.

I wave her away. "It's alright. Ain't no big deal. It ain't broke or nothing like that." I refuse to tell her I almost lost my finger yesterday. She nod her head and get up again.

"Good, grief. At least it wasn't that bad," she say, getting up from the chair and beginning to walk away. I watch her until she get at the end of the line, and then I think about how hard it is for me to like her.

Things wasn't so bad—I didn't mind the idea of her so much—fore I heard my brother on the phone begging her when I was living in they house after my last eviction. It wasn't even really bad after that. I think what really got me is that after I had been there for my brother when he got that DWI, she came back like she had all the answers for him. I was the one that told him not to drop out of school and run back to Dallas just cause he messed up. But she came to pack him—to talk him out of his education—the only education anybody in our family was ever gone get. She came to tell me I needed to find a new place cause they was leaving soon, and my brother let her.

They didn't go nowhere. They stayed in the same place—the same big house with them two extra bedrooms. Me and my boys had to move in with my momma into the house my granny left her when she died. All my money go on lights, water, and gas cause crackheads don't pay for nothing. Hard to save when you got all that on you. Momma done sold my TV and pawned the boys game station. I got to get out that place.

Ayira slide a round, metal tray on the table. "OK," she say, in her sing-song voice. "Two veggie bowls, mild salsa, cheese, and guacamole." She slide the baskets of food off the tray and put one in front of me. I look down at the bowl of food and it look real green with all the lettuce on top. I want to ask her how much this salad gone cost her, but I don't. Don't want her to think this place is better than me. She pick up a empty cup off the tray and look at mine. "What are you drinking? Are you ready for a refill?" she ask, smiling and wiggling her finger like she real anxious for me to hand her my cup. Like she know I done made my drink the ghetto way.

I shake my head. "I'm alright. I don't need no refill." She stop smiling, and I know I must be looking mean or something. I try to smile a little bit and say, "Nuh, uh, girl. I'll be peeing all day if I drink something else." She smile again and then nod her head. I wonder what she called me here for.

She go to the drink station and get her drink and then come back and sit down, sighing loud like she work real hard. I wonder how hard it is to be smart all day. To talk big all day long and not have to worry about bills and babies and being poor forever.

"I love it here. That's why I invited you. To share it. To share period," she say, mixing the lettuce into the rest of the bowl with her fork. I watch her until I see the rice and black beans and then I start doing it too. "This place, I mean," she say. "It reminds me of home in an odd, unconnected sort of way. The bukas my sisters and I used to slum. No fried yam and *dodo*, but home. My sisters and home." I feel her get still on her side of the table. I look up at her and she looking at me with a smile on her face. This smile don't seem real like all the other ones she done gave me today. This one look like she doing it so she won't cry. "I don't know how to be without them, you know?" she ask, nodding her head like she expect me to say something. "My mother, my sisters ... we ... we've always been ..." She stop herself and look back down at her bowl. She start back mixing the lettuce.

"Y'all close, huh?" I ask.

She nod. "It's different without them. I'm different without them." I nod my head like I understand, but I don't. I don't have no sisters and my brother left fore we was able to be close. "I miss how green it is at home. How fresh our fish is ... the market. My God ..." she say, holding her hands like a "X" against her heart. Like she treasuring something in her head. "Ogechi's jollof rice. I could kick myself for never learning to make it, you know?" She look serious. Like she want me to respond or something. I just nod my head. I don't even know what jollof rice is. And I ain't never seen no green on the African commercials that come on late at night. Just dust and dirt and snotty-nosed little black babies standing around white folks who be telling us how hungry they is.

"Ogechi—she's our house maid—can make anything ... food. Avocado with groundnut dressing," she say, closing her eyes real tight and letting her tongue make a sizzling sound against the roof of her mouth.

We sit quiet. I watch her rock from side to side with her eyes closed for a minute. I think about Africa and how it sound rich but it look poor on TV. I want to ask her about it, but I don't want her to know I don't already know.

She finally open her eyes and smile at me like she forgot I was with her. Like she forgot she with me in my town in my America. "My father is a diplomat and my mother.... Well, my mother is a diplomat's wife," she say, smiling like I ought to know what that mean. My face must tell her I don't cause she swat her hand like never mind and keep going. "None of us learned to cook. All of us went to university and all of us were expected to marry big men and have many sons."

"But you didn't?" I ask. I know that answer.

Her face go soft and straight. "I married a big man. He is not the big man my parents wanted, but Cedric is a really big man. I wish he knew that."

When she say that, I feel proud of my brother. Proud he picked a somebody loved him all the way across the ocean. She think he God and I'm glad.

"I appreciate you being there for Cedric this summer. He needed someone, you know? And I should've been here, but I wasn't. I couldn't stand looking him in the face so much after the baby talk, you know?" she say. She stuff a fork full of food in her mouth and look around.

I nod my head again, but I think she being dramatic about the baby. She ain't trying to understand why my brother don't really care bout having no kids. I want to tell her to open her eyes and look around our town. This ain't rich Africa. Kids ain't nothing to be planning for. In our town—on the east side where the houses crumbling and everybody on drugs—kids is accidents. I don't say that though. "He my brother. I'll be there for him when nobody else will. He'd do the same for me," I say.

She nod, trying to hurry and chew her food so she can talk. I stuff a fork full of food in my mouth. The rice and beans is cooked good, but I could do without the lettuce.

"How's it going? You find a place yet?" she ask when she ain't got no more food in her mouth.

I don't want to answer her nothing. I don't want to tell her none of my business. I had a temporary place—a comfortable place—in my brother's house—her house, and then she came. I shrug my shoulders. "I been found a place. Just getting my money together." That's all I tell her.

Her face ain't got no kind of look I can explain on it. Just looking at me with her eyes all empty or something. I look down at her bowl and her fork standing up in it without her hands on it. "I want us to be close, Miesha. I need to make my life here, you know?" she ask.

I don't say nothing. Don't know what to say. My life ain't never been nowhere but here. I watch her eyes get all watery and stuff like that, and then I finally nod. "When I get myself together. Get me a place and get out of Momma's house," I say. She looking at me like she can't wait for my next word. "We can do stuff. Go clubbing or something like that," I say, looking at her eyes. I try to smile a little. I try to mean what I'm saying.

She nod. "Your brother leaves me alone sometimes. I just get so lonely when he's gone. In Accra ... in my father's compound, someone is always there. There is no such thing as loneliness. But your brother leaves me lonely." She look like it's the end of the world. Like she can't do nothing else but be here with me. Like I'm her last hope. Her Jesus.

"Where he go, Ayira? I thought he only went to school and that's all. When I was there, he didn't never lea—"

"No, not like that." She smile a half-smile, but her eyes wet and sad. "He folds inside himself and I feel all alone. He suffers from depression, you know? I can't get him to take his medication." Her face look serious. Like she got a real problem or something like that. "I think he blames me ... about the baby business you know. I think he hides it with acceptance. I think he really wants one. All men want sons to carry on their lineage."

I think about being careful with my words. She wipe her eyes with a paper towel. I stuff some rice and beans and lettuce and stuff in my mouth. I chew it and think about how she look so broken—so different from the Ayira I saw walk through the door—different from the Ayira that put me out of her house. I think about how her skin is black—blacker than mine and how if she bleed her blood red too. She fighting tears the same way I do when I think about some old nasty man touching on my babies. And just like that, I know what to say. I know the answer to give her.

"About the depression ... he be okay, Ayira. Give him some time," I say, and I think about him begging and crying for her to come back to West Texas. He love her. Don't want to live without her, but she don't have no idea bout what his life been like. If all he do is get a little quiet sometimes, he came out good. He made it out alright. I want to tell her my brother ain't got no manhood. My momma sold it for what she love the most. I want to tell her he lost that a long time ago, but all I say is, "He'll be alright. He a man, girl. He ain't gone lie bout what he want and don't want. Stop messing with him bout kids and stuff like that. He got his reasons."

Her eyes is wide with surprise and her mouth open into a little "o." She shake her head and stretch her hand across the table and lay it on mine "But I want one so bad, Miesha. A little him to care for," she say. "He is not affectionate. Does not hold me. Sometimes I feel like I'm losing him. Almost like I'm losing home—like I'm losing Ghana. I can't lose both."

I can feel my hand twitching a little bit underneath hers. I ain't really used to nobody touching me and it make me feel funny. But I don't move cause it make me feel alive too. I want to tell her my baby daddy been gone—really gone—for two years. My momma on drugs and I live in the house with her. I got to sleep with one eye open every night just to make sure the little bit I got ain't gone in the morning. My brother been gone from me since he left home at thirteen—since he left me with our momma—since he saved himself, but I don't. That's saying too much.

I just nod and say, "Cedric strong. He carry y'all. Y'all be alright."

She smile and bite her pink heart lips. "Thank you, Miesha. That means so much coming from you. I'm sorry for never even considering you a sister. I should've called you before now. I really should have."

I pick my hand up from underneath hers and swat her words away, smacking my lips at her. "Chile, that's life. Life get in the way." I feel myself smiling without trying. I feel like I'm telling her something wise.

"Right," she say, "you're right. But I won't let it happen again." I nod and smile. She sniff and wipe at her eyes again. "How are the boys? How much do you have to go to get them out of there?"

Her questions make me nervous. I don't know if I can trust her. Everybody I trust do me wrong. So I dodge all her questions and she end up telling me bout her family. When it's time to go, I almost feel like I'm her. And when we walking our separate ways, I feel bad for not telling her nothing bout me. I feel like a thief. Like I took her and didn't give her none of me, so she nothing. She done disappeared. I feel bad for listening while she was trusting me with her hurt. I feel bad for not giving her my own to make her feel whole. I stop walking and turn back to her. "Ayira," I call. She stop and turn around. I hold up my hand—the one with the bandage. "One of my patients tried to bite the damn thing off." She look confused at first, but then she smile and move her lips. It look like she say, "Thank you, Miesha."

I'm Her(e)

Laurie Champion

You didn't leave your wife, didn't even think about leaving her, much less talk about it. "Don't mention the *D* word," you once said, as we leaned against the open tailgate of your pick-up, parked down a desolate road. I puffed my Marlboro Light and stared up at the dark West Texas sky. Where were all the stars we always sang about? Guess we weren't *deep* in the heart or at least not deep enough.

But I wasn't going to mention the *D* word. I wanted to tell you not to flatter yourself, but I slipped, said instead, "Don't flatter yourself." You mumbled something, then admitted you were making a bad joke. We laughed anyway.

We laughed a lot. "Knock-knock," you said, one morning when you heard my knock at your hotel door.

"Who's there?" I asked.

"It's I," you said. You cracked open the door.

"Yeah," I said. "It's me." You told me I should keep my pronouns straight, said something about subjects and objects and explained the difference between the use of *me* and *I*, *her* and *she*. I listened to you, watched you smirk. I stood outside the room and waited for you to open the door wider, invite me in. You finished talking, paused, and looked at me, gazed at me as though sizing me up. Not quite sure what to say, I finally twisted one corner of my mouth into a faint smile and said, "It's you," I said. "I'm here."

"This is he," you said.

"I'm hemmed," I said. I rolled my eyes and wondered why I told these stupid jokes, played dumb word games. Perhaps it was part of our agreement. Our unspoken promise to each other not to take things seriously, or *too seriously*, as you once put it.

You laughed and opened the door. I pulled champagne from a paper sack while you took clear plastic cups out of cellophane wrappers. I could see us through the big mirror on the wall beside the bathroom. You watched my reflection pour champagne in the cups. I poured slowly, careful not to overfill or spill. I handed you a full glass. "Cheers," you said and tapped your glass against mine. You cut your eyes back toward the mirror, and I did the same. We stared at our images and made weird expressions. "Your face or mine," you said.

"Hers," I said. I pointed at my reflection. We poured more champagne and sat in the chairs near the front door. A *Thank You for Not Smoking* sign was posted on the door. "Things are getting better," I told you. "Remember the last sign? Remember, it said, 'Thank for you smoking not in your room, you most valued customer.' I lit a cigarette."

"No smoking," you said. You unwrapped another cup, filled it half full of water, and set it on the table. "The usual ashtray."

You made an ashtray because you didn't want me to use your shoe again. "These are expensive shoes," you said when once I flicked ashes in your shoe. "Cole Haan."

"Cool hands," I said. "Don't you want ashes near your sole?" I continued to put ashes in your shoe. When I smoked nearly all my cigarette, I handed it to you. You emptied your shoe in the sink and threw my cigarette in the toilet.

I knew why you always stayed in non-smoking rooms. Sometimes I wanted to ask, make you admit it; other times, I didn't want to ask, didn't want to make you feel uncomfortable. Or maybe I never really wanted to know the real truth. Or *the whole truth*, as they say. Besides, you would never admit you stayed in non-smoking rooms in case she looked at the bills or made hotel reservations for you. No, you'd make a joke. You'd say it was because you don't like your rooms to smoke, and I'd laugh.

"Can I use your toothbrush?" I asked.

"Yes, you may." You handed me a disposable toothbrush, pre-filled with toothpaste. "Man," I said, "somebody was really thinking. I wished I'd invented something like this." Through the mirror, I saw you watching me brush my teeth.

"You're really sexy when you brush your teeth," you said.

When I returned to my chair, you'd filled our cups full of champagne. I told you I thought it was too early in the day to start any serious drinking, and you said it was Friday. "Good morning," you said. You held up your cup and said, "To serious drinking."

"Good Friday," I said. I sipped my champagne. I tried to think of something to say. I wanted to tell you how I felt, wanted some special way to tell you, but I was scared you wouldn't feel the same way. Or at least not admit you did. I continued to sip my champagne and lit another cigarette. I could have just said, "I love you." Maybe I should have said, "You love me" or maybe just "Love." The words wouldn't come out. I kept thinking what I would say if you didn't say you loved me, too. Perhaps I could have asked if you loved me back or asked if you loved my back.

You moved your chair closer to mine. You twirled my hair and kept looking me straight in the eyes. "You my baby," you said. I didn't know if you were asking a question or making a statement.

"Excuse me," I finally said. I got up and brushed my teeth again. "Lots of toothpaste in these things," I said. On my way back to my chair, I got a scratch pad and pen.

"What are you doing?" you asked.

"I'm feeling really neurotic," I answered. "I'm paranoid, you know." I drew hearts and squares on the tablet and held it where you couldn't see it. I tried to remember all the times we'd been together, all the beds, all the non-smoking rooms, all the cities. I scribbled, "You I Love" in the bottom corner of the paper. "How many times have we been together?" I asked.

"I don't know," you said.

"Have you and her ever been here?" I asked.

You just sat there, staring at me. "She," you said.

You said it real fast but not so straightforwardly. It sounded like you might have been asking me a question. You said *she* so quickly that at first I thought you were questioning who I was referring to. Or was it *to whom I was referring*? I should've remembered that one. Yes, that was one of my first lessons. Still waiting for an answer or for someone to do something, I tilted my head and bit my lower lip.

"She and I?" you finally confirmed. "No, not that I can recall."

"Just wondering," I said. "Where all have we been? What places? I want to get this straight. I want to get the full picture of the situation."

"Lots of places," you said. We sat there a long time, neither of us saying anything. I tried to remember all the dates, all the places. I scribbled over the page, made sure to blot out the words *Love* and *Forever*. I turned the page and made a list:

Forbidden cities (in alphabetical order):

Athens—once

Corpus Chrisi—three times, confessed to priest

Mt. Pleasant—twice, while sober

Marfa—once, while looking for the Marfa lights.

Odessa—twice

Palestine—almost

Paris—twice

Rhome—three times

Temple—once

You stood up, walked behind me, stroked my hair. You could see the list. "Are you making a grocery list?" you asked.

"I'm really sexy when I make lists."

"You're sexy," you said. You read the list out loud. "Don't forget Wichita Falls." I handed you the pen. You reached over my shoulder and wrote: *Houston* and *Wichita Falls*. You cupped your palm under my chin and stroked my cheek.

"We'll always have Wichita Falls," I said.

"Paris," you said a little too quickly, as if correcting me.

"Wichita Falls," I said. "That was a joke."

You slid your hand from my chin and wrote *Dallas*. No, this time you scribbled, said the best you could do left-handed.

"Uh, oh," I said, "you mentioned the *D* word." I put the pad down and handed you your champagne. I leaned backward, looked upside down at you.

"Here's looking at you, Kid," you said.

I was still leaning backwards, looking at you. "There's no way to make a joke of this," I said. We laughed anyway.

The Night Wind's Lullaby

Mary Russell Rogers

It was an old house when she found it, sad-eyed and empty, loved only by the night wind that whispered up the stairs to prowl the rubbish-filled rooms and riffle through piles of sheet music left behind.

Mitzi Monroe had driven past the place a hundred times and never given it a second glance, but on this morning she pulled her red Lexus coupe onto the gravel drive and took a long look.

Paint peeled from eaves and doors. Overgrown shrubbery covered stained brick walls. The broken roof sagged. The lawn had withered in the summer sun, and a termite-infested garage with an apartment above filled a corner of the parched backyard. The ugliness reminded her of places she had known when she was a barefoot girl in a hand-me-down dress.

She was accustomed to beautiful things now. She put the car in reverse, but before she stepped on the gas, Mitzi lifted her Chanel sunglasses for one more peek. Untidy hedges cast deep shadows. The board fence sagged, and the sheltered alcove by the back door almost disappeared beneath a covering of vines. It had never been grand, but once this derelict old house had been a solid anchor. She shifted into park.

When she was sure she was alone, she got out of the car, crossed the gravel drive, and stood on tiptoe to peep through a dusty window pane. Her manicured fingers never touched the glass. Her chunky necklace with clear crystal rocks the size of quail eggs sparkled in the dabbled shade.

"What a mess," she said. But she pushed through the shrubs that hid the long front porch, stepping around the beer bottles littered there. She tried the front door.

Locked.

Mitzi was on the downhill side of 50 coming up on 60 fast.

She had been locked out of lots of places. She didn't fret about such things, anymore. Money, she knew, could unlock most doors, and she had enough jingle in her jeans now to be heard coming, if not respected when she arrived.

She was a woman who usually got what she wanted and figured that covered what she needed, too. Oh, she wasn't rich; *comfortable* was a better word. Because her late husband had both a nice portfolio and an old family name (and the connections that it brings), she held a tenuous position in Fort Worth society.

No one had forgotten she had come from outside with no pedigree, no connections, and no education. In fact, she'd worked at one of the local country clubs as a hostess until she married P. Benton Monroe IV, who was called Quarto by everyone.

Once, at a debutante ball, she'd stood close to an old doyenne who ran a glittering eye over the designer gown worn by a young matron who whirled around the dance floor with a drink in her hand. The old woman took in the Harry Winston sapphires, the Judith Leiber bag, the Christian Louboutin shoes—and raised a silver eyebrow.

"Now who is she?" someone whispered. An undercurrent of low laughter and snide remarks eddied around the dance floor's edge. "No, really now, didn't she just come home from Washington or London or somewhere? Isn't she from an old family here?" the woman asked, her voice a high-pitched whine, her remarks branding her as much an outsider as the dancer.

The doyenne swallowed the last drop of scotch in her glass and sniffed. Flawless diamonds winked on her fingers, old stones in an old setting. A long rope of cabochon emeralds looped around her throat, family heirlooms she would leave to her granddaughter. Her Valentino gown was 15 years old, and she had no plans to buy another. There was no need to make a show of her station or her wealth. Her family name was emblazoned on hospitals, school buildings, and university dorms in Fort Worth and beyond.

"Honey, if your family wasn't here by 1849, you're a newcomer," she snapped. She put the empty glass on a passing waiter's silver tray and limped away, her cane stabbing the carpeted floor. She'd seen the next crop of young women make their practiced bow to society. She wouldn't stay for the dancing or midnight breakfast. She'd done it all a thousand times before, and the charm had long faded. From the doorway, her driver saw her coming and snapped to attention. He bowed as he opened the door. Her old black Lincoln was curbside.

Mitzi looked around the room and understood—suddenly and completely. She'd been married a few years by then, but for the first time, she'd heard the lock click.

She didn't bother with that door again. Oh, she hosted dinner parties for all the right people, joined the right clubs, wore the right labels in all her clothes. But Mitzi was alone in this world, and she knew it.

Now that her husband was gone, buried two years in a family plot marked by a grand marble obelisk, Monroe chiseled in two-foot letters at the bottom, her contacts had all but dried up, retreating like the water from the shoreline of a drought-stricken lake.

The invitations to lunch at the newest eateries still came, to be sure, but only occasionally, and only when someone wanted a donation for a worthy cause. She hadn't been asked to serve on a single fall gala committee since her husband died. She hadn't seen the inside of anyone's private plane bound for a ball game or an out-of-town party since long before the funeral. Shoot, she hadn't even been on anyone's lakeside picnic invitation list.

She wasn't surprised.

Of course, the solicitation letters kept coming, asking her to host a table at some charity gala, the price always in the four- or five-figure range. But she was no longer inclined to oblige. Some whispered that maybe she wasn't so well-fixed, after all. Such talk didn't matter to her, anymore. She still had a personal shopper at Neiman Marcus and still summered in Carmel, not Nantucket, where most of the others went to escape the heat of Texas in July and August.

She knew what they said about her: gold digger, social climber, no taste, no education, no connections, wrong side of the tracks, doomed marriage, her third and his second ... blah, blah, blah.

But she had hung on for 12 mostly happy years, filling a big house and lots of closets with things she wanted: clothes, jewelry, shoes, furniture, paintings, antiques—but no children and few friends.

Mitzi circled the house. No realtor's sign, nothing in the mailbox to indicate the owner's name. The house, just beyond the boundaries of one of Fort Worth's tony enclaves, had been vacant for years, and on this bright morning, Mitzi was determined to get inside.

A side door, almost hidden beneath a creeping vine, had been weakened by wood rot. A couple of kicks and it gave way. Mitzi ducked inside.

The musty odor of long-abandoned places was overpowering. She took in the shabby surroundings, the broken kitchen tile, the hodgepodge of discarded furniture. Light filtered through grimy window panes curtained with vines. Outside the sun was bright, but inside, the house was full of shadows and gloom.

She moved quickly through the downstairs rooms. Something thumped in the kitchen, and she jumped. The old house seemed to sigh, an almost imperceptible groaning, as if it were settling down for a dream, but there was another sound too, soft and hesitant, just below the surface.

She climbed complaining stairs to a surprising second floor. Sunlight streamed through dirty windows, filling a spacious room with unexpected light. A well-used fireplace stretched between two windows on one end, and on the other, a pair of French doors led to a balcony. An old upright piano stood to one side, its ivory keys chipped and yellowed. Piles of sheet music were scattered around a tattered velvet chair that must have served as a bench. Rats had been at it all.

Mitzi wandered down the wide hall, looked into each of the four bedrooms. She stopped often and listened. The house was full of tiny sounds, but beneath them all, there was a soft, frightened whisper.

Careful not to touch the filthy banister, Mitzi started back downstairs, but every step brought her closer to the realization she was not alone. She moved slowly from step to step, watching the shadows, straining to catch every sound. The wind scurried across the roof, rubbed against the chimney, and whined softly.

She was almost to the bottom when the hairs on her arm rose. She stopped and stood very still. The house seemed to breathe and moan. She peered into the gloom. There was a louder creaking. She held her breath and waited.

Something shot across the entry hall, claws scrambling on the wooden floor. She jumped, but didn't cry out. Heart pounding, she took another cautious step, and the stair creaked. A low growling rumbled through the miserable air.

Blood thrumming in her ears was an almost deafening roar, but she moved slowly into the hallway, and there near the broken door where she had entered, she saw the dog, large and black with a white star on his head, his coat, shaggy and matted. His teeth flashed, and the growling grew louder.

But Mitzi saw the fear in his eyes, the jutting hip bones, the protruding ribs. She had lived with the fear of being found out so long that she understood it as a mother understands a child's cry. She moved cautiously toward him. He backed out of the wrecked door and limped to the corner of the yard, taking another stand by the garage, barking a warning before disappearing into the undergrowth.

That night Mitzi came back to the old house and left a bowl of Kibble. She waited in her car and was surprised when the dog crept out of the house—not the shrubbery near the garage—and gobbled it down. The next day she brought more Kibble, but this time she unpacked a folding lawn chair and sat in the shade, waiting for the dog to return. He slipped from the shadows of the porch, but when he spotted her, he barked and ran away. For two hours, she sat in the shade, waiting for the dog to return. He didn't. She took the Kibble and left.

The next evening she was at the house again. This time she left the bowl of Kibble and roast chicken near the broken door, and this time, she sat very close. The dog rushed to grab a mouthful of food and then backed away to swallow it, growling all the while.

Each day she brought food and waited. Slowly, the dog began to relax, and one day, he ate from her hand. Mitzi could see that the animal's back leg had been broken and healed badly. He would always be crippled, she thought.

One day the black dog limped out of the house followed by a half-grown pup. Mitzi called the pup, but the old black dog came to her instead. He sat beside her in the shade while the spotted pup gamboled about, its ears flopping and tail whipping the air.

Morning and evening, Mitzi went to the old house to feed the dogs, but she didn't name them and seldom spoke to them. Naming and talking were dangerous business, she knew. Commitment was the next step, and then what? She had no interest in such things.

And then one morning, she found a survey crew at the house. Several small stakes with orange flags sprouted on the northern edge of the property.

"What's this?" she asked the foreman.

"Family is ready to sell," he said, shifting the wad of tobacco in his cheek. "About time. Old place is rotting down, been vacant too long, but you know how families are. Sometimes, it takes years and a few funerals before everyone agrees."

Mitzi nodded. "Have you seen some dogs?" she asked.

He shook his head. "You lose a dog?" he asked. "Now that's like losing a good member of the family, not crazy Aunt Charlotte in Muleshoe," the man said. His teeth were stained the color of old ivory, but his bright blue eyes were shrewd and knowing.

"One is old and limps," said Mitzi. "The other is young and full of play. Both are black with white markings."

"Sorry,' he said. "I did see the animal control truck a couple of blocks over. Maybe the city already got 'em."

Mitzi left the Kibble in the bowl on the back porch, but that evening after the survey crew had gone, it was still there. She sat on the steps of the old house as twilight settled over the city. The world grew darker, and a street lights began to glow. Cars still sped past the old house, but there were fewer of them now.

Day was done, but she couldn't see the stars. The dogs did not return.

She started for the car and then stopped and looked back at the sagging house, and suddenly, she knew she had to own it. She had the money. She could make it beautiful. In the morning, she would call her financial adviser and a real estate agent. Neither would understand. She didn't understand herself.

In the morning she would go to the city shelter and find the old dog before it was too late. She'd buy him a collar and give him a name.

The night wind came then, rustling through the vines, promising the earth a bedtime story full of love and loss.

Before Mitzi reached the car, the old dog limped out from a secret hiding place. This time the pup and a small girl followed him. He came to Mitzi, whining softly. The girl stood in the middle of the sun-scorched yard, as frightened as a rabbit chased by a fox. Her hair was uncombed, and her feet were bare. The torn hem of her shabby dress hung almost to her ankles.

"Well, hello there. Come here and tell me who you are," Mitzi said, and held out her hands, but the child did not move. Mitzi took one slow, cautious step toward the girl. "Come to me," she said.

The child began to run toward the street, and the dogs ran after her.

"Wait. Wait," Mitzi called. "Don't go."

The little girl had already reached the curb. She rushed into the street, the wind pulling at her tattered skirt and tossing her yellow hair. Barking, the dogs charged after her. Mitzi was running, too. The child was quick and reached the far side of the street with the pup close on her heels.

The girl turned as the old dog limped into the road and slowed his pace. Mitzi could hear the truck's gears grinding, the engine whining as it picked up speed. She called out, but the old dog with no name didn't look back. He limped forward one painful step at a time until he reached the middle of the road.

Mitzi called again and again. Frantic. Demanding. She could see the headlights as she ran into the street, waving her arms and shouting. The driver tapped the brakes, the tail lights flaring red. There was a thud, a yelp. The truck sped on.

The night wind moaned. It swept across the withered grass to kiss her face and swallowed the sorrow. It rocked the crescent moon in a warm embrace and sang a lullaby that the old house knew well.

Mr. Robinson and His Friends

Jeanne Bennett

Mr. Robinson's house dated back to 1898. A magnificent example of Queen Anne architecture, it boasted three stories topped by a six-sided cupola where one could watch the Fourth of July parade pass by. A broad porch encircled the house welcoming those visiting the doctor who first lived there.

It was almost 80 years later when Mr. Robinson bought the old place and began the job of renovation. Windows with touches of stained glass enclosed the cupola so Mr. Robinson and his friends could watch the antics of neighbors all year round. Old paint was scraped off, the new paint enhancing finely turned posts, spindles, and decorative shingles. The floor of the porch was sanded down and refinished in walnut. The work seemed endless to townspeople, but finally the very day Mr. Robinson retired, the exterior was completed. Just about everyone driving by paused to enjoy the lovely old place.

Now Mr. Robinson could concentrate on the interior. Although trained as a lawyer, he had become weary of the constant need to solve difficulties into which his complaining clients ensnared themselves. Since he found himself well off through inheritance and a sound fiscal policy, Mr. Robinson turned to his favorite occupations: reading and book collecting. He retired at the age of 45.

Soon the parlor and living room housed floor-to-ceiling bookcases. Mr. Robinson enjoyed a variety of subjects, and each time a new interest arose, he had to build more shelves to hold the books covering his latest course of study.

Envious acquaintances visiting Mr. Robinson made his passion for collection a subject of derision. John Durning, who still practiced law, said, "Henry, if you keep this up, you'll have no place to sleep."

"Well, John," replied Mr. Robinson, "my books keep me company most nights. I don't need much sleep."

The one place Mr. Robinson couldn't lodge books was in the basement, a cavern as large as the house. For some reason city engineers couldn't fathom, a cold dampness persisted. Occasionally, Mr. Robinson would venture down, hoping the basement wouldn't be so unfriendly, but it never changed. Sometimes, it seemed almost malevolent. He didn't like the basement, so he ignored it and went back to his cupola with its big leather chair and ottoman to read another book.

By the time Mr. Robinson was 73, the upstairs rooms were filled with shelves and glass-fronted lawyer's bookcases. He had become a recluse, inviting no one to visit except Miss Heather, a local librarian. A book-lover herself, she enjoyed a tour of rooms with Mr. Robinson. Everything was there: literature, philosophy, music, biographies of just about everyone, art and architecture, biology, astronomy and other sciences, a room full of poetry. There were mysteries and histories, tragedies, and comedies. From among these treasures, Mr. Robinson found new and enduring friends, meeting Tolstoy's Prince Andrew, Twain's Huckleberry Finn, discovering penicillin with Pasteur, learning about art from Robert Henri.

Miss Heather said, "Your books must fill the whole place by now. One of these days you'll have to cull a few, Mr. Robinson. When you do, don't forget the library."

Mr. Robinson laughed. "Well, you're right, Miss Heather, it's getting a bit out of hand. But I couldn't part with my friends. I keep them everywhere but in the basement. It's too damp down there. They'd catch cold. I don't think you've seen my Southwest Collection, have you? I had to convert the attic."

"No. I'd like to."

The stairs to the attic creaked loudly as they made their way up.

Miss Heather said, "You might want to have these stairs checked, Mr. Robinson. They sure don't sound too safe."

"Oh, the place is just getting old. Like me and my friends, I guess."

Only a week later, Mr. Robinson made one of his hopeful trips down the basement stairs. Their squeaking moans actually alarmed him. Something was different. He paused on the bottom step. Below him, a murky pool of water covered the floor. "What on earth," muttered Mr. Robinson.

The stairs moved perceptibly. The moans became tiny firecrackers popping. Mr. Robinson rushed up to the phone, dialed the plumber, and shouted, "It's an emergency! My house is flooding! Get here as quick as you can!"

High above, Mr. Robinson heard his friends sliding from their shelves, thumping to the floor. He rushed toward the stairs, intent on helping them. Century-old beams, buckling under their load, groaned and twisted. A door flew open, striking Scott Fitzgerald and Ernest Hemingway. Windows splintered, their shards piercing Charles and Mary Lamb. Mr. Robinson felt the floor give way, saw walls closing in. He spun about, grabbing the banister, seeking escape. It was too late, of course. Shelves and the Southwest Collection caved in, followed by Poetry, then the tremendous crush of tons of books. Mr. Robinson was under them all. Miss Heather heard the sirens. The library was only three blocks from the house. She ran all the way. The debris was already set-tling—so quickly had everything disappeared into the muddy sinkhole that was once a basement. At least that's what the city engineers concluded. Many of Mr. Robinson's friends escaped out the windows, landing every which way around the neighborhood. The house had simply vanished. Except for the cupola, which stood, alone, a proud little gazebo.

Miss Heather turned away, tears in her eyes. For years af-terward, she was the one who told the story best. And she always ended: "Sometimes, a person can have too many friends."

Bottom Land

Diane Fanning

Elspeth McCallister raised her hand, stabbed the blade into the flesh, and ripped downward in one smooth motion. The warm innards steamed in the cool morning as they slithered out of the body cavity and cascaded into the lined garbage can positioned beneath the clothesline. She wiped the blade on the checked gingham apron that looped over her neck and tied around her vanishing waistline.

Walking into the house, she deposited the knife in the chipped porcelain sink and retrieved a simmering kettle of water from the stove. Back outside, she lifted the pot up and submerged the body. She held it in place until her wrinkled arms shook from the strain.

Lowering the kettle to the ground, she attacked the carcass with both hands, pulling off clumps of sodden feathers. They fell from her fingers into the trash receptacle below. When she finished plucking, she returned the chicken to the red-stained stump where she lifted an axe and removed the yellow, clawed feet. She cradled the dressed bird in the crook of her left arm and with her right hand, snatched up the head and feet and deposited them in the can.

Specks of blood dotted Elspeth's cheeks and the bare skin on her arms. Smears and spatter soiled her apron. White feathers dusted the top of her gray hair. Butchering and cleaning a chicken for the dinner table was a messy business. It wasn't the most gruesome chore she ever did, but it was close to the top of the list.

Walking downhill to the farmhouse, she didn't turn around to investigate the crunching gravel in her driveway. In the house, she went straight to the kitchen, plopped the bird in the sink and set the oven to pre-heat. Returning to the front door, she flung it wide open.

She recognized the tan and brown uniform of local law enforcement first. Then she identified the lumbering gait and stooped shoulders of Rusty Brockman, a man she'd known since he was a little boy too small to gather eggs. "What's on your mind, Sheriff?" she hollered up the hill.

"Ms. Elspeth, you and Frank were supposed to evacuate over the weekend," Sheriff Rusty Brockman answered.

"C'mon on into the house, Sheriff. I'm fixing to pop my dinner in the oven. Soon as I finish that, I'll brew us a fresh pot of coffee," she said, turning away and disappearing inside.

At six-foot-two inches, Brockman had to remove his hat and duck to clear the doorway of the old farmhouse; nonetheless, the bristles of his red hair still slid across the top of the entryway. He followed Elspeth into the kitchen, pulled out a chair, and sat down at the table to watch her work. Her movements were precise and economical. Age hadn't seemed to slow her down. She went about the familiar task without saying a word. The sheriff knew better than to speak until she was good and ready.

After seasoning the chicken inside and out with salt and pepper, she placed it in a glass baking pan and slid it into the oven. A few minutes later, she set down two thick white mugs of coffee and a glass pitcher of milk on the table and settled into the wooden chair across from him.

The sheriff blew off the rising steam and took a small sip. "You still make the best coffee in the county, Ms. Elspeth."

"The state, sheriff—the best in the state."

"You won't get an argument from me on that," he grinned. "But listen, ma'am. Your home has been condemned. The construction on the dam project is complete. And the water's rising."

"I haven't been able to pick any of my black-eyed peas yet."

"The water isn't going to wait on that. Look out the window at the creek bed." He pointed. "The level is coming up on the banks next to your garden."

"I can see that, Sheriff, but the peas down in that there bottom land will be ready in a couple of days. It would be a waste of God's bounty not to wait till I can pick at least one mess of them.

Besides, I need to stay a while longer in case Frank pops up."

"Frank's gone? When did you last see him?"

"Thursday night. He was already gone when I got up Friday morning."

"That was four days ago," Brockman said.

Elspeth shrugged.

"Do you have any idea where he could've gone?"

Elspeth looked down at the table, fascinated for the moment with the dried blood under her fingernails. She lifted her head and said, "Well, this time of year, he goes hunting a lot with his worthless, beer-swilling buddies."

"Did he say he was going hunting? Did you ask him where he was going?"

"I used to ask him that, but a few years back, I stopped liking the answer I got."

"You didn't approve of where he was going?"

"I didn't give two hoots about where he was going, to tell the truth. But he sure got my dander up when he took to saying, 'None of your beeswax, old woman.' So I just stopped asking. Don't need that kind of aggravation."

"What if he's had an accident? What if he fell ill? How old is Frank now? 75? 76?"

"Just turned 76 last month, matter of fact," Elspeth said, and nodded.

"You really need to file a missing person's report."

"If you say so, Sheriff. Whatever you think's the right thing to do."

Brockman rose from the table and went out to his car to retrieve the blank forms. By the time he returned to the table, Elspeth had refilled his cup. He took a big slug of coffee and filled in the information he already knew. He looked up and asked, "What was Frank wearing the last time you saw him?"

Elspeth's mouth curled into an ugly sneer. "Those damned overall dungarees. Summer or winter, working or wasting time, he always wore those damned things."

Brockman chuckled as he bent back over the paperwork.

"Probably had a piece of hay bobbing in the corner of his mouth, too."

"I don't allow that in the house, Sheriff," she snapped. "Not no chewing tobacco, either. If he wanted to stick strange things in his mouth, he had to take it outside."

Rusty picked up his mug and looked at her over the rim. He couldn't figure out why Elspeth and Frank stayed together all these years. They never seemed to like each other very much. He'd never seen them smile at each other, but he'd sure watched them exchange evil glances. He brought his attention back to the report. When he finished, he turned it around and pushed it across the table for Elspeth's signature.

Placing the signed form into a folder, he pushed back the chair. "Ms. Elspeth, we'll start looking for Frank right away, but you shouldn't be waiting here for him. You need to clear out."

"Don't be worrying on that, Sheriff. I reckon the creek'll overrun the bottom land by the weekend. When it does, I'll skedaddle. Till then, I'll just stay put."

The sheriff shook his head at her stubbornness and walked out of the house. Elspeth stood in the open doorway watching him trudge up the hill, get into his car, and drive away. She circled around to the back of the house and walked down to her garden. She looked over her black-eyed peas with satisfaction and then walked over to a bare patch of earth. She stomped on it, compressing the dirt into the ground. "Well, Frank," she said, "Iffen you're gonna show up again, you'd best do it quick. Otherwise you're gonna be on your own."

⊰⊱

Two days later, Sheriff Brockman returned to the McCallister farm. As he stepped from his car, Elspeth emerged from the chicken coop with a gore-smeared axe in her hand. Rusty stopped mid-stride, his hand automatically jerking back to rest of the butt of his revolver.

The old woman halted and peered up the hill. Then she looked down at the axe and chuckled. "Just snakes, Sheriff. They were fretting my hens, eating their eggs."

"Okay," he said, easing his fingers away from the gun as he walked down the hill. "Can I take a look?"

"Sure, Sheriff," she said.

"Ms. Elspeth?"

"Yes, sir?"

"I'd feel a might bit easier if you'd put down that axe."

Elspeth laughed again and propped the handle against the side of the coop. "If there's any more snakes, you got your gun."

Inside two snake heads with dead eyes lay in nests beside regurgitated egg shells. Their black coiled bodies still glistened with recently departed life. Out in the fenced chicken yard, the hens clucked and fretted as they bustled about in obvious distress.

"Need some help with this?" Rusty asked.

"Nah. I'm going into the house for a cup of coffee. Then I'll fetch some fresh straw out of the barn and take care of it. C'mon in and have a cup, and tell me what's on your mind."

As they walked downhill to the house, Rusty said, "It's the same old thing, Ms. Elspeth. Why are you still here?"

Elspeth snorted but didn't speak until they were both seated at the kitchen table with a mugful of coffee. "Sheriff, I just can't go yet. I've gotta make sure Frank will be okay."

"I'm worried about your husband, too, Ms. Elspeth. I called all his friends and associates. Not one of them has seen Frank since last Thursday—same as you. None of his hunting buddies went hunting with him, None of the fishing buddies went fishing with him. I even hung out at the feed and supply store hoping to catch some gossip. But nobody knew his whereabouts."

"Well," Elspeth said with a shrug, "like I told you, Sheriff, I ain't seen Frank walking around since Thursday."

"Did you two have an argument that day?"

"Sheriff, we have arguments most days."

"Well, that day, that Thursday, did you argue about anything in particular?"

"Let's see," Elspeth said. "Yeah, we argued about the property I wanted to buy."

"What was the problem?"

"Lazy old Frank wanted to get a place in town with those tiny sissy yards and the postage stamp patch they call a garden. I picked out 20 acres up in the hills a bit. I thought I had a right to make that decision. This here was my family farm, so I should be able to decide what we're buying. Frank didn't think so. Said as long as we've been married, this place was as much his as mine. Then he really pissed me off."

"How's that?" the sheriff asked.

"He says, 'Didn't matter where we were going so long as there weren't no chickens.' I says, 'Old man, don't make me choose between you and my hens.' Then he says, 'Damned if I won't, woman. 'Bout time you start doing what I say.' Those were the last words he ever said to me."

"Well, what happened then, Ms. Elspeth?"

She raised her shoulders up to her ears. "That's the last time he ever spoke to me, Sheriff."

"What did he do? Walk off? Slam the door? What?"

"He knew better than to slam the door around me. Need another cup of coffee?"

Rusty shook his head, "No. No, I'd best be going. But Ms. Elspeth, I don't want to have to come back here with deputies and remove you from the property."

"No need for that, Sheriff," Elspeth said and chuckled. "The water will be up over the bottom land in a day or two. Then it'll be okay for me to leave."

"Why do you need to wait till then?"

"I just do, Sheriff. But don't worry. I got folks lined up to move my chickens and my furniture this weekend. You don't need to worry about me no more."

"Okay, Ms. Elspeth. I'm gonna hold you to that."

⸺◈⸺

The following Monday, Sheriff Brockman drove out to the McCallister place to make sure Elspeth kept her word. After he walked past the chicken coop, he was pretty sure she was gone.

Once a source of constant clucking and cackling, the chicken coop now was as silent as a barren field. He pushed the unlocked front door of the farmhouse open with two fingers. Although the living room was emptied of its furnishings, he called out, "Ms. Elspeth, are you here? Mr. Frank? Hello?"

Getting no response, he pulled the door shut and walked around back to check out the water level. The bottom land was now submerged. A few of the longer tendrils off of the black-eyed pea plants were still visible, drifting on the surface like seaweed. He hoped Elspeth had been able to get a bucketful of black-eyed peas before the garden flooded. His mouth watered as he remembered the time he came to dinner and she prepared them with lots of bacon and just the right amount of salt.

He spotted something dark just under the surface near the water's edge. Curious, he walked a few feet further down the hill. Since he still couldn't tell what it was, he ventured further down, edging sideways and taking care to maintain his balance. When he'd gone as far as safety would allow, the identification of the object still eluded him.

He picked up a long, thin, fallen branch and prodded the surface, causing the object to ride a little higher in the water. His stomach churned, spewing bile into his throat. It was a body—a body clothed in a pair of denim overalls. The over-sized bandana that usually poked out of Frank's back pocket was now cinched around his neck, its ends twisted tight in the handle of a wooden spoon.

"Dammit, Ms. Elspeth. What did you have to go and do that for?" he muttered and headed up to his car to get a forensic team on the scene ... and an arrest warrant for the newly widowed Elspeth McCallister.

Nineteen-Aught

Susan White Norman

Galveston, Texas.

Sept. 5th. Scattered nimbus and cumulus clouds.

"Sweet Sara," he began, "I feel it's my heart that's vanished. When you and I's united again, it'll reappear."

I asked Mother Bea if someone else might take down his letter, but she said I was the only nun who could make out a word he says.

He's from East Texas, and he speaks in one low creaky stream, so it sounds like "Ezexas." It's a wonder a person can survive that accent. Being a County Wicklow girl myself, I shouldn't be able to make out a syllable, but as you know, I did my postulancy in New York City, where one develops an ear for accents.

Sept. 6th. Scattered cumulus, strato-cumulus, and alto-stratus clouds. Fresh northerly winds.

I've posted off the letter to his fiancée, Sara. Nineteen, same as me, poor lamb. You've never heard the likes of the *intimate* things he sees fit to mumble in that baffling accent of his. He's a repairman on *The Mexican*, the ship that brought us over from New York. He's lost his arm to it, and he moans in the night. The arm was sliced off clean and dropped right into the Gulf. Still, he feels the cramps. He *begs* the nurses to knead it.

"There's nothing here," I say. "Naught, but air." I wave my hand through the space under the stump to show him, but he only blinks at me.

Jake, the orderly, posts up the city's weather wire each morning, although I haven't the foggiest idea what much of it means. The coastline here is a fair sight from the rugged Irish Sea. I've seen on a map that the Gulf of Mexico is curled like a kidney, but from the beach it seems a dull, flat thing.

Sept. 7th. Broken cumulus and strato-cumulus clouds. Fresh to brisk winds.

I think I've mended the ghost arm.

I took the mirror from above my bathroom sink at the convent. You should've seen the look my roommate gave out.

We brought him to the convalescing lounge, and I sat him down at the table while Jake held the mirror against his stump on the left, and ... an arm appeared. Resurrected from the ocean floor, no less! Of course, it was a mere reflection, but I rubbed it nonetheless. All the time he kept his eyes on the mirror. He let out such a moan. Afterward, he hooked me 'round with his good arm.

Sept. 8th. Strato-cumulus and nimbus clouds. High northerly winds.

Lord, have mercy on us.

It doesn't require much imagination to picture this hospital as a rickety old boat, far out at sea, surrounded by water. Water rising higher and higher every hour. Cornices, roofs, blinds, flying in all directions outside. It's gone dark now, and they all call for You. All but him. He only calls for her. He only calls for Sara.

Should I know what moves him? Will I know it finally, when I'm in Your arms? Do you hold Yourself ready to come for us, should the occasion demand?

The Fallen

Sobia Khan

She witnessed his first murder.

The boy, Omar, her grandson, in his seven years had never seen a bird lying helpless on the ground, its chest still heaving, its feathers still shivering in the wind. The bird had fallen from the apple tree in the yard. She saw the boy run into the kitchen through the back door, returning with a dirty, red curry-stained ladle. With it, he scooped up the bird along with the ground and the ants beneath. He waved the ladle around a bit, pointing it in her direction, knowing she was watching him. She tried to smile and nod. Her facial muscles twitched without any perceptible change on her face. She hoped he could sense her approval in her eyes. That was one way she could still communicate. He was going to help the little bird, she thought, how sweet.

He placed the ladle on the ground and dropped down beside the faintly fluttering bird. She peered hard through the window pane at the fallen bird trying to gauge what kind of a bird it was. She knew all the names of Texas birds and some Pakistani birds from her childhood, but it was Texas wildlife she had grown to love over the past 35 years. From across the thick window pane, she could see Omar's shadow loom over the helpless creature. She gauged the bird's color to be red. It was the same redbird she had been watching before. She wondered for the millionth time why someone had come up with such an ordinary name for a bird so unique. From her childhood in Karachi, she remembered the *guaraya*. It was a small scrawny little brown bird, but the name bestowed a sense of regality to it. Her brother had been an avid bird lover. Their father had bought a huge bird cage for her brother's 13th birthday and stocked the cage with a pair of every kind of small bird Karachi called home to. Two parrots, two pigeons, two *guarayas*, two *mainas*, *koyals*, even the small dyed birds that were popular among little children. Her brother cleaned and managed the bird cage, and he exchanged the birds with friends, but she watched them. Sometime between her teen years and her adult life, she had become a bird watcher.

"Stop day dreaming, Saba. You've been staring in the air for 20 minutes. It's odd—very odd," she remembered her mother saying.

"I'm not daydreaming. I'm watching the birds. The *guaryas* are never at rest. They constantly fly across the cage. Do you think we should let them go? I think the cage is too small for them," she replied.

"You are wasting your time worrying about silly birds. Make yourself useful." And just like that, her mother ended her bird watching. Reluctantly, Saba followed her mother to the veranda to join her aunts.

"Indeed, didn't you hear about Mali's daughter who ran away with the bus boy? Well, after he was done with her, he dropped her right off at her parents' house. The poor Mali couldn't even gather himself enough to come tend my gardenias and *chamelis* for a month. He sent his brother-in-law instead." Aunty Layla was in the middle of some story. Both her aunts, Saba, and her mother sat in the winter sunlight on the veranda sifting platters of rice for stones and hardened rice—cleaning the rice for future cooking. Cleaning rice and shelling peas were a winter ritual in Saba's mother's home. Saba hated both chores, but as a young teen, she had no choice. So she sifted and shelled and listened to the women's stories. It was funny, Saba recalled as she watched her grandson through the window, that the stories the women told were never about her aunts or her mother. They were always about others. Others who were either better than her and, hence, should be idealized and followed to the tee, or others who had mucked up their lives so badly they had become examples of what not to do. Both kinds of stories were repeated and embellished with new details and nuances at every retelling, becoming religious and sacred in tone and lesson.

"Apa, the grocery wala down the street told my cleaning girl that his neighbor's daughter ran away with an older man for two measly bottles of nail polish. *Hai hai*, what is the world coming to?" Aunty Layla exclaimed to Saba's mom and her other sister.

"What do you mean two bottles of nail polish?" Saba asked, scooping another large handful of rice toward her on the platter to sift through.

"She was so desperate and so enamored of this man that when he enticed her with nail color, it was enough for her to leave her father's home to go off with him. Disgraceful," Aunty Layla proclaimed. Saba's mother and Aunty Shireen nodded in agreement. Aunty Shireen was about to launch into another sermon on how young women of their family have always conducted themselves with honor and dignity and how they have always been beyond reproach and how future generations have to continue upholding the honor, but luckily, Saba was saved from the sermon by the radio, which started playing all her aunts' favorite new numbers. They all started humming to the tune, momentarily forgetting the horrors and scandals of the world they lived in. "*Hum Tum Aik Kamrey Mein Band Hoon*" had become somewhat a rebel song of their generation; Saba loved the tune as well and hummed along with them. The song was from the cult movie of its times, *Bobby*, a love story of two young teenagers from different socio-economic stratas of Indian society. The plot was clichéd—how the two lovers resist their familial and societal pressures, fight the good fight, and run away together, with their families eventually relenting and giving in to their love once their children's lives are in danger.

It was this song from Saba's childhood that played on repeat in her head as she watched Omar fuss over the redbird. It dawned on her that she was trapped in her room, much like what the song described from decades ago. Except she wasn't trapped with a lover. She was alone. Saba sighed and focused her attention on her grandson again. He was a rambunctious seven-year-old with her dark brown wavy hair and her big dark eyes. He was tan like his mother and had her dimples, too, dimples which made him appear sweet and innocent, no matter what mischief he was up to. Saba adored the little boy. He made her entrapment bearable.

From her place at the window, Saba saw Omar dig with his hands, press his small hands into the earth, and uproot the grass and soil. His hands will be filthy, his nails stuck with dirt. He'll need a good scrub before lunch, she thought. A few minutes later, the boy had a little cavity dug out in the earth. Like a showman performing on stage, he turned toward the window at his audience, looked at Saba, and waved to her. She would have waved back. He picked up the ladle, showing it to her one more time, showing her the tools of the trade before he performed the big act. Then he scooped the bird off the ground and into the ladle. He tossed the ladle with the redbird into the newly prepared cavity. The bird fell on its back with its furious beak pointing toward the sky. Saba became immobile, if that were even possible. She saw the bird try to move its neck. It tried raising a wing, but failed. Suddenly, the boy flipped the bird over on its stomach and thrust its beak into the dirt, flattening the bird with his pudgy hands against the base of its grave. Saba felt her own backbone snap under his palm. Omar continued the assault until Saba felt her and the bird's lungs cave in on themselves, each rib tripping on the other, collapsing like a building after an earthquake. She was in shambles.

The bird must be dead for sure, she thought. She tried calling for help, but not a whimper escaped her lips. She remembered her own brothers burying and praying over the graves of dead chicks, kittens, and rabbits. The newborn kitten, naked with a thin membrane for skin, was the first death she remembered. Her brother had bathed the newborn kitten in winter and found her dead a few hours later in the garage. They had both cried. Then familiarity with death grew as the large beaked parrot, and the orange dyed chick, and then a distant relative passed on. That's how their mother termed the unfortunate mishaps.

"They pass on, dear," her mother said after the chick died. "They move from here to another world."

"Where?" her brother asked, as he hiccupped between tears. But he never got an answer. Their mother shrugged and pointed to the blank sky overhead. That first time when the kitten died, they cupped their hands, raised them to the sky, and prayed—this would later become a ritual at every passing. They prayed the kitten live happily in the new world, not miss them too much, make good friends, and be happy in heaven. When the family member passed on while Saba and her brother were still children, they had become somewhat accustomed to the process of grieving, burying, and praying. Saba remembered playing out in the street with her cousins as the dead body of her distant uncle lay in the open courtyard of his house for viewing. People streamed in and out of the house all day. Big *daigs* of *biryani* and *qorma* were brought in to feed the grievers. Even from where Saba and her cousins sat huddled in the back alley of the house, the smell of the food wafted to them, but they remained undistracted. That was the first time they had lighted matches and played with fire.

"Watch this," Saba's slightly older cousin told the group. He lit a match and held it steady over a stray leaf until the leaf caught fire. They all leapt up in awe and fear as the leaf sizzled and then burnt itself to the ground.

"You better be careful. Someone will catch us," another cousin piped in as they took turns lighting the matches one by one.

"Nah, they're all too busy eating and grieving," the older cousin said. He lighted a match and held it to an ant he saw scurrying.

"No, not the ant. You cannot burn the ant. That's disgusting. It's cruel." Saba pushed him over with all her ten-year-old might onto the ground, and the match fell out of his fingers and extinguished. The older cousin brushed off the dirt from his white shirt, shrugged, and continued lighting matches and burning leaves until the match box was empty. Saba recalled the almost killing of the ant and shuddered. As she peered out the window at her grandson, she wondered what the burned ant would have smelled like. Would it have been like roasted peanuts or burnt popcorn? Preventing her cousin from killing a poor ant that day had been a minor victory for Saba. But today she had failed to avert tragedy.

And now her grandson. She watched the boy as he scooped up dirt into the ladle, heaped dirt and grass, worms, and ants on top of the bird. He kept burdening the small grave under dirt until it sat raised above the ground toward the sky. The child then patted the dirt into a gentle mound, the grave made, the bird dead. The ladle lay discarded to the side, an accomplice to the deed.

"Come in, Omar," her daughter-in-law called out. Omar did not move. She saw that he ignored her call and kept staring at the mound. Ah, he's going to make *dua* over the grave, pray that the bird makes great friends and stays happy in heaven, she thought. Maybe he was still the innocent little boy she wanted him to be.

"Omar, get in now." Saba heard another call out to him. Omar stood up. He was somber. He picked up the red crusted ladle and headed back into the kitchen. No, no, no, you haven't made *dua* yet. You can't go yet, she yelled out. Pray, she cried out to the silent and stubborn window pane. That's what we did. That's why we buried them and cried over them and prayed over them. She heard the kitchen door open and saw Omar sprint back into the yard. He's back, thank God. He's back. She felt herself relax. He had something in his hands, in his fist. She saw him undo his fist and take out two toothpicks. One, he stuck at the head of the mound. The other he held across the first one in the ground. The boy looked around, searching for something to tie the two tooth-picks with. He frantically looked around in the browning yard. He yanked out two blades of grass and tied the two toothpicks to-gether into a cross. As he pored over the sticks and the grave, Saba saw tiny creases marring his forehead; he was silent and focused on wrapping the blades securely.

Omar didn't see his grandmother watching him through their bedroom window. He didn't know she wept as she saw him in the yard. He was erecting a cross. She didn't understand why he would do that. She knew she should call out to her daughter-in-law and have the boy yanked away from the grave. She was tempted to press the buzzer on her wheel chair, but what good would that do, she thought. Her daughter-in-law would come in, check on her, ask her if she wanted to go to the restroom or if she wanted a drink, and not getting the arranged blinks, return to her own world. Saba had no choice but to sit and watch through a window, her progeny burying the traditions and the religion of her ancestors. A gentle drizzle streaked the window, blurring her vision again.

Saba had been watching the bird before it fell. As always, her daughter-in-law had rolled her wheelchair over to the window after breakfast and her bath so she could look out at the world. Staring at clear blue unadulterated Texas skies calmed her. Expansive, majestic, and mysterious, the sky was her companion. It looked down on her, and she up at it. The two seemed to understand each other. She didn't seek the heaven promised above it. She didn't even know if it were there; yet, she looked up at the sky every time she had a complaint or a thank you. She felt the sky was hers. She looked up and thanked often—every time she saw Omar play, when he kissed her cheek, or when she recalled her past life. Watching her grandson play with an abandonment only possible for a child made her entrapment behind the window and within her inept body bearable. The sun appeared brighter here in the suburbs than it did near downtown Dallas, where she had lived until three months ago. She willed herself to forget the familiar faces as she walked to her office on campus, or the coffee that only Riccio could make for her, or the smell of fresh books from the publisher before the semester began. And then, her son had been called to come get his mom as if she was the last child left in school to be picked up. Her son brought her to the suburbs and silently settled her into his home. She wondered at times if he had already purchased her gravesite. She wasn't religious, but she knew that she, too, would die one day. All her relatives and ancestors were buried in Karachi. She feared she would be all alone in death with no one she loved alongside her. She didn't think much more than that. For now, she shared a room with Omar, his bed closer to the door, hers closer to the restroom. Every night she skewed her eyes to the left as much as possible to see the boy sleep. She studied the postures he would huddle into or spread out to. She became a watcher again. An Omar watcher, a bird watcher, a life watcher as it sped on by without her.

She had been watching the bird before it fell. She saw the redbird swoop down from the big apple tree in the backyard down to the barren hedge, plucking a dry twig or two from the flower bed and fly back up. The nest itself was out of her sight. If she could have, she would have craned her neck a little more to the left to see past the branches and the golden leaves where the bird was building its nest. She watched Omar play with his soccer ball and ride his bike in the yard. He was an active boy, always ready to run and play. As Omar played, alternating between the ball and the bike, the bird too alternated between its nest and the flower bed to collect more twigs. She saw the petite, yet ferociously strong bird take off with the twigs, some falling mid-air, only one or two making it back safely every time. She was grateful, she reminded herself. Allah hadn't taken away her sight, and she could still appreciate the world around and away from her.

Besides the sky, the birds, and the falling leaves, she and Omar often watched cartoons together. Omar would swing her wheelchair toward the TV, wanting her to watch his favorite shows with him. He sat mesmerized by whatever cartoon show came on, and then abruptly, he broke into applause or laughter, Lego bionicle figure in one hand and a candy or some sweet in the other. But whenever he broke into applause, he jumped up, dropping both from his hands. Her heart jumped with him. And when he was afraid or when he cringed, his face got all shriveled up, the nose pinched forward, and his eyes narrowed into thin slits, and she too flinched with him.

"Look, Grammy. That's the cereal I want. Will you tell Mama to get this for me?" Omar asked. Or sometimes, he would turn and look at her, expecting her to laugh at the cartoons with him. She did laugh at them, at him, and at herself.

"Are you bugging your Grammy again?" Saba's daughter-in-law asked, often standing in the doorway to their room. She checked in on Saba and her son frequently when the nurse was not around. "Remember to press the buzzer." Saba cringed every time she heard herself called "Grammy." She would have preferred the more traditional *Daadi*, but by the time Saba had moved in with her son, Omar was already used to calling her Grammy. Saba had called her grandmother *Daadi*, as did most children in Pakistan. Her own mother had preferred the softer, more rounded off variation, *Daado*. But something had happened between her grandmother's, her mother's, and her generation. Time and space between Pakistan to Dallas, Texas, had overtaken and metamorphosed the loving term of endearment into something that didn't resonate with Saba, anymore.

"Mama, see this commercial. I want this cereal." Omar pointed to the TV.

"Yes, dear. Show it to your Grammy," she said, already walking away.

"Yes, but she can't buy it. Can she?" Omar mumbled to himself. He turned and looked at Saba, gave her a puzzled look, as if trying to seek her in her eyes, and then he turned away toward the TV. Saba sat and watched in silence, speaking many things to Omar in her head. If only he could hear her, she thought. She tried and managed a lopsided grin, again. The last three months of their lives were of conversations spoken and unheard. Still they were both happier with each other than without. Each a witness to the other.

Sitting at the window, she watched Omar kick the soccer ball into the flower bed where the bird was collecting its twigs. He scared the bird away, forcing her to return without a twig, a flight wasted. She saw the two cross each other's path and then move away from each other. The bird back in flight, and Omar kicked the soccer ball around again. Minutes later, the bird swooped back down again, continuing its search. Ahead of the storm brewing in the horizon, she silently urged the bird to finish the nest quickly. She could see the clear skies darkening, brewing, readying themselves for a downpour. The dry grass blades swayed with the wind hinting at the coming storm. She feared for the bird without a home; she feared for the incomplete nest. Maybe she will be done soon, Saba thought.

The boy was jumping under the tree where the bird was building its home. In watching the bird, she missed seeing Omar's soccer ball get stuck in the tree. He was jumping frantically under the tree waving his arms above his head trying to reach a ball several feet higher. "Mama, Grammy, my ball," he screamed. He turned to look at Grammy behind the window wall. "Mama, Mama."

"What's wrong? Why are you screaming?" Her daughter-in-law rushed out the kitchen door and asked, "Are you hurt? What happened?"

"My ball is stuck in there. See it?" Omar pointed to the tree. The ball lay snug between two low-lying branches.

"You scared me. That's nothing to worry about. Wait until your dad comes home. He can get it down for you," she said.

"No. I want it now," Omar said.

"I can't do this right now. I have food on the stove. Not now," she said, already turning and walking away. Omar turned and looked at Saba. She tried her best to look sympathetic, her eyes more convincing than her facial expressions. Omar saw the sympathy, shrugged his shoulders, and started looking around the yard. Then he disappeared. He returned with a fist full of small stones. She could see him again. He held all the stones in his left fist, then took one in his right hand, and flung it toward the ball. The stone went up a yard or two over Omar's head and fell near his feet. He took another stone and this time flung it with all his strength, willing it to hit the soccer ball. The stone almost made it. The last stone got a little further but still missed the ball. Omar disappeared from her four-by-five window into the world. He came back with more stones. Back under the tree, he started flinging the stones successively, one after another, with all his seven-year-old fury, hoping at least one would hit its mark.

It did. The ball fell to the ground below. So did the bird. Stunned, she saw the two marked and the two fall. She wanted to run out and rescue the redbird. If only she could run again, walk again, move again, anything, she thought. She pressed hard on the arms of the wheelchair, trying to lift herself. Nothing moved, not even a ripple or a hope. The ball rolled down; the bird flopped down. Both lay next to each other under the apple tree. The wind was getting stronger, blowing Omar's hair into frenzy. She pressed the buzzer on her wheel chair, keeping her thumb on it. Her daughter-in-law came running in.

"Yes? What's wrong?" she asked. She saw Saba looking out the window. She followed her eyes. "It's about to pour, and he's still out there. Thanks. I'll call him in." She moved Saba's wheelchair closer to the window, trying to make sure she had a good view of the tempestuous sky about to unburden itself. She did. She saw Omar bury the bird. When Omar ran back into the house, out of her sight, she hoped this was the end. Maybe he would call his mom to show her what he had done, and she could still save the bird. Saba hoped, even though she could sense death without smelling the wet dirt that covered the stilled bird. But Omar made a cross with the toothpicks, and she wished she were dead.

At first she didn't understand the toothpicks, and when he finally stood up, looking proudly at his handiwork, she understood that he was commemorating death the only way he had seen in his seven years—on TV, in cartoons. He had seen many crosses placed on graves on TV, but he'd never seen how his family signified and dignified death. She didn't know which was worse, his murder of the bird or her family's ignorance. She didn't blame her son or her daughter-in-law. She blamed herself. If only she could talk to him, if only she could get to him, maybe then she could save him. Tears slid down her face until finally, Omar went in for lunch. She pressed the buzzer again.

"Yes, lunch is almost ready, I'm coming for you," her daughter-in-law said. A few minutes later, her daughter-in-law came and rolled her into the kitchen. Omar was already at the kitchen table. His hands and face still dirty, he looked down at his plate, twisting the fork, ensnarling the spaghetti in front of him. She sought his eyes, waited for them. But he didn't look up. He focused on the spaghetti. Her daughter-in-law fed her lunch, paying less attention to Omar and his still-full plate of his favorite meal—spaghetti and french fries. A little while later, Omar ran off into his room.

"Wait, Omar, your lunch," his mother said after him. "Grammy, why aren't you eating? What's gotten into you two today?" she asked out loud to herself, not expecting an answer. A few minutes later, she rolled Saba back into Omar's room. The TV was switched on. Omar was on his bed asleep. Saba's daughter-in-law helped her into bed for the afternoon nap.

"Press the buzzer if you need anything. Your nurse should be back soon," she reminded Saba as she placed the buzzer under her hand. Saba skewed her eyes to look at the other side of the room and saw that her daughter-law had forgotten to cover Omar with a blanket and put a pillow under his head. *Tom and Jerry* reruns played on the TV. Saba recognized the music. On her back, she lay staring at the low ceiling. She wanted the boy to wake her up, tell her a story, talk about the bird. She wanted to go back in time—to visit her son more often, to give more in charity, to visit her brother in Pakistan—if only she were well again. She lay in an uproar, swearing by the heaven and the earth and the sky to do better, be better. Outside, the storm strengthened overhead. It had crept up close to them. She couldn't see the dark clouds harassing the house, nor could she see the thick fat drops of rain pelting the roof, but she heard them. She heard the tree moaning, the empty nest weeping. She too was crying.

She was still staring at the ceiling when Omar woke up. The rain crashed and pushed against the window, and the lightning boomed louder than the TV. She sensed Omar walk over to her bed. He inched close to her, probably to see if she was asleep. She felt his breath on her forehead. She feared the little boy. She wanted to recite some *Quranic* verses to calm herself, but she kept tripping over the words. Her memory, like her tongue, was betraying her. She opened her eyes and rolled all the way to the left so she could see the boy.

He stood by her side silently, watching her, his shadow hovering over her. She saw him extend his arms forward, and then he started gently patting her forehead. He liked taking care of her, she knew that. He kissed her forehead, his hand pressing on the wet pillow. She felt him pat the wetness from her tears a few times. She saw him look fervently around as if searching for something. He walked back a few steps and came back with another pillow in his hands. She smiled. She wanted to tell him that she was OK and that he would be okay, too. And then he pulled the wet pillow from under her neck, leaving her neck in a stretched and strained position. In that quick whipping of the pillow being pulled, the buzzer fell off the bed. Her fingers groped but could not find it. Her eyes fell open even wider. If only Omar came to look into her eyes, she could then plead mercy, plead forgiveness for not being there, plead for help from her strained position. Her neck didn't fall into place onto the mattress. It lay arched, at an angle, stiff, her airway blocked. Her mouth fell open, and she gasped for breath. Omar noticed the parabolic curve of the neck and ignored it. She saw his shadow move off of her. The new cereal commercial was on, the song filled the room with cheer. Cartoon laughter echoed in the room, as her last tear streaked down her cheek. Omar turned toward the TV, increasing the volume, the cartoon drowning out the storm and her.

The Midnight Bather

Diana López

One night, Nelda heard the garden hose below her garage apartment. Just outside the ring of porch light, a naked man rubbed soap across his neck, arms, torso, and feet. He rinsed off, and then he dried himself with a T-shirt, slipped on jeans and sandals, and grabbed a backpack. He hadn't put his T-shirt on, so when he crossed beneath the porch light, Nelda saw his back with a dreamcatcher tattoo. Then the midnight bather walked away.

She turned from the window, switched on a lamp, and drew his tattoo. She'd heard that bad thoughts fell through the center of dreamcatchers, so she wrote the worst word she could imagine, *statistic*. That's what her dad said when she got pregnant at 17. Even today, instead of hello, he said, "What's it like being a statistic?" And he'd throw out her numbers, the one-in-four teen pregnancy rate and the 36 million below the U.S. poverty line. He'd add stats for single parenthood and bad credit, too, till Nelda stopped feeling like a person with a name.

She loved her son, Sam, but he needed to eat, play, and learn things. He needed protection. So when she drew their portrait, she drew a straw in her chest with Sam sucking out her blood with its calories and will.

Statistic. She tilted the dreamcatcher sketch and wrote it again and again, making the word crisscross itself till she couldn't read it anymore, till it became a black hole. And it *was* a black hole. She could feel her frustration and regret fall into it.

—◆—

Sam went to his grandma's on Sunday, so Nelda called her boyfriend, Freddy. He wasn't Sam's dad. "Ned is Sam's dad," Nelda said aloud. She was alone, but she imagined *he* was there. Not Freddy, but the midnight bather. It helped to pretend. "That's why we got together," she went on, "because we had the same name (when you think about it) and same zodiac sign. Guess we thought we were *supposed* to be together, but in the end, all we had in common were three letters and Sam."

She went to the sink, filled it with hot soapy water, and then dumped a few plates in there. The remains of over-easy eggs had dried up on them.

"You know what Ned told me when I got pregnant? He said, 'Sorry to dump this on you. Wish I could help, but I'm off to Austin.' So now he lives in Austin. He works at Fuddrucker's and goes to UT. He makes good grades. He tells me, like I really want to know. And he tells me about his girlfriend, too, like I really want to know. He's all happy that we can 'still be friends.' Says I'm an A+ friend and a real good sport about things. Says he and his girlfriend should double-date with me and Freddy sometime. 'For Sam's sake,' he says." Nelda hurled a plastic bowl into the soapy water. Some bubbles splashed onto her shirt. "Ned's going to get his MBA. It'll take a while, so when he's done, Sam'll be seven or eight years old, and I'll be seven or eight years older, still here in San Antonio, in this apartment, I'm sure."

She imagined the midnight bather nodding. He was such a good listener.

"I had dreams, too," she said, waving her arm across the apartment where her paintings stood at the floorboards, leaning against the walls because she didn't want to punch holes and risk losing the deposit if she ever moved out.

She took a plate from the dishwater. The egg came right off after soaking, so she hardly had to scrub. If only she could clean up life so easily.

⇒•⇐

Freddy took all day to come by. When he arrived, he drank the last soda and said, "I'm quitting my job."

"Again?" Nelda asked. "Why?"

"Those places. They don't appreciate my skills."

"What skills? You dropped out of college, remember?"

"So did you. Don't forget. Three times. First you said you were gonna be a hair stylist, then a massage person, and who knows what the last thing was?"

Nelda winced. "At least I keep trying."

"Maybe."

"Maybe?"

"Yeah, maybe."

"I do!" she insisted. "It's tough with a job and a kid."

"Sure. *Maybe.*"

"You asshole," Nelda said, grabbing her keys. "Come on. Let's pick up Sam."

Freddy closed in. "Not yet. We're alone, Baby. Let's take advantage."

"But Sam's waiting for us now."

"Come on, Nelda. A quickie."

She shook her head, crossed her arms.

"Can't I have a kiss at least?"

He reached for her, kissed her, groped beneath her blouse to her bra, squeezing, in a playful but punitive way. Then she pushed him off. They headed out, but Freddy got in his own car. He wouldn't come back till he was broke or horny or bored.

Nelda drove toward her parents' house, and at the corner of Zarzamora and Culebra, she saw the midnight bather again, wearing the T-shirt now. He held a square of cardboard that said, "War vet. Need money for food."

She pulled over and beckoned him. "Here," she said, handing him a five.

He bowed gallantly. "Why, thank you, Miss. Much obliged."

He had long hair and a lean face with kind, brown eyes. His smile was beatific. He looked so much like Jesus, only greasy.

She had to admit, her imaginary version had straighter teeth and cleaner nails. But the actual man wasn't so bad, just down on his luck—like her, she believed.

She passed the intersection three more times that week. He wasn't there. Every night, she listened at her window, but he hadn't returned to bathe. So she drew him. First at the intersection with his sign. Then as a soldier. Then standing in line, though she couldn't decide what kind of line. The soup kitchen line, the welfare line, the kissing booth line at the carnival? She drew him nude, remembering his thinness, how his clavicles protruded. Then, she sketched the garden hose coiled around him. She gave the garden hose elbows, wrists, and hands for its embrace.

Nelda waitressed at a *taquería*. Her boss, Mr. Ramirez, was an older, worn-out guy—perhaps more worn-out than old. He worked the cash register. When he wasn't around, his younger brother worked it. No one else was allowed. Between customers, he read the paper. If business was really slow, he finished the paper and picked up a library book—usually something motivational like *The Seven Habits of Highly Successful People*, but lately, he flipped through coffee table books about Kahlo, Cezanne, or Klee.

She handed him a ticket to ring up.

"Want to go to Starbuck's after work?" he offered.

"We have coffee here," she said.

"I know. But there, you could get something fancy, eh? I'll pay, eh?"

She hated how he said *eh* so much.

"I don't know about fancy coffees," she said.

"I'll order for you, then. If you don't like it, I'll order something else till you find one that's good." The register spit out a receipt, and its cash drawer zipped out. Mr. Ramirez handed Nelda the change. "We can talk," he continued. "We never get the chance to talk here, eh?"

"What would we talk about?" she said. "Besides work, I mean."

He shrugged. Then he took a rag and wiped the register though it wasn't dusty. Nelda returned to her tables.

Two hours later, Mr. Ramirez said, "Tomorrow you're off. Why don't I come by? I need some new art for this place."

Mr. Ramirez was a reliable patron. A month ago, he bought a painting of Aztecs flying in army-style jeeps. At the time, Nelda was into putting native people in modern settings or modern people in native settings—like an astronaut in a *kiva*. She couldn't say what it meant though she knew that a college education would have given her the words. She wished she had them, the words, but since she didn't, she drew. She glanced at the restaurant walls with her paintings—whales jumping from hotel pools or goat-footed boys dancing with whiskered girls. The *taquería* had become a gallery for her work, each piece representing a time she had turned Mr. Ramirez down.

"I don't know why he asks me out," she told the midnight bather as she drove home. She even glanced at the empty passenger seat when she said this. "Mr. Ramirez knows I have a boyfriend. Does he think I'm going to break up with Freddy?" She stopped at a light. "Maybe I *should* break up. Freddy isn't really a catch. That guy can't keep a job, but Mr. Ramirez—he's got his own business. Maybe it isn't fancy, but lots of people eat there. We've got regulars. And he really likes my art while Freddy hardly notices. But I never think about Mr. Ramirez outside of work. When I'm lonely, I think about Freddy—not talking to him—but kissing him, sex. We've got chemistry, you know?" The light turned green, so she inched forward. "I can't believe I'm telling you this," she said to the midnight bather. Then she laughed at herself because she *wasn't* telling him—she wasn't telling anyone at all.

Mr. Ramirez stopped by the next day. As soon as Sam saw him, he ran over and held up a Hotwheels car.

"Let me see here," Mr. Ramirez said. "A Camaro, eh? That's a fancy car. Me, I just drive a plain old truck."

Sam grabbed his hand and pulled him to a heap of Hotwheels. Mr. Ramirez sat on the floor and one by one, named each car. Sam kept saying, "How about this? How about this?"

Nelda couldn't help herself. She ran comparisons. First, Freddy. He babysat sometimes but the way he might babysit a cat. He left Sam alone as long as Sam wasn't putting poison in his mouth or jumping out the window. Maybe Sam would get peanut butter all over his face or pick up dead roaches, but he was never hurt, never crying when Nelda got home. So Freddy did okay, she decided. Once in a while, Ned babysat, too. He'd take Sam to the snack bar at Target, next buy him new socks and a bunch of toys.

Then he'd start calling, asking when he could bring Sam home because they were getting bored, which really meant *Ned* was getting bored. "Guess they don't teach you how to be a dad in college," Nelda silently told the midnight bather.

Sam laughed. Mr. Ramirez had done a magic trick with the little cars, making one disappear and then reappear on Sam's shoulder.

"You're good with kids," Nelda said.

"One day, I'll have my own," Mr. Ramirez announced. "I always wanted a big family, but I was so busy getting the restaurant going. I never had time to woo the ladies, eh?"

Now *she* laughed. *Woo* was such an old-fashioned word.

He stood up. "So what have you been working on?"

Involuntarily, Nelda glanced at the midnight bather sketches. There were nearly 20 now. In the latest, he stood in a fountain, water spurting around him, the droplets gradually resembling butterflies as they fell. Some of the butterflies were whole but others had torn wings.

"Let me see. Let me see," Mr. Ramirez said as he approached the sketches.

"No." Nelda tried to stop him. "I mean ..."

He flipped through them anyway.

"I'm just brainstorming," Nelda explained. "They're not finished."

He nodded. "This man," he asked, "he is very important, eh?"

"No. I mean ... he's not anybody I know."

"Oh, so you imagined him."

"Yes, that's it."

"You're a true artist, then. Like O'Keeffe with her flowers and Monet with his haystacks and Degas with his ballerinas." He seemed proud to know the names. Nelda realized, now, why he'd been checking out those coffee table books. "You know what I mean?" Mr. Ramirez asked.

"I think so," she said, though she wasn't sure. Intuitively, she knew she was onto something, and what bugged her most was how vague that *something* was, how she didn't have the word for it.

She wasn't good with words. She wasn't good with numbers, either. And she hated how people used them—words and numbers—to pin her down. Like Ned calling her a good sport and Mr. Ramirez calling her a true artist and her dad—always her dad—calling her a statistic. He'd tell her younger sister, "Now don't turn into a statistic like Nelda."

That's why she understood the midnight bather. She knew people stuck him in categories, too, that they ran his numbers, like what percentage of war vets were homeless, when he was more than that. He *had* to be. And *she* had to be more. But how could you escape? How could you escape stats and probabilities when the world thought they were as inevitable as fate?

Sometimes, to really understand someone, like yourself, you had to draw—the same subject over and over again. Only then could you see all the angles and potentialities, the *whole* story, the variables that equations often ignored.

The next morning, she took Sam to day care and went to work her shift at the *taquería*.

A lady was sitting in the booth by Nelda's Aztec painting. "I don't get it," the lady said. "Aztecs don't fly jeeps. Is this supposed to be an ad for Mexican food?"

The way she spoke made Nelda defensive. "My boss likes it," she said, "and it's his restaurant, so he can hang whatever he wants."

"I guess," the lady said. "But shouldn't he hang something relevant? I mean, when you open your beauty parlor or massage therapy place, aren't you going to decorate with relevant pictures?"

"Who said I'm going to open a place like that?"

"You did. Last week."

"You were here last week?"

"I'm here *every* week," the lady said. "This is where I sit, and this is what I order." She tapped her coffee cup.

"Really?" Nelda tried to place her, but she couldn't. So many customers came in. So many chose this booth and ordered coffee.

The lady looked at Nelda for the longest time. "You really don't remember me?"

Nelda shook her head.

"I'm the teacher. I teach at the middle school down the street."

There it was again—another neat definition—*teacher*. You had to go to college for that. You had to be smart, too, if you meant to make others smarter. This lady, showcasing her job when she knew what Nelda's own job was, that Nelda did not have to go to school for it, did not have to be especially smart.

Nelda said, "Good for you." But her voice, its tone, said, "Who gives a shit?"

The lady unzipped her purse. "You're rude," she told Nelda. "Pretending you don't remember who I am. When I come here every week. Why do I even put up with this?" She slammed a few bucks on the table. "Tell your boss you lost a good customer today."

Nelda shrugged. She couldn't worry. Too much to do. For three more hours, she smiled, poured coffee, felt her feet swell and her back ache. She knew chores and a hungry kid waited at home. So she didn't want her shift to end, but she didn't want it to continue, either.

Then the midnight bather came in. Of course, he came in. Her apartment and the intersection where she'd seen him weren't too far. He must have been here a dozen times before the night he took a bath beneath her window.

"Hi," she said. "How are you?" This was how she greeted all the customers, only less friendly.

He chose a booth and asked for water.

She brought it for him and took the seat across the table. "I met the rudest woman this morning," she said. "She got all mad because I couldn't remember her. Apparently, she was here last week. She said she's here every week. Do you know how many customers I get? And I'm half-asleep in the morning. How could she expect me to remember her? You should have seen how she stomped out of here. You'd think she was my sister or neighbor or something. You'd think she was my *friend*."

The midnight bather took a long sip as he regarded her. He said, "I just want to get out of the heat, lady. Drink something cool.

I didn't come here to listen to your problems. Not when I've got problems of my own."

And he brushed her off, the way she brushed off eraser flecks on her drawings from the lines and shapes she didn't want to see anymore.

Quiet Miracles

Ysabel de la Rosa

For me, nature and photography are two sides of the same coin. That it is possible to hold a tool in my hands that can portray some part of the natural world's mysterious and beautiful presences has seemed miraculous to me from the moment I bought a friend's secondhand camera more than 30 years ago.

Cup of Light (A Mother's Glory)

Calla Flame

Fingers of Light

Pterodactyl in a Tree

Iris by Lamplight

Summer Garden

Lagniappe:

An Editorial Extrusion

First Names

Rachel Crawford

"Morning, Bonnie," Joe says, and sits down in a booth by the window, taking off his hat and placing it on the seat beside him. It's a straw Stetson, size 7 ½ with a 4 ¼-inch crown. I know this because I ordered it for him—I've been ordering his hats online ever since he quit driving up to Alpine to buy his own. It's the only thing the old man will let me do for him. That, and keep his coffee filled while he reads the newspaper. He drinks it black and leaves his copy of *The Terlingua Sun* and five bucks on the table when he leaves.

He's my easiest customer. He doesn't want to chat this early any more than I do—his conversations generally begin with "Morning, Bonnie" and end with a slight tip of his hat when he settles it back down over his long gray hair to walk back out into the sun and dust.

When Joe's daughter Bella and I heard our kindergarten teacher tell the class both our names mean pretty, we grinned at each other across the room. Bella was missing a tooth, like me. The first thing I said to her was "The tooth fairy left me a silver dollar. What'd you get?"

She said, "I got green money." We were friends until the year we turned 17. Bella was used to the narrow roads that wind around the sides of the Chisos, and she knew the trick of both respecting and ignoring the drop-off, but there was nothing she could do to avoid the oncoming car. She died there on the road, but I was alive when the volunteer fire department came to cut us out. It could have as easily been the other way around.

I woke up two days later in the burn center in Dallas. Joe was there with my parents when I opened my eyes. After my mother told me what had happened, Joe leaned down so his face was right in front of mine and whispered, "You're still beautiful, and your life is going to be beautiful." That was the last I heard for a long time because the doctors and nurses knew my mind needed morphine as much as the rest of me.

Today, when Joe picks up his hat and slides out of the booth, he says, "Come out to the house if you can." He knows I'll catch the meaning floating between the words. I say, "Sure, I'll come by after work," and I pull my order pad from my apron to take the next table's order. I recognize her—she's the woman who owns the souvenir shop by the highway in Study Butte. She'll recognize me, too, so I get ready to make conversation, to put her at ease when her eyes, like those of everyone else who doesn't know me well, are pulled to the burned side of my face. I wish I could explain to her that looking like I do isn't as bad as it seems. I remember hearing my grandmother talk about recovering from losing two of her fingers to a snakebite when she was a teenager—she said "You'd be surprised how quickly you get used to things when you have to," and now I understand what she meant. Some days, I even like my complicated face. Every once in a while I play with the idea of getting a tattoo that connects my scars into a pattern—a butterfly maybe.

I knew back in kindergarten I was pretty. My blue eyes and ivory skin and auburn hair made people treat me like I was made out of something expensive. I knew Bella was, too—dark eyes, coffee-with-milk skin, sleek black hair. And I knew we were smart. Straight As, both of us, at Terlingua Consolidated where our mothers taught. Her mom wanted her to be a lawyer, and mine wanted me to be a doctor.

Joe never did ask how I ended up back here waiting tables—he just seemed glad to have me around. Most people I know asked, though, and I don't blame them. The last some of them had seen of me was the caliche cloud on the road as I headed out for Sul Ross State, and most of them knew I went on to grad school in Austin. I usually answered something like "Oh, I dunno ... got homesick I guess," and left it at that. I know why I came back 15 years ago, why I'm not a history teacher like I meant to be, but nobody wants to hear over pancakes their waitress can't teach school because the state of Texas won't have a teacher with a criminal record.

I got over not being allowed to teach, even though I thought I never would. Coming back here to the desert helped. After a while, the bitterness seemed to dry up and blow away. Just like the bitterness of losing Bella, my pretty face, my mom and dad. My parents were already getting old when they had me—they've been gone for years, and so has Bella's mother. Just Joe and me left. Ghosts in the corners of the house I grew up in, ghosts on the road, ghosts walking around the valley. They're partly why I came back. I never feel lonely here.

Bella and I didn't compete or get on each other's nerves like some kids do. We figured anything good that happened to one of us happened to both. We only had one argument, and that was when we were in the fourth grade. We'd been chasing a fierce-looking little creature down the dry wash that ran behind the old pier-and-beam house my mother had inherited when my grandmother died. We knew better than to call it a horny toad because Bella's parents and mine had lived here in the valley all their lives and had taught us the names of every living thing around. We also knew the lizard might spit, but it was more docile than it looked and would calm down and let us hold it. It was too quick, though, and when I lifted my hands after slamming them down into the sand, I saw I'd trapped an arrowhead instead.

We usually had to dig for them, but this one must have been unearthed by the recent rain. It was big and smooth and whole—the kind Joe told us had probably been used for ceremonies because it wasn't chipped and worn from use. We stood and admired the sleek, black, ancient thing for a while, passing it back and forth a couple times, then ran up to the house and into my room, where Bella sat on the bed while I knelt and settled it in my bottom dresser drawer with all the others. Finders keepers, we agreed.

As I closed the drawer, she said, "I have a secret name, you know."

"Yeah?" I asked, looking up at her.

"But I'm not sure I should tell you what it is."

"How come?"

"Well, I want to tell you, but my dad says only other Apaches can know it. The magic will run out if a white person hears it."

I shot back, "You're not Apache. Your dad speaks English, and he works in a gas station. You're no more special than me."

Bella tipped her head back and stared at me through bright, narrowed eyes. "Maybe not. But I was gonna tell you. I was gonna make us blood sisters so I could tell you. But not now." And that was that. She never did.

When I told my mom about it, she looked up from the paper she was grading and said, "Bella's special, baby. Her ancestors have lived around here for hundreds of thousands of years." She paused, then added, "And so are you. Let me show you something." She stood up and led me into the living room. From the bookshelf, she pulled down volume *M-P* of the *World Book Encyclopedia* and opened it to the entry for "Pict."

She put the book in my hands and pointed to a picture of a painted warrior. He was holding a bow and arrow, and his eyes—blazing out through the centuries—were bright blue.

I reveled in the rest of the article. I read and reread it so I could tell Bella about how even Hadrian's Wall couldn't make the Roman invaders feel secure from my ancestors ... how the warriors—men and women both—painted themselves blue and fought stark naked even in the bitter cold ... how monarchs were chosen from the female royal line ... how the women owned the land and passed it down to their daughters ... how infants of women who died of childbirth were held to their mothers' mouths to catch their last breath ... how the women tattooed half-moons on their chests and suns on their breasts and light-ning bolts on their backs ... how when they smoked the same plant they used to paint themselves with, they sat back and com-muned with their gods....

I never told her, though. My ancestors' bones and pottery and arrowheads were buried across the ocean, but Bella had walked all her life among hers. Nothing could change that she belonged here in a way I didn't. I decided she was right not to tell me her other name.

It wasn't until college that I learned more of the story of Scotland and realized that's exactly what I'd read in the encyclopedia when I was a kid—a story. Some of it was good history, and some of it wasn't. But it doesn't matter. The images planted in my mind are as full of life as they were back then. That's one of the things I'd have helped students understand. You have to know the difference, but story can be as powerful and as necessary as fact.

I'm not much of a criminal—I just got caught my second year of grad school with a quarter ounce of weed, the same stuff that's legal now a few hundred miles north of here. But that's the way it is in Texas, and that's why I'm pouring coffee instead of teaching history.

When I pull into Joe's place after my shift and turn off the car engine, I think at first he's not here. Then I see him walking around the corner of his trailer, hands tucked loosely into the front pockets of his jeans, boots raising small puffs of dust with each step, hair falling in two braids down the front of his white T-shirt. He's wearing his hat and sunglasses, so he must have been outside for a while. I told him once that he looks like Willie Nelson, but Joe said, "Nah. Willie Nelson looks like me." I wave at him and step out of the car.

"Hey, Joe, what'cha know?"

"Aw, same old thing. Just fixing a leak." He looks back to the trailer, and I follow his line of vision to the spot where the skirting has been pulled back, exposing the pipes. "Daisy chased something under there last night and knocked a fitting loose." Daisy, the friendly, lazy pit bull sunning herself on the front porch steps, shifts her eyes in our direction and thumps her tail a couple times at the mention of her name, then drifts back to sleep.

"Wonder what it was."

"Dunno. Possum, maybe. Last week there was one sitting right there on the porch rail eating a frog. I walked out to scare it off and it just looked at me and kept taking bites like it belonged there. Ugly thing had *huevos*. Come on out back."

I laugh a little at the image of the ballsy possum as I follow him to the back porch where he does business. I settle into a
wrought iron chair as he walks in the back door, the screen door
creaking shut behind him. He sells weed to me at cost—medical
grade, chemical-free, and except for the drive over the border from
New Mexico or Colorado, non-criminal.

"Remember how Bella used to say *green money?*" I say, handing over my 30 dollars when he comes back out, and taking my
half-ounce bag.

"Yeah ... that's what the little bugger'd say when she wanted
us to know she was asking for bills, not coins." He smiles and sits
down in the chair next to me. "You and me are the only two people
on earth who remember that."

"Yep," I say, holding back the other thought in my head.
From the slow, careful way Joe moves on some days, I might be
the only one before long.

We sit quietly for a minute while I load my pipe. Then Joe
nudges me and points at a javelina making its slow way across
the desert floor that rolls out like an ocean from Joe's backyard. It
stops every once in a while and burrows its snout into the ground.
"Looking for roots," Joe says. "Second one I've seen today. They've
already eaten most of the prickly pear. I'm gonna have to do something about 'em. There's kids who live not far from here."

I understand his worry about the kids. I think I'd rather be
surprised by a cougar than a wild pig. Cougars usually know hu-
mans are too much trouble to mess with, but javelina are too stubborn to know they'd be better off backing off.

"Wanna come with me?"

It takes me a minute to process Joe's question. Then I realize
he's inviting me to go hunting with him. "Maybe so. When?"

"How about right now? They're on the move today, looks like."

His eagerness unsettles me—I've never known Joe to go
hunting without planning ahead, but I say "Why the hell not?"
anyway, and watch him grin as he catches the echo of the Kinky-
Friedman-for-Governor campaign slogan. I drop the pipe back

into the baggie without lighting it. I don't mix cannabis and guns, but even if I wanted to, Joe wouldn't have it. Back when we were growing up, Bella's parents and mine all had come-to-Jesus talks with us about the consequences of driving or shooting while under the influence of anything—legal or illegal. I zip the baggie into my backpack and tell Joe, "I have to get my boots out of my trunk first." No way I'm going into the valley in these tennis shoes. I can still hear my mom saying in her no-bones-about-it voice, "I don't want to kill rattlesnakes, but I will if I have to, and I expect them to have the same attitude toward me."

A couple hours later, after taking Joe's F-150 deep into his acreage, my unsettled feeling is stronger. It's getting late—a few stars are starting to break through—and we're still just sitting on the tailgate by the dry run with our rifles across our knees. It's the same wash Bella and I used to chase lizards in, just a little further south. He says we're listening for the grunts or rustling of pigs, but when he stands up and says he feels like building a fire, I'm sure that hunting's not what's on his mind.

We lay our rifles on the seat in the cab and while Joe walks around gathering tinder, I clamber back onto the bed of the truck to pick up some mesquite wood from the pile Joe brought with him. A stick snaps and whacks me on the forearm. Surprised, I stand still for a second and rub the sting. "You okay?" says Joe.

"Yeah. I must've stepped on a stick and tried to pick up the other end." I hold the wood in one arm and use the other to vault over the side of the truck and lay the wood down where Joe can reach it when he's ready.

After coaxing the fire from the sputtering, smoking stage to a blazing flame, Joe takes two empty five-gallon paint buckets from the back of his truck, turns them upside down for us to sit on, and finally tells me what he didn't want to tell me sitting on the back porch. The stars are beginning to show in pale yellows and reds and blues, and the last of the setting sun sends gold streaming down the sides of the mountains as Joe tells me he has something he wants to give me, something that belonged to Bella's mother.

"This should have gone to Bella when Linda died," he says, "but things didn't work out that way. I want you to have it." He takes a small object wrapped in a handkerchief out of the front pocket of his jeans and hands it to me.

It's Bella's mother's wedding ring—a wide silver band with a brilliant round diamond in the middle and inlaid on either side with turquoise. "Damn, Joe. I remember Linda wearing this. It's beautiful." I almost laugh with relief that Joe didn't take me out here to tell me something awful—like he was sick or dying.

"Yeah, it is. The turquoise was Linda's mother's, Bella's grandmother's. She was from New Mexico, and she had it back before people figured out how to make it synthetically. It's the real thing. The diamond was from me. I bought it in Alpine, and we had the ring made the year before Bella was born. It'll look pretty on your right hand."

When he slides the ring onto my finger, I start to tell him I'll treasure it the rest of my life, but Joe drops my hand, jumps up, and walks quickly over to the truck. He opens the door, grabs a tire iron from behind the front seat, then uses it to poke around in the firewood remaining in the truck bed. Before I can get the words out to ask him what's going on, he slams it down, over and over, into the middle of the firewood. The clang of metal on metal rings out loud in the silence of the valley.

"What the hell ...?"

"Look at your arm. Where the stick popped you."

I move closer to the fire, stick out my arm, and see the telltale mark—a tiny bead of coagulated blood, with a faint, short red line underneath it. My heart starts pounding instantly, even though I know panic will make things worse. By the time Joe carries the tire iron with the crushed rattlesnake draped over it back to the fire so I can see it, I'm light-headed and trembling. I've seen the aftermath of snakebites in other people, and I know I'm in trouble. The nearest ER is 50 miles away.

I start to kick dirt on the fire so we can head out, but Joe says, "Wait a minute, hold on. That was at least 45 minutes ago. Does it hurt?"

"No. I didn't even know it was there."

"Hold your arm out." Joe examines the mark, twisting my forearm gently to get a good look. Then he lets out a low whistle under his breath and says, "You got a dry bite, girl. You just got a kiss."

I can't believe him at first. "How do you know?"

"If you had venom in you, you'd know it. Your arm would be swollen, and you'd be hurting like hell. The only thing you have to worry about is infection, but even that's not likely."

I still can hardly believe it. "Why didn't it inject?"

"Dunno." He shakes his head. "Too surprised maybe—it's not like it had been there rattling and working itself up to strike. Not all bites envenomate. Damn. We were right next it all that time we were sitting there."

This time I do laugh in relief. "I finally earned my special name—Rattlesnake Kissed! Hahahahaha...." I'm joking, but not completely. I feel absurdly special, as if the snake really did kiss me, as if I've earned my totem, and I regret that it's lying by the fire with its head crushed.

Joe laughs too, then says, "So you've been wanting another name?"

I slowly stop laughing. "Oh ... nah, not really. I was just thinking today about how once, when we were kids, I was jealous of Bella's Apache name."

He smiles a little, but the look on his face is more complicated than nostalgia. "What else did she say about it?"

"She didn't tell me," I assure him. "She said the magic would run out—"

"—if she told a white person," Joe finishes. Then adds, like he's reciting something from memory, "Unless the white person was a blood brother."

"Yeah. Well, blood sister."

Joe shakes his head slowly. "I guess she took that to heart. But I'm sorry it came between you two. That's not how I meant it. See, when y'all were learning about the Alamo in school, Bella came home riled up because some kid called her a dirty wetback. I told her she's not dirty, and it so happens that she's Apache and the name-caller was the real immigrant. And I put together a name for her. I can't tell you what it is because—"

"It's OK, I don't have to know," I say to spare us both the embarrassment, and pull the pipe out of my backpack and light it. We sit for a while, passing the pipe back and forth, watching the moon rise over the back of the Corazon, that mountain that somebody long ago decided looks like a heart.

Maybe because my heart is still beating fast from my scare, the cannabis goes to my head quickly, and the world around us starts to shimmer with the familiar-but-strange—velvet sky, white moon, stars crackling along with the fire, my boots planted in the soft dirt, Joe's hawk-like face, soft scent of night-blooming pitaya, warm air flowing around us like water....

"Because I don't remember it," Joe says. "I got it out of a book. I know I'm native, but I don't know what kind. I grew up in an orphanage in New Mexico. I don't even know my own name. The nuns called me Joe."

I let this sink in a minute. Joe's not Joe. So maybe I'm not Bonnie.

"Joe?"

"Yeah?"

"Let's paint our faces and smoke too much and see God."

He laughs. "Why the hell not?" he says, and takes the pipe back again.

After a while, I stand up and say, "Meet me back here with something to paint with."

"All right," he says, as if what I just said made perfect sense, and we both walk out of the circle of firelight. I rummage in my backpack for my makeup bag, he collects some of the waxy, white stuff that looks like cobwebs on prickly pear leaves, but is really the home of the cochineal bug, the tiny beetle with the acid in its body that turns red when crushed.

We sit down cross-legged by the fire, facing each other. I rub my fingers in blue eye shadow and paint my face blue. Joe paints red streaks on his forehead and cheeks. He's not surprised when I take out my pocketknife and hold the blade over the fire as long as my hand can stand it. I let it cool, then slice the soft part of my left palm below the thumb. I hand the knife to Joe. Without wiping my blood from the blade, he slices his right palm. We clasp hands and bleed down past our names, past Bella, past our mothers' and fathers' bones. We don't know the alphabet our blood uses to write our names on the tectonic plates, but we hope they belong.

Cassy Burleson

Disposable Parts, Interchangeable Hearts

Sculling out early between the fog, I saw an Asian couple taking
          photos with serious cameras,
I rowed the corner slowly, held my oars with one hand and waved
          my Texas-friendly wave.
The woman looked, smiled shyly, and then agreed it was a
          diamond of a day on the way,
And as I navigated the narrow marina, knowing you were long
          gone down the St. George's,

Intent on keeping your solitude, and long gone from me in many
          ways, I saw the Asian man
Walk to her, place his hand tenderly on her shoulder, and point
          to a hawk skirting the clouds.
Misty silhouettes, they were so still ... together ... serene as roots
          as they looked at a sun rising.
Together they were, all together in the same spot in their red
          shirts, standing there on the dock,

His hand resting on her shoulder, looking with eyes of love that
          would burn through many suns,
His expressions of tenderness cutting through my heart and the
          clouds around me like a laser.
But when I told you about this, how this couple stood there in
          the glowing aura of one another,
You said, without thinking or skipping a beat, "And then he
          pushed her off." You didn't laugh.

There was the silence of 30 years wasted. The silver chord
　　　　between us gasped for air and
Snapped—at that moment I realized you are a predator, a rabid
　　　　dingo in sheep's clothing.
It happened in a millisecond, that instant when I realized that,
　　　　to you, whom I adored so long,
Women are paper dolls, cardboard cutouts with a *use-by* date,
　　　　new cards to be played ... by you.

Clothes off, clothes on, and with luck and wear, heads worn off
　　　　at the neck over mangled hearts.
It's not about you," you said. I just didn't know you meant it so
　　　　deep down ... truly deeply ....
And that's the acrid stain. For you it's never been about anyone
　　　　... but you. And won't be, ever.
Old dogs don't change their spots. So my new retirement plan
　　　　includes joining the Peace Corps

Or Doctors Without Borders—or going anywhere the enemy
　　　　is more kind and well-defined.

One Less Rat in Thomaston Tonight

The sultan of my heart is gone ... but the wharf rats scurried
        around below the washer and dryer.
Knock, knock. Nobody home. But one night, a rat as big as a
        cat streaked across our floor
In plain sight. But the fattest rat in the room was a zombie in
        sheep's clothing, a silver fox
Who sells boats and sucks the life from everyone he meets like
        West Nile virus.

His shield is love, the Great Deceiver, a lethal lone wolf who
        stalks his harem with red eyes.
And yet, we lived together, separately, me trying to please him,
        him busy trolling through five years of
Use, abuse, abandonment.... He was always busy grooming some
        savvy woman for his next fix.
But there's one less rat in Thomaston tonight. Neck snapped in a
        trap, that far less harmful wharf rat.

My hope is that the fatter rat will be ensnared by his own lies,
        lies I believed completely.
This sad glass mouse has 20/20 vision now and doesn't live in
        the same house. Her last song is a
Dirge for three nice blind mice, Tinker, Blinker, and Nod, whose
        lives were changed as he
Slapped the metal on their necks like a scythe, this Grim Reaper
        of self-esteem and souls.

Still trapped in a basement and never released, one way or the
        other, their bones going dry now
While his goals center on the continuing usefulness of good-
        but-broken women and the sweet
Cocaine of self-adoration. And so I can only hope the Big Rat's
        next victim, preening there back-

Stage now somewhere in the universe where the weather is
       warm in winters, this woman who's

Now thinking the curtain is rising on her most perfect future,
       who doesn't know she's just
Another pearl in the sandpaper trap in his gossamer web, she sees
       she's doomed and figures out
More quickly that such perfection of illusion bears the price of
       never looking behind the curtain.
This Oz weaves an ascending ladder of support, fabrication and
       control.

So yes, I'm hoping that this new *she* will recognize more quickly
       that her king of hearts has no
Clothes and slithers and saves her soul before she falls too hard
       for him.
Or barring that Illumination, will rid us all of one less rat in
       Thomaston ... tonight ...
And for many knights to come.

Cassy Burleson

Hershey's Chocolate Soldier

While purging myself of you like a liberated bulimic on a ghost
        ranch, I realized
There's been nothing worse along the way than a *pretty nothing*
        like you. And always seeing the
Bright side has had its limitations in illusion, now that I'm
        hyper-aware in this
New search for discernment. Compression released, truth is
        more important to me than oxygen ...

Its mourning kisses laid on a five-year drought once green with
        hope and your lush promises.
But truth is, still and all, not one note too many, although it lurks
        out there like a bug zapper,
Squashing my Tinker Bell *I believes*! with a pop—hiss—snap.
        Because now I know that
Truth is, after all, quite the opposite of you.

Just Sayin'

In the world we women who went to the first NOW conference
      grew up in, having a child was
The ultimate luxury because being a professional meant that, for
      one thing, we never took time
Off from work for family, and we didn't NOT go to a meeting
      because our child was sick or
Having a school play or playing soccer or just needing some extra
      Mommy time.

That would have been career suicide in our pre-NOW world,
      where men didn't do that, either ...
So in couples, it was a "career survival" negotiation. Women
      usually lost. Then there was that
Glass ceiling, where we knew, no matter how effective, efficient,
      caring or creatively brilliant we
Were, we had to move faster, jump higher, swallow lumps, and
      give credit to some manly man.

Some *he* was your boss, everywhere—at work and at home.
      Repeat that, infinitesimally ...
And that might be one reason for my shocking divorce rate.
      Maybe other issues ... just sayin' ...
But, without reservation, my daughter and her husband saying
      they don't want children
Might have something to do with my mistakes. That makes me
      infinitesimally, eternally sad.

Overall, just sad ... just sayin' .... The best thing I ever did was
      have a baby, and it was Jasa ....
And she is so *wow*, in every aspect. I respect their decision. But
      I'd really love to hug their baby.
And not having a child like her wasn't what I was fighting for all
      these years. Indeed, quite the opposite.
Just sayin' ... I'd really like to hug that baby girl and that woman
      I've been fighting for all these years.

A Poet Is Never Alone or Lonely, Even Somewhere Way Out Here or There

If you'd been here in Bastrop, I wouldn't have slept so well last
     night or been this still.
Or watched the dandelion seeds floating to the porch this
     morning, perfectly content.
Wouldn't have heard the locusts mating or the dogs barking in
     the distance somewhere
Out there across the Colorado River as wheels rumbled over
     that 1940s silver bridge.

Your noise is never noise to me but does block out some silent
     things best seen alone,
You're a river rushing forward, charming every light and heavy
     thing that comes its way.
Observing such a force, one needs to be a stethoscope occasionally,
     the dog asleep afoot,
Tuning in to silence juxtaposed against the steady rhythm of this
     still self-sufficient heart.

Take the time to see a morning glory's lilac face below, the
     sunflowers leaning into sun,
Vines intertwining rough, unpainted railings between this
     Sunday's miracle of idleness
And that green view spilling out now below cloudy skies in a
     time of too much rain ... a time
Too much of all things, except the slow eloquent drawl of God
     and honeybees buzzing.

"Wildflowers at work here," "Ship's come in" and all that jazz
     along my tranquil path.
Yet somewhere out there, a world awaits, poised to take me up
     again and squash this quiet.

But I'll be ready for it this time 'round, steeling my broken places
     against this sacred joy,
Renewed to bolster friends with cancer, parents whose own dark
     fears outweigh my own.

Yes, once I wash away all the dirt of anything but me in that big
     claw foot tub inside,
I'll leave the bed unmade, four pillows arranged against the
     window's sun,
My single cup unwashed, my trash and worries in the sink, and
     pack the pretty clothes I brought
But didn't wear, then move along more thankfully—because you
     were not there.

Twilight Fantasy

When I am old and dancing stark naked in my cardigan sweater,
And your hair is streaked with silver as you read our books in the den,
We'll be fine old Rockers worn smooth from loving hands.
      And our minds
Will be interwoven, when our skin boasts the brown,
        freckled maps of time …

We'll gaze at the embers together and listen to rain on our
Tin roof and talk about the first time we made love under a
Summer moon on the back porch so many heartbeats ago—and
Our laughter will bubble to the ceiling like children at summer camp.

Bathed in bride's lace and jasmine everywhere,
Seconds will slide into days like stones into water,
Our circular smiles drenching our hearts in full cycle.
And leaning together at last, in a whisper … we'll travel …

Familiar safaris of touch, palm to knuckles and fingers on lips,
Centered in the splendor of perfect balance. And even Death's blur,
By then, tuned and blended with the quiet harmony of our
      creaking oak
Chairs singing, under our one wide roof in spring showers
      and winter snows, until

We're two old ghosts tip-toeing down the Brazos
      after staying up way past bedtime.

Agnosia

Ashley Palmer

–A–

I feel like I need to give some background to this for Jase's sake: So we're sitting on the deck of the microbrewery down the street from her apartment when she says to me, "How am I going to know if you die?"

–B–

It was August, and we were at The Brew-B-Q. I remember he was telling me a story—some exaggerated thing that, in light of my virginal drug-taking history, I thought must have been certain death. Actually, it was something he did with *you*. But anyway, and I thought: This person is going to die, but I'm not going to know until months later or who knows how long. I mean, who would tell me?

–A–

And I say, "Well, who would tell me if *you* died?" and she starts talking about reading some book, some novel where the characters just know, and she's wondering whether she'd just know, or if we would. I guess there was this woman in the story who could feel that something had happened to the guy she was in love with. She didn't really say.

–B–

When we were in school together, back in college, we used to get these emails from the President's Office with ominous subject lines, just awful: "University mourns the death of …" and you could never tell who had died before opening them. There weren't enough characters in the subject line to fit the name.

They went to all the list-serves—faculty, staff, and students, thousands and thousands of people and so, however email works, different people would get them at different times. So I could know that some retired professor had passed on at 10 a.m., but you might not have gotten the email till 10 p.m., or vice versa.

It could be anyone in those emails—the professor at the front of a classroom or the person in the desk next to mine. The person that *used to be* in the desk next to mine. The closest I ever came to knowing the deceased was one degree of separation. It was a student who had burned himself alive in a car, and he was a student of a professor that my work-study supervisor had had for an honors class. So that's two degrees, rather.

The way that guy had died was just a rumor. They'd never say the means or method in the email. Instead it was always *suddenly* or *unexpectedly*. "So-and-so died unexpectedly in his Hometown City, USA, last Tuesday."

One weekend, I got three. *Three*. And you know how you do that with an email you're afraid of—just click on it real quickly the same way you'd tear open a letter? Just *click click click*. Or really *tap tap tap* because I was on my phone in an airport terminal.

And just, "So and so has died … the family is making arrangements … the counseling center is open at these hours … etc."

I didn't know any of them. But this could have been my cousin's best friend's former fiancé who I had this disconnected close attachment to, and here I am finding out during a weather delay at Gate 21C, and you already knew it while you were drinking your coffee that morning. All these people could know first, formally. What if I knew 'cause they knew—that collective consciousness idea, where it's supposedly easier for me to complete the crossword from yesterday's paper because all these other minds have already done it? But that's not knowing because he died; I wouldn't've felt it that way but, like, stolen it from the universe. I wanted to feel it.

Or fear is the same. The second you see that subject line, your stomach drops, and if you open it and know the person, that fear becomes confirmation that you knew. But it's not.

That was it; I stopped opening them after that, the emails.

–A–

But who *would* tell me? It's probably too much to ask parents to stay on top of that kind of thing if they're dealing with their kid dying—which, sorry, Jase that that leaves you, instead—and so I say we should make lists of these people. Because, you know, there are these certain people that are important to you but are on the periphery. They don't really know your other friends or your family. And they wouldn't be reading the newspapers from where you grew up or wherever they print obituaries, anymore.

But who are you supposed to give the list to? [Pauses.]

And what do you do with the people on the list?

–B–

Anyway, so we were on the patio of the Brew-B-Q.

And he said something about making lists of people, but there were logistical issues there, like: Who knows about the list, how often do you update it, what do you do with it, and so on. I mean, do you write this personal impersonal letter so that it covers all your close, yet disconnected friends?

It occurred to me that we could make some kind of system that involved checking in at regular intervals. Maybe just send a "10-4" type message once a month. Except, the problem was we never really saw each other at regular intervals, so that seemed incongruent. And also like a kind of commitment. It seemed like it would be enforcing a rule. But what if we drifted, like people do? Then one of us would have to issue a formal statement that you weren't going to tell each other you weren't dead, anymore.

That kind of separation is a different death. So I never suggested that solution out loud. I couldn't really. I prefer not knowing to living dead from one another. Is that hope?

–A–

I don't know. You seemed pretty serious about it, Bea. We talked about it like a joke, but after a few minutes, I could tell there was more there. And I know I'm leaving tomorrow, so there's that. Whenever I get on a plane, you freak out a little bit. Both of you do, actually.

People hear about these things, though. Plane wreck, train wreck—people talk. It's gossip. "Did you know that this guy died?"—which I said to you. That was the wrong thing to say. I quickly realized that was the wrooong thing to say.

You said, [mimics] "What?—So a mutual acquaintance that we don't even know we have is going to tell me *because it's a thing to talk about?*" and you gave me that look. I'm kind of afraid of that look.

[Laughs.]

So we were quiet for a minute until the waitress rescued us by asking about another drink order, which we had to talk to figure out, and that let us move on.

–B–

So basically, we decided nothing.

–A–

But I still thought about it. I mean, I left thinking about it to the point that I haven't turned the radio on yet on the drive back home.

–B–

After he left that night, I had this dream where three people died—each one closer and closer to me until it was him. The first was a distant relative that someone found face down in a shoddy apartment. Alcohol poisoning. A neighbor told me that while I was standing in my driveway thinking about something else.

Then there was a storm, a torrential-type thunderstorm where the rain is so heavy you can't see. All these people died. And somehow I learned that I lost two in the storm—my childhood best friend and Arie—and I began to cry.

He got caught in the rain—more than caught: he was intentionally racing a car through it. The tires hydroplaned, and the car spun and spun and careened off the road and got lodged in the mud, the front end folded up against an oak tree.

I drove down that road over what must have been the next day, sun shining of course. And the car was just one of many on the sides of the road that slid into the mud and the shade of the trees—all of it was just there for this parade of highway drivers caravanning by. Was he in there, still? I couldn't tell.

I imagined then, in the grief of my dream, having to write some consolation to his parents who I'd never met, though I was thinking mostly of his mother. I'd have to say that he was very dear to me, which is just an awful expression, and that I was sorry for the loss and how impossibly inadequate even the sound of these thoughts was. It was so horrific. I woke up weeping.

For the next week, maybe longer, I felt it all the time—the fear that seems like knowing.

–A–

It started raining about 15 minutes ago and got so hard I had to pull over onto the shoulder—you can probably hear it in the background.

I've been sitting here, watching these huge drops land on the windshield one after another. You can't tell them apart or separate them because as soon as they hit, they run into each other. And then I was thinking about snow—like if it were snowing instead, there'd be a second where the flakes would touch but still be separate before they started to melt together.

And then somehow confetti. Like, you remember when I got that interview, and you came over and threw confetti on me when I answered the door? All those little hole-punch circles were stuck in the carpet for like three months. They got in everything, man. I'd be putting on a pair of shoes and find one at the bottom. All these random places they ended up.

Except it only *seemed* random. Right? I mean, think about it—if you had enough information, you could tell where each piece was going to land. Like if you knew how the wind was blowing in the doorway of my apartment and how high you threw the confetti and how heavy they were, and if the little confettis ran into each other on the way down or if your breath blew them aside when you shouted, "Congratu-fucking-lations!" [Laughs.] As soon as they were set in motion, if you had all those variables, you could tell how they'd land.

I don't know if that answers your question or not, Bea. You're always saying that I'm gonna go first, so maybe that means you knew something from the beginning.

Maybe you just know.

But if it doesn't, if you actually get to hear this and meet my brother in a real way—which, Jase, Bea; Bea, Jase—then is my message to the friend on my list to you? I figure I am the only person who can tell you I'm gone, but maybe it's softened by you already knowing.

If it's possible, I'm sure I'll miss you. I do.

Johnny Messy Skin

Donna Walker-Nixon

Red Rover, Red Rover. Lizzie wanted them to call her over. The game the sixth-graders played at recess at the far end of the playground when she lived in Fort Worth: the game made her tingle thinking about charging through two hands held tightly together, but she wanted to run like the warm wind that brushed across her forehead as she picked up speed to break their hold. Being only in second grade, she could watch the games but never participate: those were the rules her teacher Mrs. Ingham said they must follow. Red Rover remained in Lizzie's mind the summer they moved to Allard's Crossing, when Lizzie complained, "Mama, there's nothing to do."

"Lizzie, there's everything to do. You can help me with little Grace."

Lizzie didn't like feeding her baby dolls with the grapefruit spoons Mama let her play with, much less taking care of her new baby sister, whose poop smelled like the dairy where Lizzie played with Karen when they lived in Fort Worth.

"You could read," Mama added.

Lizzie didn't want to read one more page of *Johnny Texas*, which her grandmother, Mrs. Joiner, gave her. Mostly Lizzie didn't care for the books Mrs. Joiner suggested. Lizzie and all her sisters called her Mrs. Joiner because that's what Daddy called her. To them, Mrs. Joiner meant grandma.

Honestly, Lizzie missed her best friend Karen more than she could count the words, and she missed going to sleep at night to the buzz of the airplanes landing at Meacham Field. And of course, the Airstream trailer which divided into two parts where Karen had her own house and Lizzie had hers. The only thing she didn't miss: the Putnams' dogs. When school started, Lizzie thought, I'll make new friends just like Karen.

That summer, every time they went to Turner's Store, Lizzie noted the red brick building with a black roof—the two-room country school she and Lana would attend in the fall. Lizzie couldn't help wondering why everything was completely different from Fort Worth. Stores were supposed to be like Everybody's and Leonard's with at least seven stories or, maybe, like Buddie's, where Daddy went to the back one night to buy some milk, and when he got to the front, they said a man just held up the store. At first, Lizzie didn't know what *held up* meant, but she put two and two together and figured out somebody had robbed the store.

In this country store, the gas pumps had glass bottles and contained orange soda pop gas. A green Pepsi sign with red letters hung loose from the screen door, and the Turners lived in the back. Mama said Mr. Turner would drive the bus that would take Lizzie and Lana to school. The slats of the wooden floor creaked, and Lizzie wanted to move back to Fort Worth and live with Mrs. Joiner.

When school started, there'd be a new female teacher who'd teach grades one through four. Lizzie didn't understand how one teacher could teach four grades. The night before school started, Lizzie remembered Fort Worth when Daddy worked nights and Mama sent her to the front bedroom to sleep by herself. Mama, Lana, and the rest of the family sat in the back and watched the news and weather with Harold Taft, the Dean of Texas Weathermen. In her mind pictures, the principal of the new school would look like Harold Taft: soft brown hair, eyes that sparkled when he predicted the weather, a nice comfortable old man of 45. Lizzie didn't know how to measure people's ages, but she tried to in her mind every time she met someone new. So when they walked across the newly poured concrete porch into the school, Lizzie already had a picture in mind of the teachers: she hadn't visualized the inside of the school. Instead of a long hallway, she entered through a short corridor that led to the big room. It wasn't big at all, but she learned the older students in the fifth through eighth grades had classes there. She wanted to walk all the way back to Fort Worth and Karen and Mrs. Joiner. More than anything else, she couldn't help thinking, Why'd Daddy want to own land and live on a farm like he did when he was growing up in Little Elm? But adults had their reasons.

Since the school didn't have a principal's office, Lizzie and Lana had to stand in the little room while Mama talked to an old man who was missing all of his bottom front teeth and whose two top teeth were stained brownish yellow from tobacco juice. He said his name was Mr. Cash Wilborn, and Mama said, "I've come to enroll my girls in first and third grade." From the way he nodded his head and twisted to motion to an old lady who had to be at least 86, Lizzie got the impression he already knew why Mama stood there holding Grace Kelley on her hip.

He introduced them to the white-haired old lady with yellow crust on her forehead. "Mrs. Bartles here will be your teacher," he said.

At the back of the room, a little boy with copper brown skin cried while no one paid attention to him and his daddy. Mama took Spanish when she attended junior college. She went over and said words Lizzie couldn't understand. The man smiled and said, "Gracias, Señora."

Lizzie heard the other kids whisper, "We don't got no use for wetbacks here." Lizzie didn't understand the words since everything garbled in her mind. A big girl with dirty blonde hair snickered; Lizzie did not like this girl.

Lizzie heard those words again, and this time she knew the big girl had whispered them. Mama had made sure Lizzie and her sisters dried their backs when they finished their baths. Mama whispered to Lana and Lizzie, "Did you hear what that girl said? She's old enough to know better. I don't want you to ever call him names just because he comes from a different culture." When Lizzie and Lana nodded that they understood, Mama said, "Good." Before Mama left, Lizzie heard her tell Mr. Wilborn about the big girl who called the boy names. Mr. Wilborn said he'd check into it, but he didn't.

Lizzie and Lana didn't have anyone to play with at recess, so they sat alone on the porch. Lizzie heard the big fat girl tell one of the kids, "I heard the NAACP's going to move a nigger family in. I guess they sent a Mexi-can't family instead."

Mr. Wilborn stood in the doorway; Mama would have spanked Lizzie if she used the *N* word, so Lizzie held her breath and waited for Mr. Wilborn to call the big girl aside. He only said, "Junie Small, don't go starting rumors."

"My daddy says that's what we get for electing a nigger-loving Catholic."

"He's our elected president, and we have to give him due respect, even if he's wrong," Mr. Wilborn said.

Mama told Lizzie educated people, like teachers, didn't let people say bad things, and Mama only had a junior college education. Mr. Wilborn went back in the school house. He didn't come out again until he stood on the porch and rang the bell, which meant for the kids to come inside.

While the teachers were inside, Lizzie heard one of the kids in first grade say she'd never seen a Messy Skin before. Junie Small corrected her, "It's Mexican, but you're right. He does have pretty ugly skin." So big Junie Small started calling the boy Johnny Messy Skin. Because she was the boss of the whole school, the other kids followed suit. In her mind, Lizzie called that mean, ugly girl Big Junie Small.

When she lived in Fort Worth, Lizzie liked recess. She couldn't play with Karen since they had different recess times, but Lizzie played with her friends the two Judies and Shirley. Mostly recess meant fun, except for the time Lizzie and one of the Judies saw Robert Muldoon peeing on the back side of the gym. Lizzie didn't want to tell on him, but Judy said they had to since it was only right. Lizzie wasn't sure, but in the end did what that Judy said. Lizzie felt bad for Robert Muldoon. Maybe, he just couldn't wait and thought no one was looking. And the see-saw sent a thrill up Lizzie's spine every time she hit the ground, making her almost pee in her panties. Overall, recess and playing meant fun. Not at this new school.

The big kids played scary games that made Lizzie want to run inside and read a book. Cathy, the other girl in Lizzie's grade, got to play big kid games like Crack the Whip and Annie-Over, where one team threw a softball over the roof of the small building where everyone crowded together to eat lunch. The other team caught the ball and tried to catch as many kids as they could to make them play on their side. The rules confused Lizzie, who shivered with fear that the ball could accidentally hit her head and give her a brain concussion.

Now the whole school did play Red Rover, Red Rover, sometimes. Lizzie got chosen next to last. Gary Brister, who was just a year older, held her arm, not her hand, so tight she thought her arm would crack if a kid tried to break through. Lizzie bristled with fear because the kids on the other side thought they could loosen Gary's hold easily, and they kept trying to break through when their names were called. They couldn't at first, but Lizzie had large purple bruises on her arm from his fierce hold. Finally a kid broke through, and Gary looked at her with utter disgust and said, "You're a baby." Then he had to go on the other side, and the game and Lizzie's fear continued while the teachers sat on the front porch and gossiped about students from poor families.

Lizzie didn't get to play with the big kids, except maybe once on the merry-go-round when she held on for dear life while three big boys pushed it harder and harder. She didn't want to tell them whizzing round and round scared her. When the big kids played and Lizzie got left behind, Lizzie and Lana sat on the sidewalk by themselves. Roseanne, a girl in second grade, said, "Come on. Play with me and Cindy." Roseanne had golden-olive skin, and Lizzie didn't particularly like her. Her offer gave Lizzie and Lana a chance to do something besides sit on the sidewalk next to the teachers and hear what they said about poor kids, including the boy Mama told Lizzie to be nice to.

The big kids, including Cathy, played Crack the Whip over by the baseball field, freeing up the merry-go-round. Roseanne defined the game they'd play. "Cindy has spun gold hair. She'll play princess, and I'll be her royal advisor," Roseanne announced. They would reign in the middle of the merry-go-round while Lizzie and Lana sat on opposite sides and moved it round and round with their feet. "Won't that be fun?" Roseanne asked. Cindy nodded. Lana shook her head up and down, but Lizzie didn't want to play. Roseanne said again, "We'll have lots of fun." And the game began. Of course, Lizzie and Lana couldn't get the merry-go-round to move fast enough to suit Roseanne, who ordered, "Faster, slaves. Faster." Her voice carried across to the baseball field, and some of the big kids came to watch Roseanne bark orders to Lizzie and Lana. Lizzie wanted to quit, but Roseanne said they couldn't stop now. Lizzie could only think the teachers had to know but didn't do a thing to stop Lizzie from shrinking further into the background of her thoughts in humiliation.

A week later, the kids in the big room played chase; Big Junie Small said Lizzie proved she wasn't worth a thing when they played Red Rover, Red Rover. She looked where Johnny sat at the bottom of the slide, all alone. Big Junie Small ran to him and said real loud, "I've got a new game. We'll call it Johnny Messy Skin." The one who was it had Johnny Messy Skin, like it was a communicable disease. Lizzie now hated school. Big Junie Small told everyone what to do, and the teachers didn't make her stop. They sat on the porch in rockers and drank coffee.

In October, Lizzie came down with the kissing disease, which she got from an older cousin, and Lizzie got to miss a month of school. Mama helped her with her homework and taught Lizzie a whole lot more than Mrs. Bartles. Lizzie got better, and the doctor said she could return to school. Lizzie asked if they could move back to Fort Worth, but Mama said they'd have trouble selling the farm and Daddy liked living in the country.

On her first day back, when Lizzie got on the bus, Big Junie Small teased her. "Better watch it, or Little Lizzie here will steal your boyfriends." Everybody on the bus laughed, just like they did when they made fun of Johnny when they played chase. When they got to school, they had 30 minutes before the bell rang. Big Junie Small said, "Let's play Johnny Messy Skin."

All the kids in the big room chased each other. Johnny sat on the ground and cried. Lizzie could hear Mama saying, "Don't make fun of him." The only reason she didn't want to come back to school in the first place was recess and the Johnny Messy Skin game. Lizzie was glad Big Junie Small thought she was not big enough to play their game, but then Big Junie ran over to the sidewalk where Lizzie sat.

"I'm glad you're back." Big Junie Small smiled, and Lizzie almost liked her since she was almost nice. "I guess you're big enough now. You can play Johnny Messy Skin."

Lizzie remembered what Mama said about making fun of Johnny that first day. Lizzie didn't like the game, but she also didn't like having to play with the little kids. Finally, she said, "The doctor says I have to take things easy." Lizzie lied like Mama told her never to do, unless she told someone she liked a hair ribbon that she really didn't like. "It could be a whole year before I can run and play games."

"Sure," she said.

Lizzie feared Big Junie Small would call her a sissy, but she didn't. Lizzie heard the other kids yelling, "You Got Johnny Messy Skin." He sat on the ground all by himself and cried. Cindy said, "Let's get the boys and play Red Rover, Red Rover. I'm getting bored."

Red Rover, Red Rover could be fun when the big kids didn't play. Lana would stay by Lizzie's side. But Red Rover, Red Rover was Lana's favorite game when the little kids played. Lizzie said, "You go ahead."

There sat Johnny Messy Skin on the slide. Lizzie knew his stomach felt like a knot that could not unwind. He couldn't speak good English, and he couldn't tell people how he felt. She wanted to say she'd play on the merry-go-round with him. He could push her, and she wouldn't have to run. In her mind, though, she could imagine Big Junie Small teasing, "Lizzie got her kissing disease from Johnny." All the kids would call Lizzie Johnny's girlfriend. They'd sing, "Johnny Messy Skin and Lizzie sitting in a tree. K-I-S-S-I-N-G." They'd ask when the wedding was, and Big Junie Small was just mean enough to do it, too. So Lizzie sat in the shade under the school roof and pretended she'd be sick for a long time and couldn't play anything for at least a year. Lizzie felt pride because she didn't make fun of Johnny, but she was mad at herself because Mama took a stand. Lizzie wished she could be like Mama and say, "It isn't nice to make fun of people because they're from a different culture."

Later, in history, through the thin partition, Lizzie heard Mr. Wilborn brag about Davy Crockett being his distant relative: "He fought in the Alamo and did what was right—no matter what." Mama thought well of people who went to school and completed their degrees, and she had taught Lizzie to respect teachers because of their accomplishments. After Mr. Wilborn looked the other way when Big Junie Small played her game, Lizzie couldn't see that an education made him any better than Mama with her two years of junior college. Lizzie concluded he didn't have any business bragging about Davy Crockett. She didn't know why, but she thought his claim might be not be true, and Mama had taught Lizzie and her sisters not to call a person a liar, even if you say it only in your own private mind.

A Single Day

Danielle Kilgo

Swing

Beach

Shovel

Sleep

Acknowledgments

The first appearances of previously published works are listed below:

Rosemary Catacalos — "Picture Postcard from a Painter" was included in Catacalos' collection, *Begin Here* (Wings Press, 2013); "La Casa," "Homesteaders," and "Swallow Wings" were included in her collection, *Again for the First Time* (Tooth of Time Press, 1984; Wings Press, 2013).

Tammy Cromer-Campbell — "Jeremy" photo was included in *Fruit of the Orchard/Environmental Justice in East Texas* (University of North Texas Press, 2006).

Sherry Craven — "Coleman, Texas, and Us" was first published in *The Langdon Review of the Arts in Texas* (Vol. 6, 2009-2010).

Ysabel de la Rosa — "Family Tree" and "En el estado de no estar" first appeared in Red River Review, November 2011.

Susie Kelly Flatau — "Blue Hole" first appeared as "The Spirit of the Blue Hole" in the *Story Circle Network Newsletter*.

Anne McCrady — "Camp Song," "Dusk," and "Dove Season," are from her collection, *Letting Myself In* (Dos Gatos Press, 2013).

Mary Guerrero Milligan — Earlier versions of "Lotería: La Rosa" appeared in *Blue Mesa Review* and *Daughters of the Fifth Sun: A Collection of Latina Fiction and Poetry* (Putnam/ Riverhead, 1995).

Naomi Shihab Nye — "Farming" and "Loving Working" first appeared in *San Pedro Review*; "Room for You Here" in *Molussus: World Poetry Portfolio,* No. 37 (http://www.molossus.co/worldpoetryportfolio/world-poetry-portfolio-37-naomi-shihab-nye/); "Song Book" on Poets.org.

Leslie Jill Patterson — "On Forgiving" will be published in *1966: A Journal of Creative Nonfiction* (Trinity University: December 2015).

Hermine Pinson — "Four Sisters and the Dance" first appeared in *Meridians*; "From One Music Lover to Another" was included in Pinson's collection, *Mama Yetta and Other Poems* (Wings Press).

Catherine Rainwater — "Collared by the Jaguar: Kay Sutherland (1942-2002)" appeared in *Desert Candle* (May 2006). Photograph of Kay Sutherland by Jim McCulloch.

Paula Reynolds – "A Cowgirl's Life for Me" first appeared in *Music of Your Texas Heritage Magazine*, Fall 2008.

Jan Seale— "Walking Straight," "Power," "Hypomimia (forced laughing)," and "Haiku Cycle on Pills" all appeared in her collection, *The Parkinson Poems* (Lamar University Press, 2014).

Frances Vick, "My Memorial Days" first appeared in *The PathFinder*, ed. Joyce Gibson Roach (Westlake Historical Preservation Board , Vol. 2, No. 1, Summer 2003).

Author Photo Credits

Liz Bates by Valerie Payne of Photerium, Austin, Texas

Cassy Burleson by Curtis W. Callaway

Rosemary Catacalos by Bryce Milligan

Rachel Crawford by Haley Nafe

Tammy Cromer-Campbell by Scott C Campbell

Ysabel de la Rosa by Melissa Severson

Diane Fanning by Peggy Parks Photography

Gail Folkins by Barbara Christoper

Mary Milligan by Bryce Milligan.

Karla K. Morton by Bill Mackey

Susan White Norman by Kellie Philips

Amanda Pearcy by Todd V. Wolfson

Paula Reynolds by Marty Reynolds

Mary Rogers by Jill Johnson

Jan Seale by Erren Seale

Frances Vick by Ray Bryant of Bryant Studios, Dallas

Donna Walker-Nixon by Curtis W. Callaway

Christine Warren by Tosh Brown Photography

Editors' Acknowledgments

Heartfelt thanks to Bryce Milligan of Wings Press for his years of extraordinary support of Texas women writers—and for representing the true depth and diversity of the literature of this vitally multicultural and multiethnic state.

—The Editors

With love and admiration, I revere the legacies of my grandmother Virtie Allard Joiner, who shared family lore and loved us unconditionally, and my mother Verlyn Walker, who taught us to face death without fear and to stand up for what is fair. My sisters Linda Pruden, Wendy Walker, and Monie Putty—each live out the legacies of our grandmother and mother. My shoulda-been sisters Drue Annelle Porter Parker, Mary Mahoney, Ikuko Nawa, and Elizabeth Dell create their own legacies. My stepdaughters Jean Nixon-Telfer and Nancy Garcia have stayed with me through tough times—love kept us together.

Drue Porter Parker contributed more than money to this book. She guided me through the editing process and provided love and feedback. Thus, I share her tribute to her own mother, who demonstrated the character and strength that we celebrate in this book:

> Para Porter was the first woman to get a Ph.D. from Baylor University. She took a teaching degree in the 1930s with her father telling her that there was no money to send a 'daughter' to college when she had brothers whose kids needed food. Mother worked full time, provided love and support to two young children, and still managed to complete her doctorate in the summer of 1960. Mother never forgot her rural roots or her mentor, Dr. Lorena B. Stretch. Mother always said, "My mother wanted me to be a teacher and to be the best." Mother admired John Dewey's philosophy of learning by doing and was recognized as a pioneer in early Head Start programs.
>
> —Donna Walker-Nixon

I am grateful for God's grace, good genes, and a lifetime of great storytellers, including my dad and a long line of Eds, Eddies and Edwards whose womenfolk supported them. I thank those who taught me to think, write, and believe in truth and music, including poets Marie Lively, Joseph Colin Murphey, Vassar Miller, and Anne Sexton; writer/educators such as Leon Hale, Donna M. Johnson, George Baker, and John and Suanne Rouche; my *Langdon Review* "family;" and my esteemed colleagues and students. This tribute would not be complete without the names of these true friends: Jasa, Dana, AmaSue, Sue, Karen, Anneliese, Gail, GalaDawn, Davie Ann, Jamie, Carolyn, Pam, Kathy, June, Anne, Rickey, Liz, Mia, Sara, Margaret, Jerry, and all the "girls" of '65: Judy, Eva, Donna, Shirley, Nancy and Diane. And thank you, Prince Charming, for finding me at last because I kissed a lot of frogs along the way.

—Cassy Burleson

For my grandmother, who grounded me with stories about life as the daughter of Texas sharecroppers; for my mother, who lifted me with songs about Lady Mary, Pretty Boy Floyd, and Beau Ramble; for my daughter, who is carrying our stories and songs into the future and creating her own; for my mother-in-law, whose strength lives on in her son.

—Rachel Crawford

Ashley Palmer thanks Texas for the shelter of two cities and the life-changing set of years they hosted. Thanks to Stephen Boyes and Olive Odell, my modern family, unwavering. Thanks to colleagues and friends in Waco: Lenore Wright, Theresa Williams and the informal support of the Academy for Teaching and Learning in the early stages of this project; Chad Craig, dearest friend and best reader; Hunter Hale, fellow sojourner; and Trent Dougherty, my favorite epistemologist. In Austin, thanks also to my extended family, Kendal Reddell and Brent Hamilton. Thanks to Cassy Burleson, Donna Walker-Nixon, and Rachel Crawford, the three Texas writers who invited her to her first rodeo. And finally, thanks to her darling daughter, Olive, with whom she shares a love of words and books.

—Ashley Palmer

Contributors

Christine Albert has called Austin, Texas, home since 1982, nurturing a career as a singer/songwriter. She has released 11 CDs, as a solo artist and with her husband, Chris Gage, as Albert and Gage. She has performed in 17 countries. Albert is the founder of Swan Songs, a nonprofit that fulfills musical last wishes for the terminally ill; co-founder of Austin Songwriter's Group; and national vice chair of The Recording Academy.

Rebecca Balcárcel's first book of poems is *Palabras in Each Fist,* released from Pecan Grove Press in 2010. Her work has appeared in more than 40 journals, including *North American Review, Third Coast, Oklahoma Review, Concho River Review,* and *descant.* She teaches creative writing at Tarrant County College's NE campus. Google her name to find her website, her YouTube channel called S*ixMinuteScholar,* her blog called *PoettoPoet.*

Elizabeth Bates sees the world differently every day through her one-year-old son's eyes. She appreciates this fresh perspective and the joy her son and husband bring her. In her spare time, her family travels Texas to see loved ones. They delight in eating where the locals eat wherever they go. When she has downtime, Elizabeth preserves precious memories using crafts and scrapbooks.

Jeanne Bennett launched Calliope Press in 1969 and has since published more than 25 books. She served as editor of *Granbury Showcase* and president of the Writers Bloc in Granbury. As a bookbinder/artist, her works have been exhibited throughout the United States. For the last ten years, her interest has focused on the little-known art of fore-edge painting. Her latest book is *Hidden Treasures: the History and Technique of Fore-edge Painting.*

Betsy Berry is senior lecturer in British and American Literature at the University of Texas at Austin and the author of poems, critical articles, and short stories. A story recently appeared in the *Oxford American.* She is currently writing a memoir, *The Buried Life: A Family Romance,* and a collection of short stories, *Tally Me Banana and Other Fragments Shored Against My Ruin.*

Cassy Burleson's "day job" is as a senior lecturer in Baylor University's department of Journalism, PR & New Media. She was the 2014 co-president of the American Studies Association of Texas and has worked since 1965 as a writer/editor. Her poetry has appeared in *Whetstone, Stone Drum, Green Fuse,* and as a chapter in the 2010 *Langdon Review of the Arts in Texas.* She published a second and third paper on a 16-year study of the Jasper dragging death, co-authored with Dr. Mia Moody-Ramirez, that appeared in the *Journal of the American Studies.* She received the Distinguished Professor award at the University of Mary Hardin-Baylor in 2001, was a Mortar Board Distinguished Professor at Baylor in 2010.

Rosemary Catacalos, the 2013 Poet Laureate of Texas—the first ever Latina Poet Laureate of Texas. She is the author of *Again for the First Time* (Tooth of Time, 1984; Wings Press, 2013), which received the Texas Institute of Letters poetry prize. She has been collected in the annual *The Best American Poetry* (1996 and 2003). Catacalos also has published two fine press chapbooks, *As Long As It Takes* (Iguana, 1984) and *Begin Here* (Wings, 2013). Catacalos has received Stegner/Stanford University, Dobie Paisano, and National Endowment for the Arts fellowships, and her work has been translated into Spanish, Italian, and Greek. From 1996 to 2003 she was a Visiting Scholar at Stanford University's Institute for Research on Women and Gender. Catacalos has been executive director of San Francisco's Poetry Center and American Poetry Archives, and the San Antonio literary center, Gemini Ink.

A native Texan, **Laurie Champion** moved to California to work at San Diego State University, where her teaching and research emphasize the intersection of ethnicity, gender, and class. Her short stories, creative nonfiction, scholarly essays, and book reviews have appeared in distinguished journals such as *Short Story, American Literature Southern Quarterly*, and *Texas Review*. She has edited or co-edited several collections of scholarly essays and short stories, including *5 X 5: Twenty-Five Stories by Five Texas Writers, Texas Told'em: Gambling Stories*, and *Texas Short Stories*.

Sandra Cisneros is the founder of the Alfredo Cisneros del Moral Foundation, the Elvira Cisneros Award, and the Macondo Foundation, all of which work on behalf of creative writers. She is the recipient of numerous awards including a MacArthur Fellowship. Her writings include fiction: *The House on Mango Street, Caramelo*, and *Woman Hollering Creek*; poetry: *My Wicked Wicked Ways* and *Loose Woman*; and a children's book, *Hairs/Pelitos* and *Bravo, Bruno*, with artist Leslie Greene, published in Italy. She is currently at work on several writing projects including *A House of My Own*, a book of essays; *Writing in My Pajamas*, writing tips; and *Infinito*, stories. Her most recent book is *Have You Seen Marie?*, an illustrated book for adults with artist Ester Hernández.

Cheryl Clements is an essayist, fiction writer, and movie producer. She has published in *Southwestern American Literature, Journal of the American Studies Association of Texas, Short Story, CCTE Studies, Langdon Review,* and the *Houston Chronicle,* among others. From 2011-2013 she received the George Nixon Award for Prose from the Conference of College Teachers of English. Cheryl is Professor of English at Blinn College/Bryan Campus and lives with her husband and daughter in College Station, Texas.

Sarah Cortez, member of the Texas Institute of Letters, is the author of an acclaimed poetry collection, *How to Undress a Cop*. She is the winner of the PEN Texas literary award. Her memoir, *Walking Home: Growing Up Hispanic in Houston* was published by Texas Review Press, as well as a poetry collection, *Cold Blue Steel*. Her poems, essays, and short fiction are widely anthologized.

Sherry Craven taught English at Midland College and West Texas A&M. She retired and lives in Jasper, Texas. She is published in *Amarillo Bay, New Texas, Two Southwests, The Witness, Windhover, descant, Langdon Review of the Arts in Texas, RiverSedge, The Texas Review, Concho River Review, Suddenly, Texas Poetry 2, Quotable Texas Women,* and *Writing on the Wind*. She won the Conference of College Teachers of English 2005 poetry award and published a poetry collection, *Standing at the Window*.

Rachel Crawford has worked as a waitress, guitar teacher, childbirth educator, high school and college English teacher, editor, and writer. Her poetry has appeared in *Red Rock Review, Mudlark, Lucid Rhythms, The Lyric,* and *Figures of Speech,* and she has received two Beall Poetry Festival Poetry in the Arts awards. Born in Dallas, she holds degrees from The University of Texas at Austin and Baylor University. She currently lives in central Texas with her husband Todd, daughter Haley, friendly bulldog Bella, and evil cat Marley.

Tammy Cromer-Campbell is an award-winning photographer known for her social documentary work. She received her associate's degree in photography from Kilgore College and has studied with several master photographers. UNT Press published *Fruit of the Orchard/Environmental Justice in East Texas*. Included in public and private collections internationally, Cromer-Campbell is a 2009 and 2010 Honoree for National Women's History Project.

Diane Fanning is an Edgar-nominated author with 20 published books including both fiction and non-fiction titles. A co-founder of Women in Crime Ink, she has appeared on the *Today Show*, *48 Hours*, *20/20*, *Forensic Files*, the Biography Channel, E!, and the BBC, as well as numerous cable network news and crime shows. Her most recent book is *Sleep My Darlings* (St. Martin's Press, 2013). Raised in Baltimore, she spent 20 years in Virginia and now lives in New Braunfels, Texas.

Susie Kelly Flatau is a former educator—for a Texas school district. She is a writer: author/co-author of *Counter Culture Texas*, *From My Mother's Hands*, *Reaching Out to Troubled Kids*, *Red Boots & Attitude*, and *Quotable Texas Women*. Her writing has appeared in various publications. Having spent many years facilitating creativity workshops, she is now an abstract artist.

Malou Flato, cover artist for *Her Texas*, divides her time between Austin, Texas, and Paradise Valley, Montana. Working in clay, watercolors, graphite, oils, acrylic and digital prints, she highlights the exquisite relationship between light, form, and color. Flato's work has been featured in a number of exhibitions from Texas to Wyoming. Her work is also included in many significant collections: American Bank, Coca-Cola, SBC, Shell Oil Company, Texas A&M University, Texas Commerce (Chase) Bank, and Texas Instruments.

Gail Folkins often writes about her roots in the American West. Her creative nonfiction book *Texas Dance Halls: A Two-Step Circuit* (Texas Tech University Press) was a popular culture finalist in the *ForeWord Review* Book of the Year awards for 2007, while her essay "A Palouse Horse" was a notable essay in *The Best American Essays 2010*.

Ruthie Foster's astonishing voice has taken her from rural Texas to a tour of duty with the U.S. Navy Band to New York City. After moving back to Texas, she became a regular nominee at the Austin Music Awards, winning Best Folk Artist in 2004-05 and Best Female Vocalist in 2007-08. Ruthie has added a Grammy nomination to her list of achievements and has won (seemingly contradictory) Blues Music Association awards for both Best Traditional and Best Contemporary Female Blues Artist.

Frances Hatfield grew up in Louisiana and East Texas. She studied philosophy and creative writing at the University of Dallas and graduated from the University of California at Santa Cruz with a double major in psychology and "Mythic Enactment." She studied poetry with Lucille Clifton and won the UC Poet Laureate Award. Hatfield earned her doctorate in East-West Psychology in 2000 from the California Institute of Integral Studies. *Rudiments of Flight*, her first collection of poetry, was a finalist for the Texas Institute of Letters Poetry Prize.

Tish Hinojosa grew up in San Antonio, the youngest of 13 children to Mexican immigrant parents. In 1979, she moved to New Mexico and began writing her own songs. In 1988, she achieved a national debut release (*Homeland*), and she has released 15 albums to date. Her latest CD is *After the Fair*. Tish has contributed her talent to numerous issues such as bilingual education, immigration and farm workers' rights. She has toured internationally. For the last several years, she has divided her time between Austin, Texas, and Hamburg, Germany. Her website and blog can be found at http://www.mundotish.com.

Kathleen Hudson is a professor of English at Schreiner University. She is the director and founder of the Texas Heritage Music Foundation, located on the Schreiner campus, which seeks to "preserve and perpetuate the traditions in Texas music. A 2010 Piper Professor

recipient, she is the author of two important books on Texas music published by the University of Texas Press: *Telling Stories, Writing Songs: An Album of Texas Songwriters (2001)* and *Women in Texas Music: Stories and Songs (2007)*. She is committed to the possibility that stories and songs make a difference in the world.

Guida Jackson's ancestors settled in Blackland Prairie's Peters Colony. She was born in the Panhandle, educated on the Llano Estacado and West Coast, married a South Plains medical doctor, had offspring in the Grand Prairie, Ozark foothills, Piney Woods, and Gulf Coast, where she taught. She married a Jersey Pine Barrens artist and moved to the Big Thicket. She retired to Katy Prairie with a Burns Scholar from Scotland's Lowlands. She is the author of 20 books, ranging from *Traditional Epics: A Literary Companion* to *Women Leaders of Africa, Asia, Middle East, and Pacific: A Biographical Reference.*

Donna M. Johnson is the author of *Holy Ghost Girl*, a critically acclaimed memoir. It received a Books for a Better Life Award and the Mayborn Creative Nonfiction Prize. Her work appears in several anthologies as well as *The Huffington Post* and the *Dallas Morning News*. She lives in Austin with her husband, writer Kirk Wilson.

Sobia Khan is an English Faculty member at Richland College, Dallas. Her creative work includes short fiction, flash fiction, and translations of Urdu poetry. Her work has been published in *Pakistaniaat: A Journal of Pakistan Studies*, *RiversEdge, Sojourn*, and *Parallax*, and other journals. She has won awards for her work from *Women on Writing, Sojourn Magazine*, the Dallas Public Library, and the League for Innovation. She lives between cities, languages, and homes in Dallas, Karachi, and her imagination.

Danielle Kilgo is a freelance photographer. She received her B.A. and M.A. from Baylor University. Danielle teaches photojournalism at the University of Texas in Austin, where she is pursuing her doctoral degree. Her work is featured in numerous university publications from Baylor University, Baylor Law School, New Mexico State University, and the University of Texas in Austin.

Helen Kwiatkowski holds a MFA from Texas A&M University-Commerce. Her solo exhibitions include the Fayetteville Underground, Central Texas College, the Cultural Activities Center and the Art Center of the Ozarks. In 2009, her work was included in *The Texas Biennial: An Independent Survey of Contemporary Texas Art.* She is working on a limited edition "artist book" called *I Build a Lighted House* (working title) based on her series of Little Helen paintings.

Diana Lopez is the author of the adult novel *Sofia's Saints* and middle-grade novels *Confetti Girl,* and *Ask My Mood Ring How I Feel.* Her most recent book is a young adult novel, *Choke.* Her fiction has been published in several anthologies and journals. She has appeared on NPR's *Latino USA* and is the winner of the Alfredo Cisneros del Moral Award and the William Allen White Award. Diana teaches English and works with CentroVictoria, an organization devoted to promoting Latino literature, at the University of Houston-Victoria, where she also edits the journal, *Huizache.*

Anne McCrady's poetry and creative nonfiction appear in journals, arts magazines, anthologies, and her own award-winning collections. Her most recent poetry book is *Letting Myself In* (Dos Gatos Press). Besides her writing, Anne is an inspirational speaker, storyteller, and workshop leader. A lifelong advocate for social justice and peace, she is the founder of InSpiritry—Putting

Words to Work for a Better World. She lives in Tyler, Texas.

Celeste Guzmán Mendoza holds a B.A. from Barnard College, an M.F.A. in poetry from Bennington Writing Seminars, and she is working on her Ph.D. in the Program for Higher Education Leadership at the University of Texas at Austin. She has held residencies with Macondo Writing Workshops and Hedgebrook for Women Writers. She is a co-founder of CantoMundo, a master workshop for Latina/o poets. She received the Premió Poesía Tejana Award for *Cande, te estoy llamando* (Wings, 1999). Her most recent collection is *Beneath the Halo* (Wings, 2013).

Mary Guerrero Milligan has been the librarian at St. Luke's Episcopal School in San Antonio since 1986. Her MLS is from the University of North Texas in Denton. She has worked in university, public, and school libraries. A former chair of the south Texas region of the Texas Library Association, she has been TLA's "member of the month" is a member of the Texas Bluebonnet Award selection committee. She was also a member of the Texas State Library's "Task Force on Transforming Texas Libraries for the 21st Century." She was a co-editor of two ground-breaking anthologies of Latina literature: *Daughters of the Fifth Sun: A Collection of Latina Fiction and Poetry* (Putnam/ Riverhead, 1995) and *¡Floricanto Sí! A Collection of Latina Poetry* (Penguin, 1998). Other publications have appeared in *Pax*, *Blue Mesa Review*, the *San Antonio Express-News*, and elsewhere.

Melissa Morphew has published five poetry collections. Her most recent book, *Bluster*, won the Sacramento Poetry Center Book Award. Her work has been included in *The Georgia Review*, *Shenandoah*, *Parnassus: Poetry in Review*, *Prairie Schooner*, and elsewhere. She teaches English and Creative Writing at Sam Houston State University, and she lives in the small community of Riverside, Texas.

karla k. morton, the 2010 Texas Poet Laureate, is a member of the Texas Institute of Letters and graduate of Texas A&M University. She is a Betsy Colquitt Award Winner, twice an Indie National Book Award Winner, and is the author of eight books of poetry. Morton has been twice nominated for the Pushcart Prize and is a nominee for the National Cowgirl Hall of Fame. She established a collaborative touring exhibit titled *No End of Vision: Texas as Seen by Two Laureates* where she paired photography and poetry with 2005 Texas Poet Laureate Alan Birkelbach.

Photographer **Deana Newcomb** has worked for more than 20 years as a publicity still photographer on more than 35 features films, including *Twilight;* Disney's *The Alamo*; *China: The Panda Adventure*, an IMAX production shot in China; *Robocop;* and *Waiting for Guffman.* Her work has appeared in countless publications. In her personal work, she has photographed extensively throughout South Asia, Europe, South America, Mexico, and the U.S.

Susan White Norman is a fiction writer and instructor at the University of Texas-Dallas, where she is completing her doctorate in literature and aesthetics. Fiction editor for *Reunion: The Dallas Review*, her fiction has appeared in several journals, including *The Literary Review.* She was nominated for a 2013 Pushcart Prize.

Naomi Shihab Nye lives in San Antonio. She has written or edited 35 books, including *Habibi, The Turtle of Oman, 19 Varieties of Gazelle: Poems of the Middle East, Fuel.* She edited the anthology *Is This Forever or What? Poems and Paintings from Texas,* and the popular *This Same Sky: A Collection of Poems from around the World.* A National Book Award finalist, she has won many awards, among them four Pushcart Prizes, the Jane Addams Children's Book award, the Paterson Poetry Prize, and The Academy of American Poets' Lavan Award. She is a Chancellor of the Academy of American Poets.

Ashley Palmer earned her Ph.D. in sociology from Baylor University where she specialized in the qualitative study of religion and marriage & family. She was a graduate fellow with the Academy for Teaching and Learning then worked as the center's interim assistant director, taught, and led faculty-staff seminars on new media. In 2012, she received the ACC&U's K. Patricia Cross Future Leaders Award. She is completing an M.F.A. in creative nonfiction at the University of North Carolina-Wilmington.

Deborah Parédez is the author of the poetry collection, *This Side of Skin*, and the critical study, *Selenidad: Selena, Latinos, and the Performance of Memory*. Her oft-anthologized poetry was recently featured on the cover of *Poetry*. She is an Associate Professor of English at the University of Texas and co-founder of CantoMundo, a national organization for Latina/o poets. A 13th generation Tejana, Parédez grew up in San Antonio.

Leslie Jill Patterson is a recipient of a 2012 Embrey Human Rights Fellowship; the 2013 Everett Southwest Literary Award, the 2014 Time and Place Prize (France); and a 2014 Soros Justice Fellowship. Her work has recently appeared in *Texas Monthly, Gulf Coast, Baltimore Review,* and *Literature: A Pocket Anthology*. In 1999, she founded *Iron Horse Literary Review,* and she serves as copy editor for *Creative Nonfiction*.

Amanda Pearcy, an Austin-based singer-songwriter born in Houston, "has an attractive bluesy husk of a voice that is perfectly suited to her gospel soul and country sound. She creates a hugely evocative atmosphere on every song ... with lyrics that are beautiful poetic reflections on life." Her CD, *Royal Street*, was Number 1 on the March 2013 EuroAmericana Chart.

Hermine Pinson, born and raised in Beaumont, has published three poetry collections, most recently *Dolores is Blue/Dolorez is Blues*. Her first CD was *Changing the Changes in Poetry & Song*, in special collaboration with Estella Majozo and Pulitzer-prize winning poet Yusef Komunyakaa. She has performed in the U.S., Europe, and Africa. She teaches creative writing and African American literature at the College of William and Mary.

Catherine Rainwater is Professor of English at St. Edward's University in Austin. Widely published in American and Native American literature, her works appear in books and in journals including *American Literature, Modern Fiction Studies, LIT: Literature,* and others. She is author of *Dreams of Fiery Stars: The Transformations of Native American Fiction*. She has also published literary nonfiction works, one of which won the Penelope Niven Creative Nonfiction Award in 2004.

Charlotte Renk often treks the network of trails behind her small cedar cabin, noting wildflowers, birds, snakes, and turtles. She fuses natural images with experience to craft poems and stories striving to capture the heart of truth, however elusive. Besides teaching English and humanities, she has published two books, *These Holy Hunger* and *Solidago, an Altar to Weeds*, and appeared in numerous journals.

Paula A. Reynolds has been an educator for most of her life. Her love for adventure has taken her from roundups to flying planes to running marathons. Paula is a regular contributor to *Music of Your Texas Heritage* and a freelance writer. She holds a master's degree in psychology from Texas A&M-Corpus Christi. She and her husband live in the Texas Hill Country.

Marilyn Robitaille is a professor of English and Director of International Programs at Tarleton State University in Stephenville, where she is co-editor of *Langdon Review of the Arts in Texas.* She also administers all programs associated with Tarleton's internationalization. She earned her M.A. from the Bread Loaf School, Middlebury College, and her Ph.D. from Texas Woman's University.

Ysabel de la Rosa is a fourth-generation Texan whose poetry has appeared in numerous literary journals. Her feature writing has been published in more than 45 publications in the United States and abroad. She was a finalist for the 2006 Pablo Neruda Poetry Award. Her chapbook, *Life on Interior Plains*, received an honorable mention from Kulupi Press. Her career experience includes editing, translation, and graphic design.

Mary Russell Rogers is an award-winning feature writer with the *San Angelo Standard Times* and the *Fort Worth Star-Telegram.* She lives in Fort Worth, with her husband, Charles W. Rogers, and two dogs. She is the author of *Dancing Naked: Memorable Encounters with Unforgettable Texans* and was included in *Noah's Ride*, a collaborative novel (TCU Press).

Frances Treviño Santos was a 1999 NEH fellow for "integrating U.S. Latino Literature in the secondary classroom." She received the Premió Poesía Tejana Award for *The Laughter of Doves* (Wings, 2000). A 2001 fellow of the Alfredo Cisneros del Moral Foundation, her most recent collection is *Cayetana* (Wings, 2007). She teaches American and British Literature in San Antonio.

Jan Epton Seale was the 2012 Texas Poet Laureate. She is the author of nine volumes of poetry and several books of short fiction and essays. Her writing has appeared in numerous journals and anthologies, as well as

being featured on National Public Radio. Jan's books of poetry include *Nape, The Wonder Is* (Ink Brush Press), *Valley Ark: Life Along the Rio* (50 poems with 50 photos of the Lower Rio Grande Valley), *Jan Seale: New and Selected Poems 1974-2012* (TCU Press), and *Jan Seale: The Parkinson Poems* (Lamar University Press). Her latest fiction book is *Appearances* (Lamar University Press).

Carmen Tafolla was the first poet laureate of San Antonio (2012-2014). One of the most often anthologized of all Latina poets, she is, as Ana Castillo put it, "a pioneer of Chicana literature." The author of numerous books of poetry, as well as books for children and young adults, she is the recipient of the Tomás Rivera Award for both children's literature and young adult literature, the International Latino Book Award for poetry, and the Américas Award. Her latest books of poetry is *This River Here: Poems of San Antonio.*

Emy Taylor is a Dallas-based singer-songwriter. A consummate storyteller, she takes audiences on a journey of everyday life, told from a "straightforward perspective unprotected by linguistic gloss." Taylor's first digital album is *We Are Trains.* Her music has been recognized by *American Songwriter Magazine*, and she holds a bachelor of science degree in history from TWU and a juris doctorate from Ohio Northern University.

Kathy Vargas is an internationally honored photographer whose works hang in the collections of the Smithsonian's American Art Museum, the Toledo Art Museum, the Southeast Museum of Photography, the National Museum of Mexican Art, the Museum of Fine Arts Houston, the San Antonio Museum of Art, and the Sprint Collection. She has had one-person shows in Europe, Latin America, and the U.S. She is a professor in the art department at the University of the Incarnate Word in San Antonio, her hometown.

Frances Brannen Vick is retired director of University of North Texas Press and E-Heart Press, former president of Texas Institute of Letters, Texas State Historical Association, and the Philosophical Society of Texas. Her works include *One Hundred Years of "The Eyes of Texas; Petra's Legacy; Literary Dallas* and *Letters to Alice: Birth of the Kleberg-King Ranch* Dynasty.

Loretta Diane Walker is poet and a multiple Pushcart Prize nominee. Her book *Word Ghetto* won the 2011 Bluelight Press Book Award. Her work appears in a number of publications. She received a Bachelor of Music Education degree from Texas Tech University and earned a Master's of Elementary Education from the University of Texas at the Permian Basin. She currently teaches music to elementary students in Odessa, Texas.

Donna Walker-Nixon, a recipient of the Minnie Stevens Piper award, is the founding editor of *Windhover: A Journal of Christian Literature* and the co-founding editor of *Langdon Review of the Arts in Texas.* As co-editor with James Ward Lee of the New Texas Series, she brought the journal to the University of Mary Hardin-Baylor. In 2010, her debut novel *Canaan's Oothoon* was published by TAGS Publishing. Her short story "Tented Amusements" appeared in *Journal of Texas Women Writers.* Her fiction has appeared in *Red Boots and Attitude, Writing on the Wind, Texas Short Stories,* and in *descant, Echoes,* and *Concho River Review.*

Christine Warren left a successful marketing career to explore her passion for writing and fly fishing. Her blog, *Fly Fish Chick,* has gained a loyal readership. In 2011, she released her first book, *Paddlefish,* which chronicles her experience in a 260-mile river adventure race. She is working on her second book, a history of honky-tonk music. With her husband and daughter, she splits time between Austin, Texas, and Mobile, Alabama.

 **LaToya Watkins** is a doctoral student and rhetoric instructor at the University of Texas at Dallas. Her stories have been published in several journals, including *Lunch Ticket: Antioch University, Los Angeles*, and *Kweli*. In 2012, she was the recipient of the Texas Association of Creative Writing Teachers award for graduate fiction.

 **Betty Wiesepape**, a native Texan, teaches creative writing and American literature at the University of Texas-Dallas. Betty has published two books and numerous articles on Texas literary history. Her stories, book reviews, and essays have appeared in numerous journals and anthologies. Her newest book is *Winifred Sanford: The Life and Times of a Texas Writer* (University of Texas Press, 2012).

 **June Zaner**, when her hands became too arthritic to weld and to carve stone, found that words could, by themselves, say what she needed to say. Among her publications are a poem concluding the essay, "Finessing Nature," in *Philosophy and Public Policy Quarterly*; essays in *The Tennessean* newspaper; essays in *EXplore Magazine*; and 11 poems and an essay, with accompanying photographs, in *Langdon Review*. She is the wife of Richard Zaner and the mother of Melora and Andy Zaner.

Colophon

This first edition of *Her Texas: Story, Image, Poem & Song*, edited by Donna Walker-Nixon, Cassy Burleson, Rachel Crawford, and Ashley Palmer, has been printed on 55 pound Edwards Brothers coated matte paper containing a percentage of recycled fiber. Titles have been set in Colonna type, the text in Adobe Caslon type. This book was designed by Bryce Milligan.

On-line catalogue and ordering:
www.wingspress.com
Wings Press titles are distributed to the trade by the
Independent Publishers Group
www.ipgbook.com
and in Europe by Gazelle
www.gazellebookservices.co.uk

Also available as an ebook.